SAY IT WITH A BEAUTIFUL SONG

SAY IT WITH A BEAUTIFUL SONG

THE ART AND CRAFT OF THE GREAT AMERICAN SONGBOOK

MICHAEL LASSER
AND
HARMON GREENBLATT

ROWMAN & LITTLEFIELD
Lanham • Boulder • New York • London

Published by Rowman & Littlefield
An imprint of The Rowman & Littlefield Publishing Group, Inc.
4501 Forbes Boulevard, Suite 200, Lanham, Maryland 20706
www.rowman.com

86-90 Paul Street, London EC2A 4NE

Copyright © 2024 by The Rowman & Littlefield Publishing Group, Inc.

All rights reserved. No part of this book may be reproduced in any form or by any electronic or mechanical means, including information storage and retrieval systems, without written permission from the publisher, except by a reviewer who may quote passages in a review.

British Library Cataloguing in Publication Information Available

Library of Congress Cataloging-in-Publication Data
Names: Lasser, Michael L., author. | Greenblatt, Harmon, author.
Title: Say it with a beautiful song : the art and craft of the great American songbook / Michael Lasser and Harmon Greenblatt.
Description: Lanham : Rowman & Littlefield Publishers, 2024. | Includes index.
Identifiers: LCCN 2023059209 (print) | LCCN 2023059210 (ebook) | ISBN 9781538192887 (cloth) | ISBN 9781538192894 (epub)
Subjects: LCSH: Songs—United States—History and criticism. | Popular music—United States—History and criticism.
Classification: LCC ML3477 .L3805 2024 (print) | LCC ML3477 (ebook) | DDC
    782.421640973—dc23/eng/20240124
LC record available at https://lccn.loc.gov/2023059209
LC ebook record available at https://lccn.loc.gov/2023059210

And I wish someday I could find my way
To the land where the good songs go.

—Jerome Kern and P. G. Wodehouse

For Elaine

Holding hands in a movie show . . .
May not be new,
But I like it,
How about you?
—Burton Lane and Ralph Freed

For Fran

CONTENTS

Introduction	ix
1. Craft and Authenticity	1
2. Predictable and Unpredictable	33
3. Unpredictable and Predictable	65
4. Memory and Anticipation	91
5. A Matter of Time	121
6. Your Words and My Music	147
Epilogue	173
Notes	175
Index	183
About the Authors	191

INTRODUCTION

A song is air and breath. Its music can stir our emotions, yet it dissolves as we listen. Only the words provide enough heft to give it anything like solidity even though they, too, are made of breath. Together, music and lyrics can reach the heart, but it isn't easy. It requires an equilibrium made possible only through craft. In a program of his songs at the 92nd Street Y in New York, the lyricist E. Y. Harburg said, "Words make you think a thought. Music makes you feel a feeling. A song makes you feel a thought."[1] We often underrate what the songwriters of the Great American Songbook (roughly 1920–1950) accomplished within the limits of popular music's conventions and its persistent flirtation with sentimentality. Harmon insistently yet almost apologetically calls the greatest songwriters of the Great American Songbook geniuses. Michael understands what he means. At the same time that we love songs, we also toss them away willy-nilly when something new comes along. But not all of them. Those that persist form the spine of this book.

Deena Rosenberg had songs by George and Ira Gershwin in mind, but she could have been thinking about any of the important songs of the Songbook when she wrote, "Somehow, though we take them for granted, these exquisite miniatures still affect us deeply."[2] After seventy years of rock and roll in all its incarnations and successors, the folk music fling of the 1960s, the widespread popularity of the Nashville sound, and the coming of hip-hop to Broadway, these songs refuse to disappear.

And yet the initial popularity of each of them rarely lasted for more than a couple of months. They fell from the lists of hit songs, but they remained just below the surface, never quite disappearing from the public's collective memory or the performances of some of our best singers. Lyricist P. G. Wodehouse set these words to a melody by young Jerome Kern more than a century ago. Think of it as a reassuring fairy tale:

> They had their day,
> And then we threw them away;
> And without a sign we would pass them by,
> For some other, new tune.
> So off to a happier home they flew
> Where they're always loved and they're always new.
>
> (Jerome Kern and P. G. Wodehouse, "The Land Where the Good Songs Go," *Oh, Boy!*, 1917)

We all know the music of our own growing up, but the Great American Songbook persists even though its earliest songs are now a century old.

Michael's parents were very social. On any Saturday night, they might invite people to our apartment. They'd roll up the living room rug, turn on the radio, and dance. They found those clear channel stations so they could dance to everyone from Guy Lombardo to Benny Goodman. He used to watch them. One night, as he was just entering his teen years, his mother said, "Come on, Michael. You can dance too." That night, he learned to do the fox trot and the rhumba. We can still hear at least some of these songs in Broadway revivals; showings of movie musicals from before 1960 in museums and on cable television; YouTube, where you can stumble upon the most striking conflations of singers and songs; live performances by jazz and cabaret singers; crossover recordings by both classical and rock singers; and even TV commercials. Did you know that Willie Nelson loves Irving Berlin's "Blue Skies"? The author Jody Rosen wrote recently about his deep affection for Bob Wills and the Texas Playboys, jazz musicians Louis Armstrong and Duke Ellington, and such hit songs as "Stardust" and "All the Things You Are."[3] Wills's writing and playing mixed country with Western Swing with the blues with jazz with Tin Pan Alley and Broadway. His songs fused many of the strains of American song. He made room for Broadway in Texas.

The Songbook may no longer be the center of the nation's musical attention, but take a grandchild to a revival of an old musical like

Vernon and Irene Castle dance the fox trot. Library of Congress. Public Domain.

Oklahoma!, *Guys and Dolls*, or *Ain't Misbehavin'* and watch the pleasure spread across the generations.

The Great American Songbook, mainstream American popular music written largely between the two world wars, provides the impetus and substance for most of what we have to say. Rock and roll knocked it off its perch during the fifties and early sixties, in part because it had dominated popular taste for nearly half a century and its best songwriters were aging. George Gershwin had died in 1939 at the age of thirty-seven. In 1943, Lorenz Hart succumbed to his inner demons and alcoholism. Two years later, Jerome Kern collapsed on a street in Manhattan and died a few days later. Cole Porter, despite the crippling accident that eventually required the amputation of one of his legs, persisted despite the ceaseless pain. He practiced the urbanity his songs embodied. Rhythm and Blues flourished in Harlem after the war, waiting to be discovered by white teenagers with money in their pockets for the first time in years.

A new generation of songwriters and singers couldn't match those who preceded them. Too much of the writing would not equal the combination of sentiment and wit we had grown to expect from the likes of Porter, Harold Arlen and E. Y. Harburg, and Richard Rodgers and Lorenz Hart. Although Tin Pan Alley would make room for early rock and roll by the mid-fifties, the Songbook still flourished on Broadway and in Hollywood through most of the decade. Broadway marquees flashed the word about Richard Adler and Jerry Ross's *Damn Yankees* (1955), Frederick Loewe and Alan Jay Lerner's *My Fair Lady* (1956), and Jule Styne and Stephen Sondheim's *Gypsy* (1959), while Hollywood produced musicals that featured the hits of such songwriters as Irving Berlin (*Easter Parade*, 1948), George and Ira Gershwin (*American in Paris*, 1951), Nacio Herb Brown and Arthur Freed (*Singin' in the Rain*, 1952), and Arthur Schwartz and Howard Dietz (*The Band Wagon*, 1953).

There are always great songwriters out there, but the Songbook's span of thirty years or so had more of them working at the height of their powers than at any other time. They also wrote more than those who preceded or followed. They were professionals who turned out the work at a consistent level of excellence, at least most of the time. Of the next few generations of songwriters, the lyricist Johnny Mercer complained that they didn't write enough. Beginning in the 1920s, the songwriters of the Great American Songbook didn't wait for inspiration. They had songs to write.

Mastery of technique combined with the ability to express intense emotion by merging sentiment and wit defined the best of these songs, yet overriding all of them was a sense of how American they were. In his introduction to Alec Wilder's *American Popular Songs: The Great Innovators, 1900–1950*, James T. Maher writes about the changes that first occurred at the very end of the nineteenth century: "The American popular song took on, and consolidated, certain native characteristics . . . that distinguished it from the popular song of other countries. It became a discrete musical entity."[4]

In nearly every song from the Great American Songbook, craft serves the creation of time. Songs may move forward or backward or they may stand stock still as the songwriters build each song's emotions around an inner awareness of time. Collaborators handled the merging of music by one person and words by another with aplomb and with some level of awareness of just how good at it they were. The lyricist Gene Lees first met Harold Arlen when the composer was quite old. Lees asked him, "Mr. Arlen, when you and George Gershwin and Rodgers and Hart and the others were writing for the theater in the thirties, were you consciously aware that what you were writing was art music?" Arlen looked at Lees for what Lees remembered as a long time before answering quietly, "Yes."[5] The songwriters' capacity to innovate and invent with such economy in song after song rose to the level of a particular kind of genius. Maher writes, "It is the unconscious role of the innovator to conserve in his creative reflexes both past and contemporary innovation while moving his own work in new directions. He assimilates what is fresh and stimulating, and he then explores his own intuitive sense of the further possibilities."[6]

The songwriters relished the kind of surprise that added to the emotional substance of a song. They had an intuitive grasp of where the nation and its people were. Michael once said that Irving Berlin had a genius for America, and so he did. For half a century, he could intuit what we wanted before we did. He stood beyond his contemporaries in this way, although George and Ira Gershwin came close. It was more a matter of degree than kind. How striking that a group of immigrants or immigrants' children had so keen an awareness of the new land that they or their parents had claimed as their own.

Michael is sometimes uneasy calling Arlen, Harburg, and their contemporaries geniuses. They worked within constraints they infrequently broke free of, yet they were capable of renewal and reinvention, of dazzling rhythms and rhymes, to keep millions of us engaged and emotionally charged. They were practical men and women who often prided themselves on how fast they worked. When they labored more slowly, they kept it to themselves. It took Berlin months to finish "Always" to his satisfaction. These professionals shaped a market that allowed them to flourish at the height of their abilities, not simply because their listeners expected them to but because they expected it of themselves.

Strikingly nuanced in something only thirty-two bars long, a lyric may need no more than a single word to move through time. It creates an emotional setting in which love, its loss, discovery, or survival, lives. Jule Styne, Betty Comden, and Adolph Green's "Just in Time" is a constant weave of time between present and past. The word "time" appears five times in the lyric, mainly at the beginning and end when it counts the most (Jule Styne, Betty Comden, and Adolph Green, "Just in Time," *Bells Are Ringing*, 1956). More than anything, the two characters who sing it (played originally by Judy Holliday and Sidney Chaplin) recognize their wondrous good fortune. Set to a jaunty tune, the lyrics begin with a happy ending, "I found you just in time," before admitting in the same chorus, "I was lost . . . / Nowhere to go." Both characters feel rescued from despair: "No more doubt or fear / I've found my way." Although Comden and Green relied on the past tense throughout the song, it feels immediate, very much in the present moment, shaped by such delight that the man and woman keep repeating the title line to themselves as if in joyful disbelief. Like so many other songs, it seems to embody poet Claudia Keelan's observation, "I woke up to know that time, as such, doesn't pass, but goes on and continues in a manner that links all events to other events, some already finished, some happening now, some yet to happen."[7]

Motion or stasis, not measured by the clock but attuned to the rhythms of the heart. Done so deftly and quickly and even invisibly, it attests to the mastery of craft so highly valued by the songwriters of the Great American Songbook. At the same time, these songs appear to be playing fast and loose with the way most people actually live inwardly. Love songs may rely on great (and sustained) intensity in the present, but we don't, at least not emotionally. Writing in *The New Yorker*, Paul Bloom observed, "The duration of felt experience is between two and three seconds—about as long as it takes, the psychologist Marc Wittmann points out, for Paul McCartney to sing the words 'Hey Jude.' Everything before belongs to memory; everything after is anticipation."[8] Yet within a single song a lyric may persist in the present or move back and forth nimbly in only a word or two between present, past, and future. In the guise of a single emotion, it plays off different times against one another to create its effect. It creates continuity.

This is, among other things, a book about craft and its mastery. Great songwriters preceded and followed the Songbook, but never before or since were so many so sure about how to make a song. They were so good at it that the making was nearly invisible. What William Butler Yeats wrote about poetry is equally applicable to the making of songs:

> I said, "A line will take us hours maybe;
> Yet if it does not seem a moment's thought,
> Our stitching and unstitching has been naught."[9]

The craft was essential to the songs' success. You notice it only if you look for it, but day by day why would you? This book will try to persuade you to listen more closely and thus enjoy more fully.

Similarly, the invisible style of moviemaking that came to be known as the Hollywood Style dominated during the heyday of the Studio System, from the 1930s into the early 1960s. Eventually, it lost its place to the rise of the auteur, the director who came to be seen, rightly or wrongly, as a movie's "author," the possessor of a distinctive style. In those Studio System movies—including *Casablanca*, *Bringing Up Baby*, *A Star Is Born* (with Janet Gaynor and Frederic March), *North by Northwest*, *Stagecoach*, and *Some Like It Hot*—surface polish, clear storytelling, and a star or two to lend momentum and appeal were paramount. The polish was so high that the Hollywood Style appeared to be no style at all.

Like popular songs, many of these movies were formulaic but brought new life to something familiar even though as many as six writers might have worked on a script. It was, said Joe Morton, "Hollywood storytelling at its height, so effortless, so masterful, and it's often invisible to the audience."[10] He might have been describing a song from the Great American Songbook.

At the very least, these songs appear effortless, as if they've always been around, waiting for somebody to sing them on a stage or in the shower. The best of them feel as if they're the most natural thing in the world. And yet they were made by men and women who lacked the ambition or ability to tackle an opera (rest in peace, George Gershwin and Stephen Sondheim) or a novel but who were very good at what they could do. They saw themselves, not as great artists, but as masters of craft who were also shrewd business people. Perhaps the best word, though they would have been suspicious of it, is artisan.

The performing arts are always interwoven with commerce, none more so than popular music. Irving Berlin wrote, "My ambition is to reach the heart of the average American, not the highbrow nor the lowbrow but that vast intermediate crew which is the real soul of the country. . . . My public is the real people."[11] He had a habit of talking straight to his listeners:

> Let the dance floor feel your leather,
> Step as lightly as a feather.
> Let yourself go.
>
> (Irving Berlin, "Let Yourself Go," *Follow the Fleet*, 1936)

Those who wrote the songs understood how lucky they were (and how adept). They delighted in the popularity of their work, the broad audiences they reached, the large amounts of money it earned them, and the fine singers who feasted on what they had written.

During World War II, the emotions of parting and separation were especially sharp. The ballad "I've Heard That Song Before" by Jule Styne and Sammy Cahn is surprisingly uptempo as it seems to exist only in the present, but the brief lyric shifts often from time to time (Jule Styne and Sammy Cahn, "I've Heard That Song Before," *Youth on Parade*, 1942). It moves quickly and easily from the present to the past and back as the narrator listens to a band playing a familiar song she remembers well. The lyrics say, "forever more," but the song and its promise are both in the past. All that remains is memory and the desire to hear the song again, "and I'll remember just when / I've heard that lovely song before."

We began to work on this book in 2021, a century after the Songbook's opening salvo. That's when Irving Berlin wrote "Say It with Music" and "All By Myself"; James F. Hanley and Grant Clarke wrote "Second Hand Rose" for Fanny Brice to sing in the Ziegfeld Follies; Ted FioRito and Gus Kahn wrote "Toot, Toot, Toosie" for Al Jolson; and Richard A. Whiting, Kahn, and Raymond Egan wrote "Ain't We Got Fun" about married lovers.

Things were changing. By the middle of the decade, Milton Ager and Jack Yellen were writing flapper songs ("Ain't She Sweet"); Fred Ahlert and Roy Turk, among others, were writing blues-like torch ballads ("I'll Get By"); Berlin had written "What'll I Do," "All Alone," and "Always," three of his most important songs; Rodgers and Hart and the Gershwins had triumphed on Broadway (*Garrick Gaieties* of 1925 and *Lady, Be Good!*); and the Harlem Renaissance would soon reach far beyond Uptown with songs by James P. Johnson, Thomas "Fats" Waller, Duke Ellington, and Andy Razaf. The Songbook had arrived. By the end of the decade, Al Jolson was singing Berlin's "Blue Skies" in *The Jazz Singer* on the screen. Sheet music, recordings, radio, and then talking pictures—all putting the same songs in America's collective ear.

Michael wrote his first two books about individual songs and how they came to be written, and the next about a larger theme that shaped popular music mostly during the first half of the twentieth century. No matter what he wrote, though, the Great American Songbook was at the center of it. They are the songs (and songwriters) he most admires and enjoys. This book is about the Songbook itself and how its composers and lyricists shaped its songs. We are still the beneficiaries of what they accomplished.

We've tried to identify some of the things that mark the Songbook as both distinctive and enduring and devote at least part of a chapter to each. Many of them overlap, even interweave, so they show up more than once. Among them in no particular order: the mastery of craft, especially rhyme; the delight in wordplay and wit; the way in which songs create a sense of theatricality; the manipulation of time; the importance of unpredictability and the rise to authenticity; the essential nature of collaboration; and the relationship such as it is between lyrics and poetry. We could write a paragraph about each of them now, but we prefer to have you discover them in the chapters along with songs to illustrate.

When we have to use technical language to make a point, we make our explanation as brief and clear as possible. We aim at the general intelligent reader, not the expert. We try to be persuasive and we do our very best to avoid the density of so much academic prose. We'd like people to read the book, enjoy it, and learn something from it.

What we write about isn't exclusive to the Songbook. You can hardly escape time, memory, or unpredictability regardless of what you're writing. Stephen Sondheim told an interviewer, "A song exists in time."[12] He was talking, not about the use of tense in a lyric, but rather a song in performance. Alexandra Petri, a *Washington Post* columnist, added, "It is not like a poem you can stop and start and read at any pace you like and return to if you fail to grasp its meaning the first time. A song is delivered in time, and it has only as long as it lasts to tell you what it is trying to say, whether you hear it or not."[13]

But these songs have their own approach. They follow a series of conventions and rely heavily on syncopation, loose jazzy rhythms, and the merging of elevated romantic language with everyday talk enriched by wit. Unlike most of those who came after them, they knew how to write with a sense of humor.

For anybody who cares about the music and lyrics from these years, Alec Wilder's *American Popular Song* and Philip Furia's *The Poets of Tin Pan Alley* are essential reading. We've learned from both of them, but we've consulted them infrequently for this book. They organize by individual songwriters, while we approach the songs guided by the Songbook's various elements.

Michael and Harmon set out to get at some of the essential qualities of the Great American Songbook through a mix of observation and close reading. If what we write is recitative, the songs are the arias. This is not mainly a work of research but of personal testimony—what we've learned from over forty years of blissful immersion in thousands of American songs. To echo what one of our greatest songwriters wrote only four years into his career, "Come on along!"

Michael Lasser
Rochester, NY
Harmon Greenblatt
Northbrook, IL
May 2023

RECORDINGS

(Most of these recordings are available on YouTube. Sometimes they're film clips or videos of live performances. When there are numerous recordings available, we chose one we liked or that was popular when the song was new. Occasionally there were no recordings available. —ML, HG)

INTRODUCTION

Frank Sinatra, "There Goes That Song Again," 1943
Rebecca Luker, Matthew Scott, "The Land Where the Good Songs Go," 2010
Sydney Chaplin, Judy Holliday, "Just in Time," 1956
Ginger Rogers, "Let Yourself Go," 1935
Harry James and His Orchestra, Helen Forrest, "I've Heard That Song Before," 1942

1
CRAFT AND AUTHENTICITY

In an interview with the NPR radio host Terry Gross, Ken Emerson, Stephen Foster's most recent biographer, described the American popular song beginning with Foster as "deeply, even proudly, inauthentic."[1] It borrowed from European and African American music, everything from the polka, waltz, and march to ragtime, jazz, and the blues. Eventually, songwriters merged these various elements into a popular music hybrid that was, by its very nature, American. And that takes us to the Great American Songbook.

The nation's varied population—and its equally varied music—means that most of what we call American is a hybrid. If America were a dog, it would be a mutt. We recast what we receive into something new, but we don't throw anything away. The professional songwriters smoothed off the harder edges of each particular strain to make it more respectable and acceptable. They then merged it with other kinds of music. And that's the story of Tin Pan Alley in a nutshell.

In her book about the coming of Modernism to Paris at the turn of the twentieth century, Sue Roe writes that the newly arrived young artists responded "to the mood of artistic self-consciousness which . . . came to characterize the modern age."[2] The years before World War I were a time of artistic and cultural upheaval in this country as well; it didn't start with the Charleston in the mid-twenties. Rather, it reignited itself in the years after World War I. What was going on in Paris was also going on in different ways in the United States. Here we had the urban artists known as The Eight; the Armory Show of Modernist art in 1913; the rise of ragtime, jazz, and the blues; the Modernist poet Ezra Pound's rallying cry, "Make it new"; and more. Yet popular music was much less self-aware and much more conservative than the other arts. Self-consciousness in Tin Pan Alley and Broadway during these years was not the American bag. It was a commercial undertaking that achieved artfulness and a different kind of modernity almost despite itself. Roe's point about artists' increasing self-consciousness also requires a broader view. Painting was probably the first of the arts to emphasize its own medium, but other forms followed quickly in the 1920s, when the Great American Songbook first flowered. Its songwriters were determined to move past the Tin Pan Alley formulas of the pre–World War I years to write songs with broad appeal yet rooted in a combination of sentiment and wit. They wanted to be inventive. They prided themselves on their craftsmanship. They put everything they had into their songs. Money was part of it, but look at what they accomplished. Working within a conservative framework, Philip Furia explains, song lyricists adapted "the techniques of modern poetry, as well as those of society verse, and wedded them to music. The lyricists of Tin Pan Alley took the American vernacular and made it sing."[3]

Pound, whose book of essays *Make It New* appeared in 1934, was committed to promoting Modernism in contemporary writing, but if one popular song from the early twentieth century stands as an exemplar of Pound's motto, it has to be Irving Berlin's "Alexander's Ragtime Band." Berlin wrote it in 1911, eleven years before Eliot's "The Waste Land." His biographer James Kaplan calls it "a thrilling song with a thrilling lyric, about the thrill of the new: a great new American artform, ragtime.... Even more, it was a celebration of America itself, a paean to—and very soon, a symbol of—emerging American cultural superpower."[4] It soon became for Berlin and perhaps for other songwriters as well "a breakout anthem of modernity."[5] Yet at the same time, Berlin was a traditionalist. Long after we understood how offensive the language and attitudes of minstrel shows were, he continued to see minstrelsy as a form of essential American entertainment. He also kept an image of Stephen Foster on his office wall. He combined these two strains in a single song in 1914, "Simple Melody," one of his numerous contrapuntal duets (which he preferred to call "double songs"). Its first melody is sweet and old fashioned. It conjures up the feel of a nineteenth-century sentimental ballad. Its second melody evokes ragtime, the sensation of the day, American music's first twentieth-century sound. He then combines the two to create an implied capsule history of American song—only seven years after he wrote his first song.

The sheet music cover for "Alexander's Ragtime Band." Duke University. Public Domain.

In the early twenties, Berlin wrote "What'll I Do," a deeply affecting melancholy ballad. He said of it, "I established the syncopated ballad and I have shown that the metre can be 'chopped up' to fit the words."[6] Yet he set this innovative approach to a slow waltz.

Berlin's eagerness to write successful songs—sometimes as many as forty a year—reflected his deep desire to become and to be recognized as an American. His drive to remake himself served as an unarticulated

Tin Pan Alley. In Search of Tin Pan Alley. Public Domain.

subtext in many of his songs, regardless of subject matter. Writing about love became his pathway to the future.

Tin Pan Alley emerged in the last few years of the nineteenth century when several music publishers opened offices in a row of brownstones on West 28th Street between Fifth and Sixth Avenues in Manhattan. Today, what remains of it is located in the Brill Building on Broadway near West 49th Street and other nearby office buildings. But initially, the young go-getters who saw an opportunity to make a buck included Leo Feist, Edward B. Marks, and Jerome M. Resnick. Increasingly, the songwriters and performers were Jewish, and so were the publishers.

Tin Pan Alley resisted the artistic revolution brought on by social change. Popular music was never part of Modernism, but it did respond to its own time in its own way. It devised a particular kind of modernity. It kept the syncopation and rhythms of African American music but softened the edges. It also replaced the formal language of the sentimental ballad with the talk of ordinary people. Not simply by quoting it but by lifting it to song through the songwriters' growing awareness of the music in language and their mastering of craft to let them somehow capture the music in words without losing their origins in the streets of New York.

The music felt freer, looser, and more spontaneous, yet closer to the longings of ordinary people. Syncopation became the hallmark of American song in the first half of the century. You can hear America balanced on the cusp of the modern in its popular songs. It even affected the way parents calmed crying babies in the middle of the night:

> That ragtime walk with baby, baby,
> You rock and rock with baby;
> Like someone older, rests her head upon your shoulder.
> You don't have to change the baby's lullaby
> She won't cry. Don't you try.
> Eyes you're rubbing. Toes you're stubbing.
> Ragging the baby to sleep.
>
> (Lewis F. Muir and L. Wolfe Gilbert,
> "Ragging the Baby to Sleep," 1912)

Nobody ever talked about an avant garde popular song. Yet commercial songs flourished during a time of massive cultural change, everything from national boundaries to moral certainties. By the 1920s, we were singing to a new urban beat, informed by ragtime and jazz, and attuned to the clang and clamor of growing cities. Together, ragtime and jazz were the sound of the new century. Despite the conservatism of Tin Pan Alley songs, the songwriters led the way forward by appropriating the hot, sexy, jagged sounds of African American music and making them accessible to an expanding white population. America was eager to put the dark, distant memories of the Civil War behind it. The lost generation of World War I had enough to face up to.

Ira Gershwin, one of the giants of the Great American Songbook, understood that sincerity was never enough for a lyric, nor was conviction. "Given a fondness for music," he wrote,

> a feeling for rhyme, a sense of whimsy and humor, an eye for the balanced sentence, an ear for the current phrase, and the ability to imagine oneself a performer trying to put over the number in progress—given all this, I would still say it takes four or five years collaborating with knowledgeable composers to become a well-rounded lyricist.[7]

Similarly, when the lyricist Sheldon Harnick (*Fiddler on the Roof*) was at the beginning of his career, his mentor E. Y. Harburg told him that it would take at least two years to become a truly professional lyricist. "He was wrong," Harnick said years later, "It took me four."

Ira Gershwin was in every way a professional. Although DuBose Hayward wrote the libretto and most of the lyrics for *Porgy and Bess*, he was not a lyricist. Ira Gershwin pitched in to help and actually wrote the lyrics to some of the songs. At one point, George, Ira, and Hayward were talking about the song "I Got Plenty o' Nuthin" when Hayward said he'd like to finish it on his own. When he saw the results, Ira thought that many of the lines looked good on paper but were clumsy when sung:

> It takes years and years of experience to know that such a note cannot take such a syllable, that many a poetic line can be unsingable, that many an ordinary line fitted into the proper musical phrase can sound like a million.[8]

Usually contented to read a book or sit by his pool and play tennis with his friends, Ira once observed that he would not have written as much as he did if George had not been so ambitious. When George was ready to work, Ira was ready to follow. He wrote the words to fit his brother's melodies, a character or situation in a story, or a performer with a defined public personality. It may have been a task he loved, but it was a task nonetheless. Not a direct expression of self. Ironically, that's what gives

Ira Gershwin in 1925 or earlier. Time 6 (July 20, 1925). Public Domain.

the songs by the Gershwins and their contemporaries their lasting appeal. Ultimately, they combined sentiment and wit with jazz-inflected melodies in song after song, as they attuned their songs to recognizable emotions and polished the results until they gleamed.

"A feeling for rhyme," Ira had written. If anything, he understated its importance. Rhyme has always been essential to songwriting, especially during the Songbook. It is a vital part of what makes songs succeed even though English is notorious for having fewer rhyme words than other languages. For "love," popular music's most important word, English has only five rhymes, most of them not especially promising: "dove," "above," "glove," "shove," and "of." That explains why the word, so common in songs, usually lands anywhere except at the end of a rhyming line. Yet sometimes a lyricist can pull it off. Oscar Hammerstein II wrote one of the best-known lines to rhyme "love":

> Give me my rose and my glove.
> Sweetheart, they're suspecting things.
> People will say we're in love.
>
> (Richard Rodgers and Oscar Hammerstein II, "People Will Say We're in Love," *Oklahoma!*, 1943)

Perhaps that's why so many lyricists stretch the limits as far as they can with triple and quadruple rhymes. These songs also rely on patterns of sound and thus movement, especially alliteration and assonance. Anything to match the flow of the music in the sound of words. Alliteration refers to the repetition of consonant sounds, assonance to vowels; they are almost as important as rhyme. Without them, how could we have added tongue twisters to the language. "Peter Piper picked a peck of pickled peppers" has fun popping the alliterative "p" plus the assonant "picked" and "pickled," and also "peck" and "peppers." Before you know it, you've stumbled your way to the end of the line. As the poet E. E. Cummings wrote, "I am abnormally fond of that precision which creates movement."[9] The same is true of the lyricists of the Great American Songbook.

Songs usually rhyme where they're supposed to and as we expect them to, and their images were well worn long ago. They were the stuff of love poetry centuries before Tin Pan Alley songwriters tucked them under their arms and snuck off to use them again. Whatever works. Most of their rhymes fit into thirty-two-bar refrains divided into four eight-bar choruses. The first, second, and last are closely related melodically; the third chorus, known as the release or bridge, introduces a new melody for eight bars. In other words, AABA. Hundreds upon hundreds of songs rely on that pattern without departing from it. At most, they vary it slightly.

A lot of choruses are four lines long and follow a specific pattern of rhyme, known as rhyme scheme. Sometimes the second and fourth lines rhyme (ABCB), sometimes the first and third (ABAC) or the first and third as well as the second and fourth (ABAB), and sometimes the first and second and then the third and fourth (AABB). Sometimes the first three lines rhyme followed by a closing line that rhymes with the closing lines of the other choruses (AAAB). It's also important to note that the rhymes are exact. None of this time/mine stuff. That may also help to explain why so many of the rhyming words are one syllable long.

Since the 1960s, popular music has borrowed regularly from folk music. The line between them sometimes blurs. Late in his life Pete Seeger appeared onstage with Bruce Springsteen. Both men wrote and sang protest songs throughout their careers. Acoustic guitar meets amplified; it was a natural bond. Perhaps the urge to authenticity in recent popular music helps to explain the connection. The electronic drive in the music and the "honesty" in the lyric are what matter. It is a strikingly different aesthetic.

When E. Y. Harburg rhymed "prowess" with "mowess" in the song he wrote for the Cowardly Lion in *The Wizard of Oz* (1939), he was making a verbal joke, the sort of thing he did with such apparent felicity. The lion, a great sissy, is bemoaning his lack of courage. Nearly two decades later, teenage songwriters had begun to write for teenage listeners. Week after week on Dick Clark's TV show *American Bandstand*, teenagers evaluated the new releases. Time after time, if they liked a song, they said it was good to dance to. Nothing less, but nothing more. By the time Neil Sedaka and Howard Greenfield collaborated on "Oh, Carol" in 1958, rhythm superseded melody and words. Whatever you wrote had to fit the rhythm, no matter what:

> I am but a fool.
> Darling, I love you,
> Though you treat me cruel.
>
> (Neil Sedaka and Howard Greenfield, "Oh, Carol," 1958)

This is no example of wit, merely an example of grammatical distortion to make the lyric fit the music. It's also not quite an exact rhyme. The inventiveness and exactitude of the great lyric writers no longer seemed to matter very much.

We assume that authenticity is a virtue and its opposite is not. But is its opposite merely contrived or phony? Authenticity often implies spontaneity even though you can also call it shooting from the hip. Is the opposite of spontaneity something planned or is it craft designed to shape and express the content more convincingly? Is it okay to sacrifice craft for authenticity? Or authenticity for craft? We don't doubt that their songs matter to confessional songwriters and their audiences, but the songwriters of the Great American Songbook also cared about their work. They practiced their craft with conviction; they served the song. It had certain needs and requirements. They set out to meet them with discipline and inventiveness within the familiar limits and occasionally beyond them. They believed in form. No matter how romantic their songs might be, the writers were in their way classicists. Classicists, Joan Acocella wrote in *The New Yorker*, believe "that experience has order, that life can be understood."[10]

Who knows how deeply these songwriters thought? They did understand that love was an emotion that could be expressed, even manipulated, briefly, simply, and in an appealing way. They understood it and its varied emotions as well as anybody, but they also believed in reaching as broad an audience as possible. There was no way to reach that audience without finding a familiar language that would draw a listener into an emotion. Conviction requires more than personal belief. Young love was often their subject, but it rarely smacked of adolescent angst or the self-consciousness of I need, I want, I love. The songwriters of the Great American Songbook might create a character who suffered from narcissistic melancholy, but there was nothing that felt like self-indulgence in their work.

Even in the occasional song that appears not to be about love, a passing reference to it is all it takes to connect it to the larger body of songs. Pollyanna songs sometimes ignore love in the service of the sunshine that appears from behind the clouds. The same is true of the few protest songs that appear in mainstream popular music: a song like "Brother, Can You Spare a Dime?" from the Great Depression. More often than not, these songs appeared in Broadway musicals where characters have a story to tell that might include more than love. In the show *Out of This World*, the god Mercury instructs an ordinary young woman: "Use your imagination, / You'll see such wonders if you do" (Cole Porter, "Use Your Imagination," *Out of This World*, 1945). In the final chorus, Mercury predicts the future with a promise of love: "And soon you will dance / On the road to sweet romance." The song seems to exist out of time because a god sings it; he seems to know the future. Perhaps it's better to say that it exists in all times because he sings it to a mortal woman.

Although Alexander Pope, the eighteenth-century English poet, is not one of our favorites, Michael remembers learning along the way that he would prop himself up in bed every morning to write heroic couplets. He was extending his mastery. Such people as Ira Gershwin and Cole Porter would have understood. Even George Gershwin, so intuitive a composer, kept a notebook in which he jotted scraps of melody whenever they came to him. When it was time to make a song and neither brother had an idea,

George would try out some of his brief notations on Ira to see what reaction he got. After hearing several, Ira in his diffident way might say something like, "Play that one again. I think I might be able to do something with it." I assume that means that he could hear potential speech in it even if he hadn't yet translated a hunch into words.

Whatever these men and women were writing, they were also selling. Composer Douglas Moore said that Irving Berlin "caught and immortalized in his songs what we say, what we think about, and what we believe."[11] Berlin often said that he believed in the judgments of what he called the "mob," his word for the American public. He meant it in an approving way. If a song reached them emotionally, they would then buy the recording or sheet music. It was more complicated than having a feeling and setting it to a tune. These songwriters created a sense of character (especially when they wrote for a show or movie), but, with exceptions, their songs were impersonal. They wrote, not about themselves, but about us to us. If it was on our minds or in our hearts, it soon ended up in a popular song. Each song's narrator was the liaison between song and listener. That's what makes the songs the extraordinary social mirrors they are. That's how they persuade us to care. George Gershwin told his friend, the playwright S. N. Behrman, that he "wanted to write for young girls sitting on fire-escapes on hot summer nights in New York and dreaming of love."[12] Many of Ira's lyrics were a little more sophisticated than that, but Berlin did it time and time again.

Craft doesn't diminish authenticity, it strengthens it. Has anyone ever superseded the emotionalism of Shakespeare's great sonnets in which he worked within the constraints of the form? They feel genuine, as do the best songs of the Great American Songbook (on a different level), also shaped by craft. Michael's students often defined verisimilitude as being lifelike. That's correct but oversimplified. It's really the effect of being lifelike. It's a form of make believe that we believe—at least for a moment. As Oscar Hammerstein wrote, "We could make believe I love you, / Only make believe that you love me" (Jerome Kern and Oscar Hammerstein, "Make Believe," *Show Boat*, 1927). A novel is nothing more than squiggles on a page, a song nothing beyond sound waves in the air. But they can suggest the quality of being alive. Because they persuade us to believe, they move toward artfulness and authenticity by means of craft.

One afternoon in 1932, the composer Vernon Duke, E. Y. Harburg, and some of their songwriting pals were sitting around a table having lunch.

Duke looked over at Harburg to say that he had to write a song about Paris and wondered if Harburg wanted to write the lyrics. Harburg, whom everybody (including his children) called Yip, was agreeable, but he'd never been to Paris. He stopped at a nearby office of Cook's, the famous travel agency, to pick up some brochures to study. And then he applied his craft. The result was "April in Paris" (Vernon Duke and E. Y. Harburg, "April in Paris," *Walk a Little Faster*, 1932). It may be in one sense inauthentic, but listeners were taken by it. Through craft and allusion, it emerged as a great standard.

The English Romantic poet William Wordsworth defined poetry as the spontaneous overflow of emotion recollected in tranquility. Despite his belief in that sort of literary eruption, other poets and GAS songwriters would say that only craft can create the effect of sincerity in a poem (or song) about genuine emotion. When someone asked the poet T. S. Eliot about getting his emotions on paper, he explained that they lay somewhere in the past. The act of writing was not about the emotion but about the struggle to capture it on the page, and that required a mastery of poetic technique and language.

Sincerity requires skill; it's never enough on its own. Without craft, it becomes mere earnestness, one of the dreariest of virtues. Oscar Hammerstein II succumbed from time to time, especially in his attempts at anthems. Such a song as "You'll Never Walk Alone" makes the case for avoiding earnestness. We find it banal and sentimental without being moving: "When you walk through a storm, / Hold your head up high" (Richard Rodgers and Oscar Hammerstein II, "You'll Never Walk Alone," *Carousel*, 1945).

Nothing could be more different than the rousing, good-humored, believable "The Farmer and the Cowman Should Be Friends," also with lyrics by Hammerstein: "I don't say I'm no better than anybody else, / But I'll be damned if I ain't just as good." One lyric feels like a denatured greeting card; the other is about people having a good time together despite the barely concealed tensions between the two groups. It feels true—authentic (Richard Rodgers and Oscar Hammerstein II, "The Farmer and the Cowman Should Be Friends," *Oklahoma!*, 1943).

That said, some songs from the Great American Songbook are personal; they rise from the individual experience of the songwriter: Irving Berlin's "White Christmas" and Johnny Mercer's words for "That Old Black Magic," among them. "White Christmas" has several back stories. One says that Berlin was in California at Christmas, probably in 1938. Although he was an unobservant Jew, he had married Ellin Mackay, a

Roman Catholic, and had come to enjoy his family's celebration of Christmas. Stuck in Hollywood, he missed home. The song's melancholy at Christmas may have had a deeper source as well. In December 1928, Ellin Berlin gave birth to their second child, a son they named Irving Berlin Jr. Early on Christmas morning, the infant's nurse found him dead from sudden infant death syndrome. For both Berlin parents, Christmas became a source of persistent personal anguish.

Mercer wrote "That Old Black Magic" as an expression of sexual passion at the resumption of his longtime affair with Judy Garland.

Songwriters can create something very personal, with a feeling of authenticity. We're suggesting that there's more than one way to achieve it. In a time when people see authenticity as a bedrock of character and behavior, it's important to say a word for the inauthentic, especially when it produced a body of such remarkable songs. At the center of it were African American and Jewish songwriters in the late nineteenth and early twentieth centuries, who influenced American song for the next fifty or seventy-five years. They had different roles to play, but between them they created a distinctive American music.

The Great American Songbook borrowed from ragtime, jazz, and the blues to create a new popular music in the first half of the twentieth century. The music moaned and wailed and cried out in ecstasy, its syncopation and hot rhythms urging us on in dances with such suggestive names as the shimmy, slow drag, shag, strut, and jitterbug. African Americans provided the raw material; Jews did much of the translating and polishing. It continues to amaze us that without the contributions of ex-slaves and perennial pariahs, we would have no music of our own.

Jeffrey Melnick writes that the Jewish songwriters of Tin Pan Alley figured out "how to use the sounds of blackness as the basis of their own creations."[13] They were proud to be New Yorkers. They saw the city as "bustling yet spiritual, merry yet deeply romantic."[14] Although they were writing songs to please popular tastes and borrowing from every available source, a particular authenticity emerged from these manufactured popular tunes, most of which were here today and gone tomorrow. Those that survived we call standards. Did these songwriters take advantage of African American songwriters and their inability to get their work published? Certainly they did, but the music also genuinely attracted them.

African American music is authentic in its reflection of the memories and daily experiences of a people; it grew up from deep memories of Africa and the sorrows and sufferings of slavery. Such brutal experiences grew deep roots. African Americans sang about (and fought for) an America that might be, certainly not the America they knew. They were out to survive and create change. Their songs helped to mark the path.

The Jews, though, were out to succeed, to put down their own roots, to diminish the view of themselves as "the other," the perennial outsider. The older generations of Jewish immigrants were white but perhaps ominous, with their long beards, strange dress, mysterious worship, and odd language. Soon, though, their children and grandchildren learned the song styles of the new century and turned them into something hot, sexy, and syncopated—something irresistible—that white Americans would accept as their own. They became America's chameleons to prove that shape shifting was no longer required for safety.

The African American activist, author, and sometime song lyricist James Weldon Johnson wrote, "Interesting, if not curious, that among white Americans, those who have completely mastered these rhythms most completely are Jewish Americans."[15] They may have made African American music respectable, but they also kept it alive. Maybe that's because the transformation was incomplete. Enough of the heat remained, but they coupled it with craft. By the time they finished, African American music had become an essential part of being American, and a combination of syncopated tunes and Yankee Doodle gab lay at its heart.

The inauthenticity of Tin Pan Alley's borrowings could be crudely racist, especially in the offensive "coon songs" whose popularity lasted for thirty years around the turn of the twentieth century. But it also could have a kind of grandeur—less so than the authentic sorrow songs and work cries of African American music, whose improvised call and response gave songs tone and texture—but grandeur nevertheless. Ragtime emerged in the last years of the nineteenth century. It spread from saloons and whorehouses along the Mississippi near St. Louis until itinerant musicians began to play it anywhere they could find a piano. White musicians and orchestras soon joined them. Before long, the music reached New York and made its way to Broadway.

At the turn of the century, African American songwriters for Broadway musicals insisted on writing new vernacular songs rooted in ragtime. They saw it as an authentic Black music. These men often met in a rough neighborhood on Manhattan's West Side known as the Tenderloin. It was an area of the city where different kinds of people rubbed elbows. Blacks and whites sat next to one another in theaters and danced with one another in disreputable clubs. When the dancing got hot, nobody cared about skin color. The goings-on were provocative. The whiff of danger enticed respectable people.

Such important early African American songwriters as Bob Cole, Will Marion Cook, James Weldon and J. Rosamond Johnson, and Bert Williams would gather in Tenderloin hotel lobbies and lounges to work, perform for one another, and consider the future of their music. Not far away, Blacks and whites in subterranean dives would "hug up close to your baby." As the whiskey flowed and the music grew hotter, the dancers might toss off their clothes and grind their hips together without missing a beat.

The Tenderloin's population was varied. It included a smattering of recent immigrants, but mainly it was Black. Tin Pan Alley was just to its south, so the songwriters lurked in its shadows, always ready to pounce. They would listen to what their Black counterparts were writing and singing, and then they would do what every songwriter used to do: they took what they wanted for their songs. Write a recognizable Tin Pan Alley tune, add syncopation everywhere you could, and shape a lyric about the delights of dancing to this sexy, liberating music. No wonder respectable elders were horrified. The president of New York City's police board was outspoken: "'Rag-time' dancing in public is to be stopped."[16] Imagine the heat in 1910 in:

> Hug up close to your baby,
> Sway me everywhere:
> Show your darlin' beau
> Just how you go to Buffalo,
> Doin' the Grizzly Bear.

(Irving Berlin, "Grizzly Bear," 1910)

The board's president and his supporters weren't very successful. Suddenly everybody was dancing as part of what people were calling the Dance Craze. It lasted from 1911 through World War I and was so insistent that people danced not only in dives but at work during their lunch break, on their way home in hotel ballrooms, and later that night in posh nightclubs. People were doing these new dances to something they called the one-step; it was easy. If you could walk, you could do it, always to the sound of syncopated "ragtime songs."

The songwriters in the Alley were still writing thirty-two-bar songs with an AABA structure, but their lyrics boasted that ragtime was everywhere. You couldn't escape its irresistible syncopation, and most of all it made you want to dance. They turned authentic African American ragtime into hundreds of inauthentic ragtime songs. Nobody wrote more (or more important) ragtime songs than Irving Berlin. In 1914, the producer Charles Dillingham asked Berlin, still in his twenties, to write his first Broadway score and the first score based on ragtime. The loose combination of revue and musical comedy called *Watch Your Step* starred Vernon and Irene Castle, who brought their elegant approach to raffish ragtime dances to Broadway. Berlin gave them such danceable rag-a-ma-tag numbers as "The Dancing Teacher," "Show Us How to Do the Fox Trot," and "The Syncopated Walk."

Berlin was right on the money when he wrote a song called "Ev'rything in America Is Ragtime" in 1916. These ragtime songs (none more important than Berlin's "Alexander's Ragtime Band") sent the waltz to the cedar chest in the attic, put a new emphasis on youth, and extended ragtime's life by another decade. They were the popular American embodiment of the spirit of modernity.

The appropriation of African American music by white songwriters raises troubling questions a century or more later. Were they opportunists who simply stole what they wanted? They had to have known that they had access to music publishers and audiences that African Americans did not. Were they genuinely drawn to the music but "translated" it into sounds and sentiments that white audiences would accept? Ragtime songs borrowed syncopation from ragtime; blues songs the subject matter, worldview, and blues scale from the blues. The composer Harold Arlen, more influenced by the blues than any other composer of the Great American Songbook, freely admitted that he never wrote a blues. Or were the Jews in Tin Pan Alley trying to make their way in a new world—a matter of survival? Like all stories involving race and various ethnic groups in America, there is no simple or single answer.

We've been making the case for the value of the Great American Songbook's "inauthentic" songs, but we also believe that they achieve their own authenticity. These songs are willfully inauthentic; they revel in their inauthenticity. Most of the songwriters did not write about their own experiences. Their task was to align the lyrics with the implied emotionalism in a melody; make music and words appealing, accessible, and memorable; and freshen what listeners had encountered in a thousand other songs. Their task was to merge the sounds of music and talk in a song that people liked enough to buy.

It's a trick that requires a high degree of skill, a bit of magic but without the indirection of the master magician. When people asked him which came first, the music or the lyrics, the lyricist Sammy Cahn answered, "The phone call." Yet from that pragmatic beginning, these composers and lyricists invented something with its own authenticity. The movie director Jim Jarmusch makes the point with bald-faced confidence:

> Nothing is original. Steal from anywhere that resonates with inspiration or fuels your imagination. Select only things to steal that speak to your soul. If you do this, your work (and theft) will be authentic. . . . In any case, always remember what Jean-Luc Goddard said: "It's not where you take things from—it's where you take them to."[17]

Therein lies the authenticity of the Great American Songbook.

In "The Lady Is a Tramp," the narrator's outspoken self-awareness raises the song to the level of authenticity. Richard Rodgers and Lorenz Hart wrote it as a spoof of Manhattan's High Society during the Great Depression when sugar daddies and gold diggers barely knew the country had a problem. High Society, the descendent of the Gilded Age, came with its own rules of public etiquette and propriety. Appearance and reputation were everything. What gives the woman in the song such appeal is the delight she takes in disregarding them with flair and a flourish. She makes no bones about it:

> I don't like crap games with barons and earls.
> Won't go to Harlem in ermine and pearls.
> Won't dish the dirt with the rest of the girls.[18]
>
> (Richard Rodgers and Lorenz Hart,
> "The Lady Is a Tramp," *Babes in Arms*, 1937)

She tells you she's a tramp in language you recognize. It's one person talking to another. She may be a little more outspoken and flamboyant than most of us, but she's no less real. In the melody and the lyrics, Rodgers's melody and Hart's lyric, the "lady" springs to life. Rodgers's music underscores her free and independent spirit. He uses a rapid tempo with syncopation at the start of each of the first three lines, relying almost entirely on major chords. The music moves. It provides an ideal setting for a woman who not only behaves in ways expected of her but has a style uniquely her own. She doesn't care about fashions or trends or the manners of the day. She does things on her own terms and pays whatever price she has to. At night and in private, when everybody who seems to follow the rules is in bed with somebody else's spouse, she's "all alone when I lower my lamp. / That's why the lady is a tramp."

The lyric gives us a revealing, richly humorous, and ironic portrait of someone who rejects pretension. In a case of reverse irony, she embraces the label that everyone else uses to mock her. They call her a tramp, a label she takes as her own. She relishes the fact that she always tells the truth: "I'm not so hot, but my shape is my own." For Hart, who often seemed more interested in dazzling technique than content, the song is his finest example of creating a character within a single song. She is nothing if not authentic.

Not long before his death in 1864, Stephen Foster had written one of his most beautiful songs, "Beautiful Dreamer." The familiar refrain begins:

> Beautiful dreamer, wake unto me,
> Starlight and dewdrops are waiting for thee.
>
> (Stephen Foster, "Beautiful Dreamer," c. 1862)

It's impossible to imagine walking into a bedroom in the twenty-first century and saying these words to anyone. In fact, by the end of the nineteenth century, that kind of elevated lyric was disappearing from popular music. For every "I Love You Truly" (Carrie Jacobs Bond, 1901) that looked back to the nineteenth century, there were dozens of down to earth lyrics like "Won't You Come Home, Bill Bailey" (Hughie Cannon, 1902), "All Goin' Out and Nothin' Comin' In" (Burt Williams and George Walker, 1902), and "In the Good Old Summertime" (George Evans and Ren Shields, 1902).

They reflected the way Americans had begun to speak and behave. Ragtime and especially ragtime songs played a role in the change, as did changing sexual attitudes. A good girl could sit on the porch with a beau to do some spooning. She knew exactly how far to go. Also adding to the change: the large numbers of working-class immigrants who were learning the English of the streets and the work place. Everywhere from dingy saloons to elegant hotel ballrooms, people were dancing to "Alexander's Ragtime Band" and "Ev'rything in America is Ragtime." People were calling Irving Berlin the King of Ragtime even though he never wrote a rag, only ragtime songs.

Big cities often divided into ethnic enclaves, but eventually the immigrants who lived near the Five Corners, in Little Italy, or on the Lower East Side began to venture out of the neighborhoods. Especially if they were young and wanted more than anything to become American. They and sometimes even their parents began to hear themselves (sometimes including the accents) in the Tin Pan Alley songs performed in barrooms and vaudeville houses.

As Tin Pan Alley transformed popular music into a music publishing business on the West Side of Manhattan, and as the technology for publishing and distributing improved and grew less costly, the goal was to write a song that would reach the widest popular audience. Many of the songwriters in those early years were Irish or Jewish, but they aimed what they wrote at everybody who might want to listen. Unless they were playing comic ethnic songs on a wind-up phonograph, listeners found nothing but American talk and American sentiments.

Two years after he wrote his first song, Berlin (born Israel Baline in Czarist Russia) took time out from writing ragtime songs to take a stab at his first comic ballad. A forward young woman takes advantage of her parents' absence and the new telephone in the house to contact a beau. It turns out that she's not as faithful as he had hoped, but for now, he's thrilled by her invitation. Berlin, George M. Cohan, and their Tin Pan Alley and Broadway buddies were writing hit songs that defined what the conversational lyric was and how it sounded. Mostly it sounded like us in rhyme:

> Call me up some rainy afternoon,
> I'll arrange for a quiet little spoon
> Think of all the joy and bliss
> We can hug and we can
> Talk about the weather.
>
> (Irving Berlin, "Call Me Up Some Rainy Afternoon," 1910)

At the turn of the twentieth century, song lyrics had begun to crackle with slang and wordplay, helped along by the upfront styles of cocky Cohan and observant, innovative Berlin. The songs have an irresistible element of joy. Even the love songs preferred pizzazz to passion. Romantic language would soon reemerge in love songs, although it would be less florid and more closely tied to everyday talk. No matter how high the moon, the characters in songs had to speak a language that paralleled our own. Through the first half of the twentieth century, we could hear ourselves in such songs as "Cuddle Up a Little Closer, Lovey Mine" (1908), "What Do You Want to Make Those Eyes at Me For?" (1916), Ain't She Sweet?" (1927), "Walkin' My Baby Back Home" (1931), and "I Had the Craziest Dream" (1942). You can hear the talk in the titles.

Of these five, "Cuddle Up a Little Closer" is the most revealing. Written in 1908, it balances on the cusp between the old century and the new. The verse feels old fashioned and consciously literary, its melody reminiscent of the now-dated sentimental ballads that Foster and others had written so successfully. The song's story, first emerging in the verse, feels mannered and overly formal:

> Then she deigned to rest,
> On his manly chest,
> Her dear heart with its flowing curls.
>
> (Karl Hoschna and Otto Harbach, "Cuddle Up a Little Closer, Lovey Mine," *Three Twins*, 1908)

The narrator in the two verses is an observer; he speaks directly to the listener as he describes a dramatic situation. Only in the refrain does one lover speak to the other in an up-to-date language of wooing. It feels like talk from the early twentieth century lifted to song. The first verse relies in part on the high seriousness of nineteenth-century song, but the refrain is slangy, flirtatious, and seductive:

> Like to feel your cheek so rosy,
> Like to make you comfy, cozy,
> 'Cause I love from head to toesie
> Lovey mine.

The verse to a song often goes unnoticed or unappreciated. Singers omit it and listeners don't remember it even when they can sing the refrain word for word. The refrain is all that follows from the verse; many call it the chorus. At the same time, some refer to the verse as the introduction. Yet it plays an essential role. It comes first; it precedes the refrain, the part of the song where the narrator's emotions are on display. But it sets the stage. It reveals what motivates the narrator, what set of emotions or circumstances compel the character in the song to burst into song. It also has few rules. It can be as long or short as the songwriters want and its melody is different from the refrain to follow. It can ask a question that the refrain answers. It can take a point of view and use the refrain to elaborate. Or whatever else the songwriters have in mind. In other words, it gives the expression of love its sense of context and drama. It brings it closer to reality.

Rather than being nothing more than an expression of deep feeling, the refrain derives emotionally from the verse. By the time it begins, we know what's behind it. We know if the narrator sings both verse and refrain, or if they involve two different people. The verse may speak to us, but the refrain may speak to a specific individual. We may also learn something about the role of time in what follows. A song may be simple or complex, it may skim the surface or delve into a lover's heart, whether 1920s jaunty or 1930s/1940s heartsore. The verse starts us out toward the emotional destination.

These songs are not straightforward personal expressions of how "I" feel or what "I" remember or regret. That is, they're not about the songwriter. But they can build on a more complex set of emotions and the ways people express or respond to them. The songs achieve authenticity through craft rather than autobiography.

Authenticity in these songs also grows from their theatricality; it isn't as simple as an outpouring of emotion. Whether a song is a duet, dramatic monologue, or soliloquy, tension creates emotional movement. Without it, nothing gets off the ground. In other words, a song is often a single moment in an implied narrative. Sometimes we learn about the past that led to it, sometimes not. Sometimes, despite its brevity, a song covers past, present, and future in only a moment—from memory to the current moment to speculation that ranges from despair to hope. Even in something that seems to be as still as a single lyric, tension usually lies in the verse and release, and their relationship to the rest of the song.

At the end of the first act of Stephen Sondheim and James Lapine's *Sunday in the Park with George*, the French post-Impressionist painter Georges Seurat (Mandy Patinkin) nears the completion of his masterwork, "A Sunday on the Island of Le Grand Jatte" (Stephen Sondheim, "Sunday," *Sunday in the Park with George*, 1984). "Order," he says and some of the people he has painted move into place. "Design," made possible by order, adds more of the pieces—essential but still inadequate. "Tension," he adds, and more pieces move, often quarreling in the process. Finally, he says, "Balance" and "Harmony," and moves his mistress Dot (Bernadette Peters) into place. In a moment, the painting will be complete. Order and tension have created balance and, ultimately, harmony.

In songs, too, order and tension create balance and thus completion. Order emerges from the music's structure. The melody sets limits but also creates a setting for the lyricist's flight of language. Order lies in the AABA pattern of most refrains and also helps to set the placement of rhymes. Within those limits the lyricist is free to add words that depict the emotion in terms of human experience. The result is balance between the abstract and the concrete: the harmony between music and words but also the tension. One made of air, the other earth. One lifts, the other holds firm. Tension also exists within a song in the use of repetition and change. It lies in the ways a verse and a refrain contrast yet merge within the song, and how a release also contrasts yet merges with the A sections that precede and follow. What may appear static—a single moment of emotion—is always in motion. That's where the mastery of craft matters. In the following three songs, a soliloquy, a dramatic monologue, and a duet, tension shapes the expression of emotion for the characters who have stories to tell and emotions to express.

In the 1972 movie adaptation of *Cabaret*, the composer John Kander and the lyricist Fred Ebb changed the soliloquy "Maybe Next Time" from a previously written torch ballad into a character song (John Kander and Fred Ebb, "Maybe This Time," *Cabaret*, 1972). It is an exercise in a character's self-delusion. The English writer and wit Samuel Johnson long ago described a second marriage as "the triumph of hope over experience."[19] The nightclub singer Sally Bowles has never married, but Johnson's witticism describes her in a nutshell. Liza Minnelli portrays Bowles and performs the song in the movie, but Kander and Ebb had written it for the comedian and singer Kaye Ballard in 1964, two years before *Cabaret* opened on Broadway.

It was not in the original Broadway score even though Minnelli was singing it in nightclubs and on television by 1966. In the movie it's as introspective as the flighty and not especially talented Bowles can be. She works in a seedy club that slides all too easily from the decadence and corruption of the latter-day Weimar Republic into the emerging horror of Nazi Germany. Sally remains oblivious to the world around her, and rejects her English lover's plea to flee Germany with him.

The structure of the song is almost conventional, but instead of AABA, Kander has written an ABAA melody, with the release coming earlier than usual. The release or bridge is the B section, in which the melody and even the content may change before it returns to the final A. The song works well as a stand alone torch song, but within the show, it becomes Sally's passing moment of self-awareness. She is finally honest with herself as she hopes that her lover will stay even though none of her other affairs lasted. While she cannot escape her failures at love, she dreams in the release that "he will hold me fast." Unfortunately for Sally, the dream soon collides with reality again: "Not a loser anymore" like "the time before." As she nears the end of song, at the edge of desperation, she finds a way to affirm hope even though it's blind. She insists that "all the odds are in my favor"; she insists as she looks to the future that "something's bound to begin." All that remains for her is an insistence on hope that is little more than a pipe dream.

Dramatic monologues work differently from soliloquies. Their intensity is sharper because there's always a listener, someone the narrator talks to. In the verse to Cole Porter's "What Is This Thing Called Love?" the narrator speaks honestly about himself (Cole Porter, "What Is This Thing Called Love?" *Wake Up and Dream*, 1929). He was a "humdrum person" until "love flew in through my window wide," but then it "flew out again." For a little while, though, he had come alive, but now he's back to "leading a life apart."

Confused and bitter, the character raises five questions in the eight-line refrain that he can't answer. They grow out the story he tells about himself in the verse as he tries to understand "What is this thing called love?" in the refrain. He speaks to her directly: "I saw you there one wonderful day. / You took my heart and threw it away." Despite his anger, he knows that he's a fool, but he cannot solve the mystery. The refrain ends as it began, its sense of drama intact in the repetition of its opening question.

"Make Believe," the first of Jerome Kern and Oscar Hammerstein's three aria-like love songs from *Show Boat*, is the score's courting duet between Gaylord Ravenal, a riverboat gambler with a reputation as a ladies' man, and Magnolia Hawks, daughter of Cap'n Andy Hawks of the Cotton Blossom, a Mississippi River show boat (Jerome Kern and Oscar Hammerstein II, "Make Believe," *Show Boat*, 1927). Each of the score's love songs is a duet, and each defines a moment in Magnolia and Gay's relationship: "You Are Love," when they first profess their love for one another, and "Why Do I Love You?" after they marry and have started a family. In "Make Believe," what starts as an attempt at a pick-up soon changes into something more substantive and truer in the guise of pretending (Jerome Kern and Oscar Hammerstein II, "Make Believe," *Show Boat*, 1927).

"Make Believe" appears early in the first act when Gaylord first strikes up a conversation with Magnolia. As they flirt and chat about making believe, he glides into the song's verse, designed to appeal to young, innocent Magnolia. It begins a conversation that suggests this is nothing more than passing chatter:

Jerome Kern. Musical Courier 77, no. 13 (1918). Public Domain.

> And if the things we dream about
> Don't happen to be so,
> That's just an unimportant technicality.

The structure of the refrain that follows is unusual. It consists of two A sections, although the second A changes in its final two lines to create a sense of drama. First, though, Gaylord offers to make believe he loves Magnolia and invites her to make believe that she loves him. What starts as nothing more than a passing moment changes when, struck by her beauty and freshness, Gaylord invites her to pretend too. He reassures her in the more conversational line, "Others find peace of mind in pretending," that soon rises in emotion: "Might as well make believe I love you." Charmed by her, he takes a step forward. It may sound very romantic, but there's also an element of seductiveness and need in it: "Others find peace of mind in pretending; / Couldn't you? Couldn't I? Couldn't we?" He entices her with pretending until he takes a riskier final step in the refrain's closing lines. He is an appealing man and she is falling under his spell. Is the seduction advancing or does he realize that his feelings are changing? At this point, the song begins what Kern calls an interlude. It's closer to dialogue than the rest of the lyric. It also gives implied stage directions to both characters. When Magnolia looks away, he realizes that he's gone too far. She reassures him, though, as she sings for the first time:

> We only pretend,
> You do not offend,
> In playing a lover's part.

She has grown up on the Cotton Blossom and recognizes acting when she sees it. At the same time, she may be falling for him. You see it in the way they behave toward one another, the things they say, and the way the emotions in the song advance despite the misstep by Gaylord. Order and tension create balance, especially in the song's final lines. The space between them is an emotional fulcrum. They sing the refrain together as the duet soars before ending on a quieter conversational note: "Might as well make believe I love you, / For to tell the truth, I do."

In the late 1930s and thereafter, musicians made Jerome Kern and Oscar Hammerstein II's aria-like "All the Things You Are" into a jazz standard. Ironically, Kern didn't especially like jazz and had little feel for it. Kern and Hammerstein wrote the song for their last Broadway collaboration, *Very Warm for May*. The show ran for only fifty-nine performances in late 1939 and early 1940 even though it had a gorgeous score that included "All in Fun," the haunting "In the Heart of the Dark," the lighthearted "Heaven in My Arms," and especially "All the Things You Are."

Kern's melody feels hushed as it hearkens back to the composer's operetta-like musicals. Even his and Hammerstein's landmark show, *Show Boat*, had at its heart the three romantic duets that feel as if they derive directly from a European operetta but given an American twist. Kern had studied in Germany when he was young and operetta was in vogue on the Continent as well as on Broadway. Meanwhile, Hammerstein established himself by collaborating on several major operettas: with Rudolf Friml, Herbert Stothart, and Otto Harbach on *Rose-Marie* (1924), and with Sigmund Romberg on *Desert Song* (1926) and *New Moon* (1928). Kern writes with the lush romanticism we expect from operetta, while Hammerstein's lyric comes very close to turning purple: "You are the promised kiss of springtime / That makes the lonely winter seem long" (Jerome Kern and Oscar Hammerstein II, "All the Things You Are," *Very Warm for May*, 1939).

The two lines exemplify the "pathetic fallacy," a term coined by the nineteenth-century English writer John Ruskin to protest against the sentimentality of the poetry of his time. It means that the writer gives human feelings to objects in nature. Ruskin did not intend it as a compliment. There's nothing conversational about Hammerstein's lyric. It's the exception to prove the rule, especially because Hammerstein wrote in the same show:

> You're with me night and day,
> And so the dopes all say
> That I'm that way 'bout you.
>
> (Jerome Kern and Oscar Hammerstein II, "All in Fun," *Very Warm for May*, 1939)

By the time he began his sixteen-year collaboration with Richard Rodgers, he had learned to write a love song that felt much more natural. It suited the characters and their circumstances. Its believability gives it the aura of authenticity: "You start to light her cigarette / And all at once you love her." Order and tension once again create balance (Richard Rodgers and Oscar Hammerstein II, "All at Once You Love Her," *Pipe Dream*, 1955). By linking songs to listeners, the conversational lyric plays an essential role in the emergence and authenticity of the Great American Songbook.

Even Cole Porter, who wrote very sophisticated, sometimes surprisingly artificial lyrics, could make you believe them. They possess a level of self-awareness uniquely his own. Yet they border on the self-conscious. No one would ever say anything about a beguine in just this way:

> It brings back the sound of music so tender,
> It brings back a night of tropical splendor,
> It brings back a memory ever green.
>
> (Cole Porter, "Begin the Beguine," *Jubilee*, 1935)

That Porter wrote both words and music helped. He had both in his ear as he worked. He needed to find a language that would match the erotically charged yet languid sound of a beguine. Despite the apparent inauthenticity, the merging of melody and words creates a distinctive sound. The language though stylized is simple; it passes quickly as Porter repeats, "It brings back" three times. Only at the end of each line does he reach for an effect. Yet "tender," "splendor," and "ever green" are the language of emotion in these lines. They probably would feel odd in a fox trot or in swing time, but in the exotic setting of a beguine, they feel right. They're not exactly conversation, but the lines remain rooted in talk.

In other words, the conversational lyric does not limit songwriters to everyday chit-chat. The goal is to add style to speech to lift it to the level of song. The music is their guide. It's not only setting words to a melody, it also means matching the right word to the right note, the right set of words to the right musical phrase.

Unfortunately, the lyrics readily available online are often incorrect. They're usually accurate word by word, but they're off line by line. That matters, as does the often-missing or incorrect punctuation. The errors undermine the craft. The lyricists knew how to divide their lines guided by the suggested emotion in the music, their sense of the music inherent in language, the emotion and point of view they needed to articulate, and the sounds of individual words. It's as complicated as it sounds, but they had the conversational lyric to keep them connected to human experience and the melody to rely on and guide them forward.

For the 1925 song "Dinah," colyricists Sam M. Lewis and Joe Young laid out the lines less with a sense of the sentence but more with how to maximize the effect of rhyme, internal rhyme, rhythm, and movement:

> Dinah,
> Is there anyone finer
> In the state of Carolina?
> If there is and you know 'er
> Show 'er to me.
>
> > (Harry Akst, Sam M. Lewis, and Joe Young,
> > "Dinah," *The Plantation Revue*, 1925)

The clever final rhyme of "know 'er" and "show 'er" begins as it should at the end of a line. But then Lewis and Young place their rhyme word at the start of the next line to make room for a connection between Dinah and the song's loving narrator: "Show 'er *to me*" (emphasis added).

The line is also shorter than every line in the chorus except the first, which consists of one word. Varying the length of musical phrases can make a melody more interesting but also poses a greater challenge for the lyricist:

> I'm just breezin' along with the breeze,
> Trailin' the rails,
> Roamin' the seas.
> Like the birdies that sing in the trees . . .
>
> > (Seymour Simons, Richard A. Whiting, and Haven Gillespie, "Breezin' Along with the Breeze," 1926)

Even a songwriter as sophisticated as Porter turned to the same device in the verse to "Down in the Depths." It provides a melancholy wail as the short lines break the sentences into something hard to say because they're so filled with pain.

> Manhattan—
> I'm up a tree.
> The one I most adored
>
> > (Cole Porter, "Down in the Depths," *Red, Hot and Blue*, 1936)

And then Porter delivers the punch line: "The one I most adored / Is bored with me."

As the lyricist, Porter heard something in his melody that led him to break these lines. He has no rests there, and singers usually sing straight through those divisions: "The one I most adored is bored with me."

Paying attention to a lyricist's delineation can help to bring a singer closer to the intent and emotional substance of the song. Porter wrote the song for a woman to sing, and Ethel Merman introduced it. One reference in the lyric identifies the character as a woman: "In my pet pailletted gown."

The character looks inward during the verse, but in the refrain she also observes the outside world as a contrast to what she's going through. The musical phrases lengthen as a result:

> While the crowds at El Morocco punish the parquet
> And at "21" the couples clamor for more . . .

In addition, the accompanist in several recorded versions of the song (including Merman's) emphasizes the backbeat (beats two and four) to suggest that the narrator is not the cool customer she would like to be but rather someone whose world is in a state of upheaval.

Examples abound throughout the Great American Songbook of lyrics that reflect the way in which the lyricists heard the music as they set words to it. To capture Manhattan's frenetic pace, Irving Berlin merged a driving, staccato melody of short lines with quick lyrics and little punctuation:

> Manhattan madness,
> You've got me at last.
> I'm like a fly upon a steeple . . .
>
> > (Irving Berlin, "Manhattan Madness," *Face the Music*, 1931)

Near the end of the song, he pulls off a neat trick to create a pause that anticipates the following line so it does what it says it does.

> Watching seven million people
> Do a rhythm
> That draws me with 'em.

He follows "rhythm" with a rest and then syncopates the next line. The next to last line emphasizes "rhythm," and the pause emphasizes and accelerates "that draws me with 'em."

In one of his and Al Dubin's few romantic ballads, Harry Warren wrote the music to the gentle "September in the Rain." The refrain begins with a flowing melodic line, followed by a line that breaks into three parts. The rest of the song goes back and forth between the two. Dubin laid out the lines as he heard them in the melody, but first he used an internal rhyme in the first line as if to hear it in two parts. That implied division leads to the very short rhyming lines that follow:

> The leaves of brown came tumbling down,
> Remember?
> In September,
> In the rain.
>
> (Harry Warren and Al Dubin, "September in the Rain," *Stars Over Broadway*, 1937)

For "remember," the music carries the note for "ber" for a full two beats into the next measure. It's almost as if it should read "ber in the rain." At a result it accelerates the musical line after the longer "the leaves of brown came tumbling down." Warren also ends the two preceding brief lines ("Remember? / In September") with unaccented beats. Everything here is leading to the emphatic word "rain" that Dubin would tie to the note at the end.

In "Button Up Your Overcoat," colyricists B. G. DeSylva and Lew Brown divided the lines to Ray Henderson's melody in unpredictable ways. Another lyricist just as adept might have begun the refrain with three lines that grow progressively shorter: "Button up your overcoat when the wind is free, / Take good care of yourself, / You belong to me." But DeSylva and Brown gave the song a more 1920s punch with all those imperative opening words ("button," "take") and one-syllable words. What starts as good advice almost immediately becomes good advice from a lover:

> Take good
> Care of yourself,
> You belong to me.
>
> (Ray Henderson, B. G. DeSylva, and Lew Brown, "Button Up Your Overcoat," *Follow Thru*, 1926)

Harry Warren's verse to "Jeepers Creepers" uses a very narrow range of notes to lengthen the melodic line while creating the effect of speed:

> I don't care what the weatherman says,
> When the weatherman says it's raining.
>
> (Harry Warren and Johnny Mercer, "Jeepers Creepers," *Going Places*, 1937)

At the same time, Mercer's lyric follows with fast-moving exclamatory lines followed by slightly longer questions that shape the refrain:

> Jeepers creepers!
> Where'd you got those peepers?

In all the ways that lyricists use to merge lyric with melody, how they hear the music plays an essential role. Most of the time the lines divide as you would expect. The composer writes a musical phrase of so many beats. The lyricist sets syllables to them but sometimes may hear something distinctive in the music and divide the line accordingly:

> You've got to give
> A little,
> Take
> A little
> And let your poor heart break
> A little.
>
> (Billy Hill, "The Glory of Love," 1936)

Most singers sing the lines straight through as if Hill had written: "You've got to give a little, take a little / And let your poor heart break a little." But Hill heard the music differently, as if "give" and "take" are longer notes followed by brief rests and a drop off in emphasis on "a little." Of all the singers we've heard do the song, Jimmy Durante, of all people, comes closest to what Hill appeared to have had in mind. The result is a surprise, not in the content of the song but the way in which Hill lays out the lines and the appeal of hearing Durante sing a romantic ballad. Over and over again, the relationship between the predictable and the unpredictable is central to the way in which the songs of the Great American Songbook work.

RECORDINGS

Alice Faye, "Alexander's Ragtime Band," 1938
Musical Theater Project, "Simple Melody," 2012
Al Jolson, "Ragging the Baby to Sleep," 1912
Alfred Drake, Joan Roberts, "People Will Say We're in Love," 1943
Neil Sedaka, "Oh, Carol," 1959

Mabel Mercer, "Use Your Imagination," 1956
Barbara Cook, Stephen Douglass, "Make Believe," 1966
Ella Fitzgerald, "April in Paris," 1957
Renee Fleming, "You'll Never Walk Alone," 2008
Ensemble, "The Farmer and the Cowman Should Be Friends," 2002
Bing Crosby with Marjorie Reynolds, "White Christmas," 1942
Ella Fitzgerald, "That Old Black Magic," 1961
Max Morath, "Grizzly Bear," 1963
Lena Horne, "The Lady Is a Tramp," 1949
Jan DeGaetani, "Beautiful Dreamer," 1987
Betty Grable, "Cuddle Up a Little Closer," 1943
Mandy Patinkin, "Sunday," 1984
Kristin Chenoweth, "Maybe Next Time," 2015
Leslie Hutchinson, "What Is This Thing Called Love?" 1929
Jerry Hadley, Frederica von Stade, "Make Believe," 1990
Allan Jones, Irene Dunne, "You Are Love," 1936
Edna Best, Howett Worster, "Why Do I Love You?" 1928
Laura Osnes, "All the Things You Are," 2015
Tony Bennett, "All in Fun," 2004
William Johnson, "All at Once You Love Her," 1955
Ella Fitzgerald, "Begin the Beguine," 1956
Bing Crosby with The Mills Brother, "Dinah," 1931
Johnny Marvin, "Breezin' Along with the Breeze," 1926
Ethel Merman, "Down in the Depths," 1935
Jeffry Denman, "Manhattan Madness," 2007
Peggy Lee, "September in the Rain," 2009
Zelma O'Neal, Jack Haley, "Button Up Your Overcoat," 1929
Louis Armstrong, Jack Teagarden, "Jeepers Creepers," 1958
Benny Goodman and His Orchestra, Helen Ward, "The Glory of Love," 1936

2

PREDICTABLE AND UNPREDICTABLE

Predictability produces profits. Up to a point. When it comes to songs, people generally like what they already know. Yet Irving Berlin once said that if you lead listeners in one line to expect something in the next, make a point of surprising them. In his 1921 song "All by Myself," Berlin wrote, "I'd love to rest my weary head on somebody's shoulder," followed by the surprise in what seems to be a straightforward song about lost love. Suddenly it becomes something more: "I hate to grow older / All by myself" (Irving Berlin, "All by Myself," 1921).

The line doesn't answer all questions, but it adds new resonance to what the narrator endures.

In the first decades of the twentieth century, before such inventive composers as Richard Rodgers, George Gershwin, and Harold Arlen, and such equally inventive lyricists as Lorenz Hart, Ira Gershwin, Cole Porter, and E. Y. Harburg spiked the brew, most songs were largely formulaic. This new generation that first flourished in the 1920s set out to renew the familiar in ways that still fit with what audiences demonstrated they wanted. Even so, no matter how much was familiar in a new song, the results had to sparkle. Whatever it took.

One day in the fall of 1926, on a whim George Gershwin popped into a store to buy a rag doll. He was in Philadelphia for try-outs for his latest show, *Oh, Kay!* George's lyric-writing brother Ira was there, too, as was their star Gertrude Lawrence, along with the rest of the cast and crew. On another impulse, George handed the doll to Lawrence that night just as she went out to sing "Someone to Watch Over Me" alone on stage. The prop increased the song's and the character's feeling of vulnerability. Curled up in a corner of a sofa, Lawrence sang to the doll at each of the show's 256 Broadway performances.

Gershwin had originally intended the melody for an uptempo rhythm number but, playing around at the piano one day, he slowed it down. He and Ira realized immediately how much better it sounded as a tender, sad, but hopeful ballad. The theater reviewer Percy Hammond wrote that on opening night the song and its performance had "wrung the withers of even the most hard-hearted of those present."[1]

George's melody relies heavily on repeated notes and uneven rhythms (George Gershwin and Ira Gershwin, "Someone to Watch Over Me," *Oh, Kay!*, 1936). He did the same thing in numerous other songs, as early as "Oh, Lady Be Good!" in 1924, and as late as "They Can't Take That Away from Me" and "A Foggy Day (in London Town)" in 1937. Here the repeated notes and their strong rhythmic accent act like a musical springboard while preparing the listener for the melodic, harmonic, and rhythmic complexities to follow.[2]

The melody buoys up the lyric of longing that Ira added to George's music. George found an ingenious way to reach the note to which Ira set the word "watch." The music is coming out of a downward-moving sequence:

> . . . longing to see:
> I hope that he
> Turns out to be . . .

in which the emphasis falls on the first note in each line. In the next line, though, the melody rises: "Someone who'll watch over me." This syncopated line begins after the first beat. That moves the emphasis from "someone" to "watch." It is also the highest pitched and most forceful note in the line.

The narrator has a "certain lad" in mind to love. She hasn't found him yet, but he's also "the big affair I can't forget, / Only man I ever think of with regret." Is the affair real or imagined? Something real that she's eager to resume? Her perceptions lean back and forward in time as she also anticipates adding "his initial to my monogram." A "lost lamb," she pins everything on him in the hope that he will "turn out to be / Someone who'll watch over me."

Time slips forward and back in the song to add uncertainty to longing but also weaves it and hope together in what emerges as an unusually poignant but determined ballad. It reaches from the present of longing to the imagined moment of discovery to a longer future of being permanently watched over. It is an inward-looking song anchored in time by the presence of its narrator, yet, within the lyric, it is always in motion.

The songwriters in the early days of Tin Pan Alley were usually under contract to the music publishers. If a publisher like Marcus Witmark or Leo Feist said that he needed a song about Hawaii because such songs had caught the popular imagination (as they first did around 1916), you didn't need to travel there to know what to write. You twanged some Hawaiian guitars to flavor a new tossed salad of palm trees, bright flowers, tropical breezes, and couples in elegant gowns and white dinner jackets dancing under the moon and stars. Love was love no matter where you put it. Make it rhyme for thirty-two bars and hand it over.

Milman Parry was a classicist who proved in the 1930s that Homer was actually an amalgam of many "authors" whose stories were passed along orally. They invented and improvised; it's likely that no two tellings were exactly alike. Parry wrote, "In a society where there is no reading and writing, the poet, as we know from the study of such peoples in our own time, always makes his verse out of formulas. He can do it no other way."[3]

The songwriters of the Great American Songbook were not especially well educated, but they were also far from illiterate. Like the oral poets (and unlike most poets) they told their stories for everyone except that they recorded them in words and musical notation. Like those ancient poets, though, they relied on formulas, but formulas transformed by inventiveness and craft to reach those who listen. More than poets, novelists, or playwrights, they came as close as a modern industrial nation could to an oral tradition. They would have disagreed with Henry David Thoreau, who wrote in Walden: "We are in great haste to construct a magnetic telegraph from Maine to Texas, but Maine and Texas, it may be, have nothing important to communicate."[4] The songwriters in each of their songs wanted to say one thing to everyone.

Predictability makes songs feel comfy. Rather than creating conflict, more often than not they gratify the expectations. Unlike much great art—painting or poetry or music—mainstream popular music rarely confronts the listener. It's more likely to reassure. Even in a song about the loss of love and the painful emotions that accompany it, we know how to listen. What we recognize can move us, but it infrequently surprises us. The language and imagery of despair is something we know whether or not we've endured it. We learned about it in part from popular songs.

Their melodies are easy to follow and their lyrics trade in familiar emotions. Everything needs to be accessible. The miracle is not that so many songwriters continued to work within such restrictions for so long but that so many of their songs were good. Some of our greatest songs make only minor adjustments within the conventions. Others push the limits to see what they can get away with. Others don't push at all but they're good songs anyway.

The composer Harry Ruby and the lyricist Bert Kalmar may not have been widely known beyond people in show business, but they collaborated on hits in the 1920s and 1930s that audiences might still recognize. They didn't innovate dramatically, but they wrote singable melodies and lyrics that make them accessible and likeable. You hear one of them two or three times and you can spend the rest of the day humming it to yourself and singing most of the words.

Both men were native New Yorkers; they knew how to work the town. By the time they were in their teens, they were writing songs and sketches for Broadway revues. They soon turned to writing scores for successful musical comedies and then moved to Hollywood for the sunshine and paychecks. They wrote "Hooray for Captain Spaulding" for Groucho Marx and "I Wanna Be Loved By You" for Helen Kane, the "Boop-Boop-a-Doop Girl," to sing in Broadway musical comedies. Marx later performed "Captain Spaulding" in the movie adaptation of *Animal Crackers*.

There's nothing especially original about most of Ruby and Kalmar's songs beyond their wacky special material for Marx. They're safe, predictable—and irresistible. What bounce they have! The collaborators' most successful romantic ballad, "Nevertheless (I'm in Love with You)," has a sure sense of rhythm and a lilting melody that carry the listener effortlessly through the song. Despite its conventionality, it's a good song. It was a hit when it was new in 1930 and then again in 1950, and that doesn't happen for a lot of songs (Harry Ruby and Bert Kalmar, "Nevertheless (I'm in Love with You)," 1931).

The lyric repeats the title line at the end of each of the three A choruses. Most of the rest of these sections list opposites preceded by "maybe." The narrator knows only that despite these possible flip-flops, he loves her: "Maybe I'm right and maybe I'm wrong, / And maybe I'm weak and maybe I'm strong." Emphasizing "maybe" would have been obvious, but Kalmar and Ruby were smart enough to shift the emphasis to the end of each line, to the words that express the opposites: "right," "wrong," "weak," "strong." The "maybe" lines build in emphasis to lead to the closing line of each chorus, the emphatic "nevertheless." No matter what happens, the narrator is determined to see it through. Emphasizing "maybe" (which some singers regrettably do) changes the emotion and attitude of the song. Right from the beginning, the narrator knows with certainty how he feels. That's why the emphasis needs to remain where Kalmar and Ruby put it—on "nevertheless."

Typical of the Songbook's lyricists, Kalmar also weaves a series of deft internal rhymes through the refrain. Nothing especially showy but they work well and provide a bit of acceleration because all the rhyming words are within the lines. Many of the lines have two sets of rhymes: "Maybe I'll win and maybe I'll lose, / And maybe I'm in for cryin' the blues." The lines are revealing. This is no open-throated blues, wailing about personal misery and betrayal, but the hint is powerful. The indirection of "in" for "in for cryin' the blues" implies the narrator's doubt about the other person's feelings for him. The song is not especially complex, but during the Great American Songbook most songs reflected great attention to craft as the creator of emotion.

If you think that "Nevertheless" is simple, consider "Three Little Words," a 1930 hit for the Rhythm Boys (featuring a young Bing Crosby). It feels as if Kalmar and Ruby dashed it off in twenty minutes. Maybe they did, but it works. It's very hard not to tap your toes to this engaging bit of fluff. A three-line chorus (A), another three-line chorus (A), a four-line release (B), and then a final four-line A to end it: a coda that lets the melody wriggle loose for just a moment. None of the three lines in the first A section rhymes with one another, but they do rhyme with their comparable lines in the second A. "Oh, what I'd give for / That wonderful phrase" rhymes with "That's all I'd live for / The rest of my days" in the next stanza. It's another way to use rhyme to propel a song (Harry Ruby and Bert Kalmar, "Three Little Words," *Check and Double Check*, 1930).

Composers and lyricists alike knew how to move a song along. The relative intensity of the release affirms the importance of those three words, the subject of the song. For the last chorus, Ruby pushes the melody out of the way and Kalmar meets him word for note without a single rhyme. It's a peroration and the most dramatic moment in a playful little song about anchoring love in three words and eight letters, helped along by the assonant short "i" of "little," "which," and "simply": "Three little words, / Eight little letters / Which simply mean, / 'I love you!'" The closed vowels help to keep things on the go. Sometimes tiny things give you something larger.

Although "Three Little Words" is a lighthearted uptempo fox trot and "Nevertheless" a sadder, slower ballad, the music in both songs has interesting similarities to achieve different ends. Aside from their use of an AABA structure, both songs rely on a short-short-short-long pattern of notes within the lines. It creates necessary movement in an airy song and equally necessary movement in something much sadder and slower. For "Nevertheless," the pattern of notes appears twice in a single line: "Maybe I'm weak and maybe I'm strong." The emphasis lands on "weak" and "strong." The song may move like a lazy stream, but it never comes to a stop. Similarly, in "Three Little Words," the title line emphasizes not "three" but "words," and, for example, in "maybe I'm weak and maybe I'm strong," the emphasis lands, as it should, on "weak" and "strong." The song skips along.

Yet because the songs are so different from one another, there are important musical differences as well. The rhythmic pattern may be the same, but in "Nevertheless" the short notes are on the same pitch; in "Three Little Words," they're all on different notes. "Nevertheless" glides and "Three Little Words" bounces. "Nevertheless" also uses minor keys often while "Three Little Words" relies almost entirely on major keys. Those differences are essential to how the music creates the mood of each song, from the melancholy to the madcap. Before going out on his own, Ruby had worked as Irving Berlin's musical secretary. No wonder he learned to trust simplicity.

Those who wrote for the Great American Songbook were not inventors so much as reinventors, the best of them stretching the limits so a song resembled an amoeba more than a circle. Cole Porter added elegance and smart talk that no one had heard in a popular song before; George Gershwin borrowed African American syncopation and the improvisational feel of jazz while his brother Ira immersed his lyrics in a mix of classical allusion and chit-chat ("My nights were sour / Spent with Schopenhauer"); Savannah-raised Johnny Mercer forged a unique blend of rural nostalgia and urban hip.

Meanwhile, no one could ever put Irving Berlin in a songwriting corner. Was he the master of all styles or was his own style a constant adaptation to the needs of whatever he was writing so that he became America's greatest musical chameleon? He was a street kid who wrote street songs years before he mastered Broadway. It turned out that there was no kind of song he could not write; he gave many of them the feel of spontaneity that at their best rose to the level of inevitability: "What'll I Do," "Cheek to Cheek," "Let's Face the Music and Dance," and "How Deep Is the Ocean?" among others.

Now that we've said so much about the way in which songs usually stick to the thirty-two-bar pattern and create variety within it, it's time to turn to Harold Arlen because he so often broke with expectations. Arlen brought an unusual sensibility to his writing. He understood that he had to work within the constraints of popular music, but he was always trying to stretch limits without shattering them. He wrote such conventional thirty-two-bar melodies as "Happy as the Day Is Long" and "I've Got the World on a String," but no one pushed against the thirty-two-bar format more forcefully than he. "That Old Black Magic" is seventy-two bars long; "One for My Baby," forty-eight bars; "The Man That Got Away," sixty-two bars; and "Blues in the Night," sixty-eight bars. Arlen let some of his best melodies find their own length.

The son of an Orthodox cantor, he discovered jazz as a teenager and was influenced by ancient Hebrew chants on one hand and jazz and especially the blues on the other. Born Hyman Arluck in Buffalo, New York, Arlen grew up in the synagogue, singing in the choir. He called his father's chanting of the ancient melodies the greatest improvisations he ever heard. Arluck, who changed his name when he started a jazzy dance band in his teens, once played his father a recording by Louis Armstrong. The cantor listened to Armstrong's gravelly scatting and asked, "How did he learn to sing like that?"

Arlen eventually moved to New York City, hoping to become a musician and singer. He landed a part in *Great Day*, a new musical by Vincent Youmans, Edward Eliscu, and William Rose. When the rehearsal pianist Fletcher Henderson was out sick one day, Arlen offered to take his place. He improvised a catchy vamp to let the dancers know that their number was about to begin. The show's African American choral director and former Broadway composer, Will Marion Cook, told Arlen he had a song there.

Soon after, composer Harry Warren introduced Arlen to the lyricist Ted Koehler. They turned that vamp into Arlen's first important song, "Get Happy." It was an unlikely combination of revivalist hymn and polyanna song: "The sun is shining, / Come on get happy, / The Lord is waiting to take your hand" (Harold Arlen and Ted Koehler, "Get Happy," *Nine-Fifteen Revue*, 1930). Arlen's music relies on unconventional chords. They give his melodies the loose sound that most Americans came to know through jazz. In effect, Arlen is messing around with the harmony

Harold Arlen who, with lyricist Ted Koehler, wrote "Stormy Weather." Library of Congress.

to give his song a gospel-y sound, as if it connects back to its origins in spirituals and work songs.

Arlen's music often relies on the blues scale, although he denied, correctly, that he had ever written a true blues. It may have been part of the reason that his songs for the Cotton Club revues fit their setting so well, and why he felt so much at home in Harlem. After watching him work with African Americans at the Cotton Club in the early 1930s, the lyricist

Cotton Club. Public Domain.

Ralph Freed wrote, "He was really one of them. He had absorbed so much from them—their idiom, their tonalities, their phrasings, their rhythms."[5]

Arlen and Koehler wrote scores for the Club's all-Black revues before they left New York for Hollywood. Their songs in the midst of the Harlem Renaissance include "Happy as the Day in Long," "Ill Wind," "Between the Devil and the Deep Blue Sea," and "Stormy Weather."

One of the best songs we know that doesn't vary the typical AABA pattern is Cole Porter's "I Get a Kick Out of You" (Cole Porter, "I Get a Kick Out of You," *Anything Goes*, 1934). Porter wrote it as the opening number for his 1934 hit, *Anything Goes*, where it initially served as a "friendship song" between Reno Sweeney and Billy Crocker (Ethel Merman and William Gaxton), old pals who run into one another by accident. Only in later revivals did it become a soliloquy for Reno after she meets the man of her dreams on shipboard crossing the Atlantic. It comes down to us as a song about unrequited love, more pulsating than palsy. That change required moving the song to a later spot in the play.

Even though the song's structure is conventional, within each section of the refrain, Porter is up to his typical inventiveness, especially the emphatic word "kick" in the first and fourth lines, the changing rhyme schemes from chorus to chorus, and the ever-shifting internal rhymes.

> I get no kick from champagne,
> Mere alcohol doesn't thrill me at all,
> So tell me why should it be true

Porter was always determined to have the last laugh. In a bit of lyrical showmanship, he closes out the chorus: "That I get a kick out of you?" He also has "alcohol" do double duty; the word adds a cacophonous "c" to the sounds in "kick" while also rhyming internally with "me at all." Porter emphasizes the rhyme by placing the assonant short "i" in "thrill" between the rhymes and using the word for an additional emotional kick. All this may be invisible to casual listeners, but it's working on them, holding their interest, moving them forward, and increasing their pleasure—the play of sound in both music and language, blended into this new third thing. A song. This mastery of craft, so complete that it becomes invisible (except in the hands of a show-off like Lorenz Hart), is one of the hallmarks of the Great American Songbook.

The lyric also begins negatively—"get no kick" and "doesn't thrill"; only in the final line does its outlook change, but even then it's part of a question that suggests confusion. After rhyming "if" and "sniff" in line two of the second chorus, Porter extends the game by adding an internal rhyme in a single word in the third line: "That would bore me terrific'ly, too." This contracted four syllable word is the one that matters. Notice where Porter places it, surrounds it with open vowels ("bore," "me," "too"), and bends the line to the music to put even more emphasis on "rif" than usual.

The release is conventional in structure, but it's also more negative in viewpoint: "You obviously don't adore me." Then back to the assonance in the final stanza, where Porter adds yet another internal rhyme. The second line has four different rhyme words: "Flying too high with some guy in the sky," followed by a fifth and sixth repeat of that same long "i" sound in the next line: "Is my idea of nothing to do." And that brings us back to the word at the start of the recurring title line: "Yet I get a kick out of you." "Kick" gives the song a kick.

Porter sets all this to a swooping melody that rises and falls:

"I get no kick from champagne" rises.

"Mere alcohol doesn't thrill me all" continues to rise before leveling off.

"So tell me why should it be true" moves partway down to where the four lines began.

"That I get a kick out of you" completes the descent, especially the three quieter notes after "kick."

This is nothing more than a brilliant song about how "I" feel about "you," but Porter brings the full arsenal of his craft and inventiveness to bear. The narrator is dumbstruck by his feelings but, fortunately, not mute.

Despite his gift for innovation, Ira Gershwin argued that clichés were an essential part of lyric writing. Many of them began as vivid images or clever expressions that died of overuse. Good writing avoids them, but Gershwin makes a distinction between literary writing and writing lyrics. He says that he'd never use a line like "things have come to a pretty pass" if he were writing an editorial, but he likes it at the start of "Let's Call the Whole Thing Off" (George Gershwin and Ira Gershwin, "Let's Call the Whole Thing Off," *Shall We Dance*, 1936). He's right to say that "the phrase that is trite and worn-out when appearing in print usually becomes, when heard fitted to an appropriate musical turn, revitalized, and seems somehow to revert to its original provocativeness."[6]

Because songs are brief and accessibility is essential, because songwriting had been formulaic in the early days of Tin Pan Alley, and because

George Gershwin in the 1920s. Bain News Service. Public Domain.

the imagery of romantic love was both old and familiar, songwriters turned to clichés because everybody gets them. The best songwriters also manage to bring them back to life. After setting the opening cliché to George's punchy tune," Ira adds:

> Our romance is growing flat,
> For you like this and the other,
> While I go for this and that.

We think that Ira has already hooked even the most casual listener as the cliché leads first to a line that ends with the surprising use of "flat." It's an unanticipated word, followed almost immediately by the engaging use of "this and the other" and "this and that." His snappy monosyllables are the verbal equivalent of George's percussive musical line. He's also setting you up for the wordplay to follow.

Ira adds another element of unpredictability. He's written a comic lyric defined by wordplay, but it's really about trying to hold a love affair together. Set to George's tripping melody, his lyrics play with different pronunciations of the same word. He comes up with a songful of them, from potato/po-tah-to to vanilla/vanella. It's more than bantering. The verse provides a dramatic setting for this conversation between lovers who may be anticipating marriage. The verse concludes, "It looks as if we two will never be one."

Just because a song is airy doesn't mean it doesn't matter beyond a passing moment. The couple is about to end things because they can't agree about anything—including something as insignificant as the pronunciation of words. By the end of the second A section, the narrator realizes what's at stake. The song climaxes as the release begins with an octave leap from "but" to "oh," followed by his recognition that if they part, "then that might break my heart." The final A offers reconciliation through compromise. He offers to wear pajamas "and give up pa-jah-mas." He's learned that they need each other and had better stay together. The dash through the pronunciations gives him a chance to come to terms with what he's got and how much he wants it. You see it affirmed cleverly in the last two lines where he repeats the same word three times without changing the pronunciation: "Better call the calling off off, / Let's call the whole thing off!" It's a final bit of verbal trickery in a song that Walter Rimler, the author of *A Gershwin Companion*, says calls up "feelings of instability and yearning."[7]

The musical accents that Ira had to match must have been a challenge. For instance, George usually accented the first beat of every measure. Here, though, he moved the emphasis to the second beat. That helped Ira find his solution: "potato" and "vanilla" where the accents fall on the second syllable. For the release, though, George turned to a much smoother melodic line that had to have been easier to set words to: "But oh, if we call the whole thing off, then we must part." Some of the musical lines are more lyrical than others, but the song never strays far from the animated rhythm and snappy wordplay that give it drive.

"They Can't Take That Away from Me," also by the Gershwins, is just as full of verve and vibrancy as "Let's Call the Whole Thing Off," even though the man and woman know that their marriage will soon end (George and Ira Gershwin, "They Can't Take That Away from Me," *Swing Time*, 1937). The Gershwins wrote it for Fred Astaire to sing to Ginger Rogers on a ferry boat ride to New Jersey to gain a quickie divorce. They married because plot complications required it and now they plan to end it. Fred's been drawn to Ginger from the start but she's resisted him: a typical Fred and Ginger situation and the classic setup of romantic comedy going back at least as far as Shakespeare. Her resistance begins to melt, and this song helps to apply the heat: "The way your smile just beams / The way you sing off key." The couple in "Let's Call the Whole Thing Off" saves its marriage just in time; this couple isn't ready to take that step. As is often the case, wit grounds the sentiments in reality to give them greater believability and charm. In song after song regardless of emotion or tempo, that brilliant polish characterizes the Great American Songbook "on the bumpy road to love."

Deena Rosenberg got to "But Not for Me" before we did, but we had it in mind as soon as we realized that we'd have to write about clichés. She wrote about it in 1991 in her brilliant book *Fascinating Rhythm: The Collaboration of George and Ira Gershwin*. Ira Gershwin used clichés through most of the lyric, but they are clichés subverted and reinvented to create unpredictability and wit and undermine sentimentality. Reinvented but never discarded. The song confronts loneliness, one of the major themes in the Gershwins's romantic ballads. At the same time, the clichés help Ira avoid a direct statement of love except in the opening lines, and then he undermines it: "They're writing songs of love, / But not for me." He begins with a general observation that everyone would understand, but then he personalizes it. He immediately creates a narrator with a point of view. From then on, any reference to love is indirect or, in Rosenberg's word, "oblique" (George Gershwin and Ira Gershwin, "But Not for Me," *Girl Crazy*, 1930).

The narrator's way of personalizing the clichés, transforming them into conversational lyrics, leads to the song's emotions expressed in archaic language—"Heigh ho! Alas! and al- / So lackaday!" The lover is serious, but Ira limits the melancholy by giving the narrator the ability to make fun of himself. At the end, the lyric moves past cliché to painful memory: "Although I can't dismiss / The mem'ry of his kiss," but then uses "guess" to undermine not the genuine emotion but the potential for sentimentality, "I guess he's not for me." A song set insistently in the present takes only the slightest peek ahead to a bleak future. The lyric never submits to the enticements of excessive romanticism but remains conversational. "Lyrics," Rosenberg wrote, "are not prose but stylizations of speech."[8] She had to invent a clumsy word to make her point, but she's dead right. Ira's understanding of clichés doesn't mean that he was incapable of making fun of them in songs. They were useful but they were also a perfect foil. Ira, with his keen sense of words and their placement, was the right lyricist to do the twitting.

In "Bidin' My Time," Ira was content more than once to take a swipe at songs that he thought used clichés but never rescued them from the obvious. While others are doing all the silly things the lyric lists off, the narrator is content to wait for whatever's coming:

> Some fellers love to Tip-toe Through the Tulips;
> Some fellers go on Singin' in the Rain; . . .
> But—
> I'm bidin my time,
> 'Cause that's the kind of guy I'm.

> (George Gershwin and Ira Gershwin, "Bidin' My Time," *Girl Crazy*, 1930)

Another apparently nonsensical song is the Gershwins's bit of whimsy titled "Blah, Blah, Blah." It's hard to imagine any other lyricist coming up with such a title. Porter was too elegant, Hart too obsessively inventive, Hammerstein too sentimental. Ira Gershwin uses nonsense to mock the clichés of songwriting. He knows he needs them but that doesn't mean he doesn't understand what he's doing, His narrator has written a song to his beloved after studying "the rhymes that all the lovers sing." That's the giveaway; the suitor is sincere but he's not much of a songwriter:

Blah, blah, blah, blah, croon,
Blah, blah, blah, love.

> (George Gershwin and Ira Gershwin, "Blah,
> Blah, Blah," *Delicious*, 1931)

Only when you get to the end do you realize that Ira has written a proposal of marriage that combines nonsense with cliches:

Tra la la la, tra la la la la, cottage for two—
Blah, blah, blah, blah, blah, darling with you!

A few years later, for the revue *Life Begins at 8:40*, Arlen, Gershwin, and E. Y. Harburg concocted a similar song. Because it resembles "Blah, Blah, Blah," our hunch is that Gershwin was largely responsible for the lyric and its eagerness to make fun of love song clichés: "Mmmm, surrender. / Mmmm, so tender." The next two lines drive home the point: "What can you say in a love song / That hasn't been said before?" (Harold Arlen, Ira Gershwin, and E. Y. Harburg, "What Can You Say in a Love Song," *Life Begins at 8:40*, 1934).

These songs mix nonsense and cliché except for the rhyming words that glue them together. Like nearly every lyricist from the Great American Songbook, Ira Gershwin was besotted by rhyme. He was always looking for a way to be unpredictable by upending the obvious. A master of rhyme, he once wrote a song about the impossibility of rhyming. A man in love with a woman named Angela wants to do what lovers have always done: write a song professing his love and praising his beloved. But where is he going to find a rhyme for "Angela"? Most names are easy, as he demonstrates again and again, but Angela flummoxes him. In the end, though, he finds a clever way around his dilemma. Leave it to Ira to come up with clever rhymes and then fix everything at the end. For "Lucy," "her kiss is juicy"; for "Chloe," "her breast is snowy"; for "Irma," "She's heaven on terra firma." Only then does he turn defeat into triumph: "And yet, what does it matter / If Angela's heart rhymes with mine!" (Kurt Weill and Ira Gershwin, "A Rhyme for Angela," *The Firebrand of Florence*, 1945).

Before he worked with the composer Kurt Weill, Gershwin always wrote words to fit a melody. Weill, though, preferred to have the lyrics before he composed. They worked out a compromise made more difficult because Weill was in New York and Gershwin had settled in Beverly Hills. Weill wrote eight bars of music to which Gershwin set words and then added eight more bars of lyric. Weill set them to music and added another eight bars of melody. And so on. Eventually, Weill moved to Hollywood to simplify and accelerate the process. Having read Ira's mock romantic lyric for "Angela," in which having hearts rhyme is the closest he comes to expressing love, Weill wrote music that Gershwin called "lively and graceful."

In a funny way, songs of mockery lend themselves to Ira's precision and arched eyebrow. In his lyric to "By Strauss," set to George's exuberant Viennese waltz, the narrator asserts his affection for any waltz by Strauss:

> Away with the music of Broadway!
> Be off with your Irving Berlin!

It's worth noting who ends up as his punch line:

> Oh, I'd give no quarter
> To Kern or Cole Porter,
> And Gershwin keeps pounding on tin.
>
> (George and Ira Gershwin, "By Strauss," *The Show Is On*, 1936)

It's hard to imagine this song's being written after the arrival of rock and the emergence of the folk song revival. The songs of the sixties and thereafter make little room for humor, wordplay, or wit.

The mix of the common and uncommon is essential to the success of songs from the Great American Songbook. What could be more predictable than a pollyanna song? Winter gives way to warmth, rain to sunshine, snow to daffodils. The narrator in Irving Berlin's "Blue Skies" affirms that the skies are "smiling at me," but only after he admits that he was "just as blue as I could be" (Irving Berlin, "Blue Skies," *Betsy*, 1927). Nobody fails to recognize the moment, except unlike the song's narrator, we know it will soon pass. We're smarter than the narrator but we're also happy to bask in his pleasure while it lasts. Sustaining belief in make believe for three minutes isn't the worst thing a listener ever did.

As good as "Blue Skies" is, another pollyanna song might be better, Jimmy McHugh and Dorothy Fields's "On the Sunny Side of the Street." Even though most songs are predictable and conventional, composers and lyricists create something inventive, innovative, and playful within those limits. If jazz feeds the music, everyday talk nourishes the lyric. Many of the men and women doing the writing lived affluent but more or less conventional adult lives, yet somewhere within themselves they nurtured antic spirits—at the very least a desire to do something they hadn't done before.

Just as Berlin had a gift for drawing forth rich emotion from the simplest language, so the lyricist Dorothy Fields had a gift for colloquial English that does much the same thing. Her lyrics connect song to listener. They speak the same lingo. This song's narrator lives in the shadows until she meets someone who brightens her life by teaching her to say (and believe):

> Grab your coat, and get your hat,
> Leave your worry on the doorstep.
>
> (Jimmy McHugh and Dorothy Fields, "On the Sunny Side of the Street," *Lew Leslie's International Revue*, 1930)

A minimal amount of rhyming here, but look what happens in the second chorus: "Life can be so sweet, / On the sunny side of the street." The "eet" rhyme stretches through the second and third A sections to add to the song's natural swing, culminating always in the alliterative "sunny side of the street." They keep the song (and the listener) tripping along. Fields also uses alliteration so the lyric fits the spirit of McHugh's bouncy rhythm and its use of alternating long and short notes. She makes McHugh's octave leap in a single line feel natural and spontaneous: "Grab your coat and get *your hat*" (emphasis added).

The song offers good advice by relying on the imperative. The lyric doesn't make suggestions; it points out necessities. You can't wait around for something good to happen; you have to act. The first lines of the refrain are insistent: "grab," "get," and "leave." Only in the third line does "just" diminish the imperative but makes good by showing how simple the task is. All you have to do is aim your feet and suddenly you're standing in sunshine. The lyric's first surprise comes in the middle of the third line: "Just direct your feet." The mock formality of "direct" adds to the feel of playful conversation.

Fields rooted her lyrics in American talk. We often speak in imperatives even though we're not issuing a command: "Pass the salt," "Please make the bed," "Remember to walk the dog, honey." The song's release is more lyrical, but even here Fields turns to wordplay at the end—a combination of internal rhyme and alliteration—to take us back to the familiar melody of the final chorus: "This rover crossed over." "Rover" is the most dazzling word of all. It's a superb example of a conceit—something designed to call attention to itself—and does so with a brief rest right after it. When it succeeds, a conceit also provides illumination and depth. The song's outlook doesn't change until the release when it shifts from a lesson learned to its application. The person who heeds the advice feels stuck in one place until she takes one step. Lo and behold, she's become a rover, something the person giving the advice has already been.

The narrator may have crossed the street but he is also more contented than he has been in a long time. He's no longer summarizing what he learned; he's acting on his own. The "rover" has crossed the street into the sunshine. The song offers optimism and joy during the early years of the Great Depression.

The first two choruses repeat what he's learned (though with uncommon flair), but then "I used to walk in the shade . . . / But I'm not afraid, / This rover crossed over." He puts in a claim on what he's done; he is not merely a rover, but "this rover." Yes, of course the word is there to fill a two-note space and rhyme with "over," but it does so with such confidence that to hear it is to recognize its pull of inevitability. It's the one word in the lyric that surprises yet also feels absolutely right. It reflects Fields's craft and her intuitive feel for the capacity of language to stir us to everything from hopeless giggles to racking sobs.

To recognize Fields's ability to adapt her use of witty conversational language song by song, you have to look no further than her erotic love ballad "I'm in the Mood for Love." The composer Jimmy McHugh gave her a limpid melody to set words to. The narrator, perhaps female because in 1935 that would have made the song more daring and because Francis Langford had the hit recording, sings insinuatingly, "Funny, but when you're near me, / I'm in the mood for love" (Jimmy McHugh and Dorothy Fields, "I'm in the Mood for Love," *Every Night at Eight*, 1935). What makes the line striking, though, is Fields's use of "funny." Is the narrator surprised by her effect on him? Is this their first time together? Is she startled by her own outspokenness? It took some confidence and perhaps a dash of chutzpah on Fields's part, but she had both in full measure.

The combination was also part of how she got into show business. Her father Lou, half of the famous vaudeville team of Weber and Fields, did everything he could to discourage his daughter. To feed his aspirations to gentility, he had become a producer rather than a "Dutch comic" who relied heavily on exaggerated German-accented malapropisms for his laughs. As a result, Dorothy was teaching school. Finally, she'd had enough. She stood before her father's desk to tell him that she wanted to write song lyrics. He looked up long enough to say, "Ladies don't write lyrics." She replied in that out-of-the-corner-of-her-mouth, wiseacre way of hers, "I'm no lady. I'm your daughter."

She wrote a few unsuccessful songs with the composer J. Fred Coots who then introduced her to the composer Jimmy McHugh with whom she worked from the late 1920s into the 1930s.

In "I'm in the Mood for Love," the closer the narrator is to the man she's talking to, the more her desire rises. Yet much of the lyric is strictly the stuff of love ballads. It continues from the verse into the refrain: "Heaven is in your eyes / Bright as the stars we're under." In a lesser song, romance and wit might have collided. Here, though, Fields's wit makes the song feel spontaneous. Words like "heaven" and "stars" can make a song feel disconnected from real people's feelings, even phony. Wit keeps it connected to reality. The speaker's nerve matches Fields's own. The result is a song in which pleasure adds even more spice to the ardor and turns what might have been a soliloquy into a one-sided conversation.

In the refrain's first four-line chorus, the narrator states her feelings in an unadorned way. She's in the mood for love because she's standing close to him. But she begins two of the four lines with conversational interruptions, "simply" and "funny." Each line—in fact the whole refrain—turns from abstraction to talk. "Simply" suggests spontaneity. It also uses understatement to confirm the intensity of the feeling. All it takes is for her to be near him. The momentary reflection, "funny," suggests that the recognition and what's funny in it are new to her. That may be, but the word's greatest effect lies in its insinuating quality. It might be nothing more than a bit of conversation, or it might be a way to advance a flirtation that probably won't stop with flirting.

Each of the choruses begins with the hyperbole of love lyrics before the narrator sings euphemistically about putting their hearts together and asserts that they can temporarily escape their troubles, even during the Depression: "But for tonight, forget it! / I'm in the mood for love." The line is slangy and erotically charged, but just as songs often nod toward marriage, so Depression songs often portray love (and sex) as an escape from troubles.

Michael once had the chance to interview the lyricist Sammy Cahn. Cahn had a very strong sense of the exact pronunciations that led to rhyme. To make his point, he spelled out three different words for him to say, "your," "yore," and "you're." He pronounced them identically. That's when Cahn had him. "No, dammit!" he said of the third word, "It's yooou're!" He was that meticulous. It was the sort of shaping that was so important to the Great American Songbook. The songwriters got the small things right.

By mastering the intricacies of rhyme, lyricists learned all that it can do for a song in only thirty-two bars. Rhyme, along with internal rhyme, alliteration, and assonance, sustains and extends connections through movement. The web of sound in the lyric and music holds a song together. At the same time, a lyricist might vary the pattern to enhance the merging of syllables and notes, words and music. Even a sappy song can become more interesting through variation. On a dance floor in a garden, a young woman bumps into a young man and apologizes. That changes everything for him:

> Suddenly I saw
> Polka dots and moonbeams
> All around a pug-nosed dream.
>
> (Jimmy Van Heusen and Johnny Burke, "Polka Dots and Moonbeams," 1943)

Van Heusen syncopates the first two lines—(Beat) "A country dance was being held in a garden" and then (Beat) "I felt a bump and heard an 'Oh, I beg your pardon.'" These are also the only lines in the chorus that rhyme. The lyricist Johnny Burke, in sync with Van Heusen's melody, begins the first line with the word "A" to further delay the narrator's appearance. In a single line, he creates a familiar idyllic setting for dancing followed by something unpredictable: a slight mishap, enhanced by a bit of conversation. "Suddenly" is the word that turns the refrain from chance to serendipity in the lyric's shortest line.

Each of the choruses except for the release repeats the final line in slightly modified form, from "all around a pug-nosed dream" to "sparkled on a pug-nosed dream," to the song's final line "when I kiss the pug-nosed dream." The incremental repetition summarizes what happens in the song. The song ends happily on this single night of dancing, but Van Heusen's shifting between major and minor keys keeps the melody slightly off balance. The music doesn't want the listener (or the narrator) to take anything for granted until that kiss at the very end of the song.

The lyric has one especially innovative moment, easily overlooked: "moonbeams" nearly rhymes with "pug-nosed dream," but it doesn't feel as if does. What precedes the rhyme sound diminishes the effect: because "moon" and "nosed" are the accented syllables, they draw attention away from the possibility of rhyme. The consonants in both words are heavy and have little to connect them. Meanwhile, Burke places "nosed" on Van Heusen's emphatic note. The melody has been gliding effortlessly up and down the scale until it suddenly leaps up from "pug."

Unpredictability is no guarantee of a good song. Some of the Songbook's biggest hits follow all the rules. "I'll Walk Alone," the biggest seller and probably the most important love ballad of World War II, follows a typical AABA pattern with the identical first, second, and fourth choruses separated by the release. It appears to be a textbook example, although the composer Jule Styne shortened the final chorus. Cahn added to the sense of ending by having the narrator dream of a contented future in the song's closing lines: "Till you're walking beside me, / I'll walk alone" (Jule Styne and Sammy Cahn, "I'll Walk Alone," *Follow the Fleet*, 1944). Cahn varies the rhyme scheme slightly throughout the refrain and occasionally uses repetition instead of rhyme. Even with the variations, the result stays very close to Tin Pan Alley tried and true as Styne weaves an inviting melodic line except for the release.

The most notable rhyme shifts come in the first lines of the refrain:

> I'll walk alone,
> Because to tell you the truth,
> I'll be lonely.

"Alone" and "lonely" are where you might expect a rhyme to be, but the connection relies on assonance. The "on" sound appears in the second syllable of "alone" and the first of "lonely," thereby throwing off the rhyme even more. Meanwhile, "truth" in line two has the same long "u" sound as the rhyme word "you." It's an example of assonance as the patterns of sound continue throughout. "Truth" is one of the most important words in the lyric. The narrator is going to be speaking only the truth. The subtle shifts are effective, partly through Cahn's use of repetition to complement Styne's legato melody.

Because songs are so brief, the joining of a single word to a note or two can imply a great deal. Like most of his songwriting contemporaries, Cahn was very good at that sort of thing. His placing of "truth" on an emphatic note allows the narrator to underscore that everything she says is so. Yet the legato style of most of the chorus, along with Cahn's lyric, gives the song a contemplative quality, as if she's writing a letter. The opening line of the three A sections ends on the same word, "alone," with its unaccented final syllable. The quiet ending of a song that declines after "walk" suits its thoughtful mood.

Styne's tempo also matters. He marked it as "slowly," but it's far from being a dirge. The narrator has learned to live with the loneliness and anticipates having her love "walking beside me." But the release is more dramatic. She pledges fidelity now and in the future; it is the song's emotional climax. The music for these few lines is less legato than the other choruses; it moves dramatically by relying more on minor keys to underscore the narrator's grasp of the dangers her beloved faces despite their love. Cahn's adept placement of words matches Styne's handling of change. For instance, the first three lines of the release—I'll always be near you, / Wherever you are, / Each night in ev'ry prayer."—move quickly until they climax in the emphatic "night." A rest follows before the music subsides in intensity. From there to the end of the release, the music begins the transition back to the final legato A chorus: "Just close your eyes and I'll be there."

The song is filled with loneliness and longing, but this is 1944 rather than 1942. The narrator has found a way to live with her fears. When the song returns to the final A chorus, the outlook is different. In the first two A sections, the narrator offers personal conviction—"I'll walk alone." Now, though, she pleads forcefully with her lover. She asks him to pledge to her what she has pledged to him: "Please walk alone, / And send your love and your kisses to guide me." In a song set resolutely in the present, she now turns to the future. By shortening the chorus and emphasizing the final tonic chord, Styne gives the song a dramatic ending. Despite the drama, though, the song ends quietly on "alone," although its use of the tonic adds a hint of intensity as she reaffirms her loyalty and love.

The most potent songs from World War II trade in loss and loneliness. Songwriters had an audience in mind for their love ballads: the women who remained behind while husbands and sweethearts were fighting in North Africa, Europe, and the Pacific. In Duke Ellington and Bob Russell's "Don't Get Around Much Anymore," the lyric for the verse creates a dramatic context immediately. But Ellington had written the music in 1938 for a jazz piece he called "Never No Lament." He didn't care much about most of the lyrics that eventually attached to his music. Supposedly he once asked Irving Mills, his publisher, manager, and sometime lyricist, what one of his new songs was about.

Four years after "Never No Lament," by which time the United States had entered World War II, Mills recognized a potential melody within the longer work. Although the resulting song has a familiar AABA thirty-two-bar structure, along with recognizable allusions and themes—going to a dance, feeling lonely—its lyric is innovative and unpredictable though still immediately accessible. Recordings by the Ink Spots and Ellington's orchestra made it to the top ten lists the following year.

Mills eventually asked Russell to add a lyric (Duke Ellington and Bob Russell, "Don't Get Around Much Anymore," 1942). Ellington's music is jaunty; its original title suited it well. But this is one of those songs where the music and lyric feel as if they're at odds with one another yet somehow interweave. Ellington keeps the song moving with sudden leaps of an octave or more. In the refrain's opening line, for example, "Missed the Saturday dance," descends an octave from "missed" to "dance." The same pattern continues in the next line: "Heard they crowded the floor." "Missed" and "heard" intensify her discoveries—and underscore her loneliness. She wasn't there.

Syncopation drives all three A choruses. Each begins on the offbeat to give the words greater force—(Beat) "Missed," (Beat) "Heard," and (Beat) "Couldn't." The first three lines begin emphatically before the arc of each line descends. The final line has a slightly different syncopation. "Don't," the line's first word, sits between the first and second beats as the words and the narrator's emotional weariness reflect the downward arc of the remaining notes: "Don't get around much anymore." Even with Ellington's lively melody, the song gives off a feeling of regret or weariness matched by Russell's lyric.

The release, a more plaintive melody largely without the syncopation that gives the song its drive, shifts from describing events to introspection. Withdrawing from the world, the narrator finds, makes her mind "more at ease." The four lines are also more conventionally melodic.

The woman who speaks prefers to "keep pretty much to myself." It sounds diverting enough except for her need to repeat the way she passes the time day after day after day, played off against her underlying dread. That's what she tries to fend off, what the best wartime songs were so good at suggesting without giving in to it.

The songs of 1942, the darkest year of the war, were especially bleak:

> Thought I'd visit the club,
> Got as far as the door.

This is a place she knows, a place where she is known. That's what would make it unbearable: "They'd have asked me about you, / Don't get around much anymore." Russell's elliptical lyric sounds the most common themes of World War II ballads—parting and separation, loneliness and longing, and the dream of return—but the omissions, the details and emotions left unsaid, draw the listener more fully into the song to make it distinctive. We have gaps to fill between the lines, made more compelling by their brevity.

The lyric omits everything between the time the narrator decides to "visit the club" until she approaches the door. We never encounter her feelings directly, only the emotional distress just beneath the surface: "They'd have asked me about you." Those people are probably friends who knew the couple before he left for war; they would mean their solicitude as a source of comfort, but she can't bear it. And then the unadorned conclusion, compelling in its rueful clarity: "Don't get around much anymore."

Millions of women were going through the same sort of emotions in the 1940s, but the narrator is also distinctively herself. That's what makes her so convincing. She never indulges in self-pity. Despite her loneliness she has a clear eye. She heard that a dance on Saturday night was packed but she "couldn't bear it" without her lover. It is much more intense than merely not wanting to go without him, something more immediate, more penetrating. In her imagination, she speaks across great distances to the man she loves.

When we hear this song, we imagine the narrator walking tentatively to the door and then backing away. Better to be on her own even if it means being alone. The women in a substantial number of wartime ballads prefer to stay home, especially in 1942, early in the war, away from friends who seek to comfort but only deepen the longing. We might say that the songwriters were describing depression, but it's more likely that they had found a way to dramatize the emotions of the women who listened on the radio. A narrator within a song speaks for them in ways that feel honest and sympathetic. Popular songs can be more than hyperbolic escapism; they can tell truths when they matter. Michael used to give a talk about the songs of World War II. Audience members who had lived through the war would soon start to sing and cry.

Music is one of the Great American Songbook's most important subjects. We have hundreds of songs about music, song, singing, dancing, and rhythm. They are among our most romantic and rhapsodic. A melody soars with the coming of love and lingers long after the love has ended. As image and metaphor, music may embody love or it may be love's accompaniment. Because of its abstraction, music written in time soon feels outside it. Its rhythm and flow may parallel ours, but they're not the same thing. As the music rises, the lyric's task is to keep it connected to what people remember, know, and dream on. In songs about song, the image can carry us to the heart of the matter. As the poet Bink Noll once wrote in a note to Michael, "Facts give vision responsibility."

The liveliest of these songs are about themselves. Like ragtime songs before them, they concentrate on themselves with hardly a passing reference to love. They're about what music does to the listener, especially when it's hot, driving, and sexy. Before *Flying Down to Rio* (1933), her first movie with Fred Astaire, Ginger Rogers was a featured player at RKO Radio Studios. The studio inserted her in *Flying Down to Rio* because the actor already cast in the role took ill. Rogers played a band singer named Honey Hale and Astaire was cast as Fred Ayres, the band's accordionist. By then Rogers was a seasoned professional. She had played in vaudeville, done a turn on Broadway as a leading lady, and had some minor roles in movies. When RKO signed her, the studio saw her as a featured player, not a star. But "Music Makes Me," the hit song "Carioca," and her first time dancing with Astaire (he got fifth billing; she got fourth) changed everything.

As Rogers sings "Music Makes Me," everything is always moving (Vincent Youmans, Gus Kahn, and Edward Eliscu, "Music Makes Me," *Flying Down to Rio*, 1932). Dressed in a low-cut gown, she is irresistibly sexy as she sings about the music she can't resist and what happens next. It "makes me do the things I never should do." She confesses that she's "a sinner / And music is my crime."

These songs may include a reference to love, but they usually keep it brief. Their purpose seems to be placing the song within the usual limits of the Great American Songbook. Mention love and you can write almost anything else you want. In Burton Lane and Frank Loesser's "I Hear Music," love appears only in the release, which is half the length of the other three choruses. It's also the song's climax. The first two choruses list off the music the narrator hears—a morning breeze, a sparrow's singing, and coffee perking on the stove—but the release changes the focus for a necessary moment: "There's my favorite melody, / You, my angel, phoning me" (Burton Lane and Frank Loesser, "I Hear Music," *Dancing on a Dime*, 1940). We like the tension between the hyperbolic "angel" and the up-to-date "phoning."

The next two songs, "The Song Is Ended" and "Let's Face the Music and Dance," stay alive in the present. It's the music that gets the narrator moving—right now. The allure of carpe diem ("seize the day") keeps the beat going just beneath the surface. It's a different approach from carpe diem's typical seductiveness. Elsewhere, it surfaces to shape more romantic emotions, perhaps most famously in Andrew Marvell's deceptive eighteenth-century poem "To His Coy Mistress." It is an exercise in seduction in which the seducer suddenly confronts his own mortality. In Berlin's "The Song Is Ended," though, a lover recognizes what he has lost and realizes now that the melody had told him the truth. On this beautiful night of heavenly dancing, the music warns him. Aware that his lover has deserted him, he sings, "Summer will pass away, / Take your happiness while you may" (Irving Berlin, "The Song Is Ended [But the Melody Lingers On]," 1927).

The darkest of these carpe diem songs promises trouble ahead and "teardrops to shed," but it stakes a claim on the present down to its ambiguous title. Despite what's bound to come, "Let's face the music and dance" (Irving Berlin, "Let's Face the Music and Dance," *Follow the Fleet*, 1935). Berlin writes a reassuring list at the start of the song, "But while there's moonlight and music / And love and romance," but three of the words are nothing more than abstractions. It's only with the next line that the listener understands their purpose. They lead to the line that matters, "Let's face the music and dance," an ironic pun that leads to a life-affirming determination to dance. In its acceptance of difficult times and its determination not to succumb to them, the song remains one of the great romantic anthems of the Great Depression, a demonstration of how the Great American Songbook took on the troubles of its time without joining folk singers in protest. Berlin wrote it for Astaire to sing and Astaire and Rogers to dance to. It is a performance number, but the dramatic context adds a further element of darkness and a scintilla of hope.

The number begins on the patio of a large country house. Astaire dressed in black tails wanders outside. Everyone ignores or snubs him. Isolated, alone, and dead broke, he draws a pistol. Before he can use it, he sees the elegantly gowned Rogers about to jump from a high balustrade. He draws her back from the edge and eventually into a dance. First he sings and then seems to hypnotize her into the dance. There's nothing joyful in what they do, but as the dance ends, they leave together:

> So while there's moonlight and music
> And love and romance,
> Let's face the music and dance.

Many songs rely on music as a central image for expressing the narrator's emotional point of view. In others, it serves as essential background for whatever is happening. The emotions and circumstances change from song to song, but music plays its necessary role in the lyrics. In this song, two people dance together. He looks at her and hears music, not because they're dancing but because the music somehow embodies her. Yet only he has heard this singular refrain. He longs to tell her but he's unable to speak: "I alone / Have heard this lovely strain . . ." Even so, he still has questions and the need for answers:

> Must it be
> Forever inside of me?
> Why can't I let you know?
>
> (Jerome Kern and Oscar Hammerstein II,
> "The Song Is You," *Music in the Air*, 1932)

The song was originally performed as a duet so both lovers must suffer from the same mysterious reluctance to speak.

In one song, "The song is you," but in another, "You are the song." Love survives "as long as there's music for sweethearts to sing" (Jule Styne and Sammy Cahn, "As Long as There's Music," *Step Lively*, 1944). What starts as observation about the essential role that music plays in sustaining love eventually becomes personal. The narrator's observations give way to speaking directly to the beloved who becomes the song that love requires. Even when they're apart, loneliness will amount to little "as long as there's music and you are the song."

Although the imagery in these songs barely changes from song to song, it serves different emotional ends. The title of "Music Maestro Please" sounds as if the song will be upbeat; it isn't (Allie Wrubel and Herb Magidson, "Music Maestro, Please," 1938). The title of "The Music Stopped" sounds as if the song will be melancholy; it isn't (Jimmy McHugh and Harold Adamson, "The Music Stopped," *Higher and Higher*, 1943). In "Music, Maestro, Please," someone trying to forget hopes the band will distract him. He sits in a nightclub near the bandstand, orders a drink, and tries not to think of her. He calls for ". . . any old thing / To help me ease the pain." In "The Music Stopped," the lovers are so absorbed in one another that they continue to dance after the music stops and the musicians leave. People stare at them but they continue to dance "because the lights were low / And we were in love."

In a time when sex was handled discretely, dancing was a way for a couple to get close to one another. The lights dim, the music starts, and the lovers hold one another as if they are alone. The "soft lights and sweet music" are essential, but only with "you in my arms." Lights and melody will bring "you closer to me." The lyric is dream-like because it is a dream of sorts—a reverie in which he asks for what he wants: "So give me velvet lights and sweet music / And you in my arms" (Irving Berlin, "Soft Lights and Sweet Music," *Face the Music*, 1932). Light, music, and dancing are a connection to reality here. When they continue to dance after the music stops, the other people stare at them. The lovers are caught up in the moment but at least one of them notices.

Dancing close when it still meant something is an important part of a lot of these songs because it almost always brings sex into the mix with romance. In 1951, some radio stations banned the playing of the tango, "I Get Ideas" because of the lines, "When we are dancing / And you're dangerously near me, / I get ideas" (Lenny Sanders and Dorcas Cochran, "I Get Ideas,"1951). Ten years earlier, Frank Loesser had placed his lovers on a jammed dance floor on which "There isn't an inch of space / For being discrete" (Burton Lane and Frank Loesser, "Dancing on a Dime," *Dancing on a Dime*, 1941). But "the crowded floor is perfect for / A nice romantic time." The narrator confesses at the end that he couldn't wait to get out on the floor with her: "For I knew it all the time, / That I'd be close to you / Dancing on a dime."

Another song by Irving Berlin also conjures up the magical moment, not by sending a couple onto the dance floor to move with the music but by developing a changing point of view and redefining music (Irving Berlin, "Say It with Music," *Music Box Revue of 1921*, 1921). The first verse speaks to the listener: "Music is a language lovers understand." In the second verse, one lover speaks to the other: "Sentimental speeches never could impart / Just exactly what I want to tell you." As in "As Long as There's Music," the lover can't find the words, but he does understand that "a melody mellow / . . . / Helps Mister Cupid along."

These romantic ballads are rarely innovative. They set aside the clever wordplay for something more straightforward. Burton Lane and Alan Jay Lerner wrote one of the loveliest and most interesting of them in 1979 for a Broadway flop titled *Carmalina*. Lane's exquisite melody feels hushed, an ideal setting for a song of reflection and reminiscence in the service of need.

The song's title, "It's Time for a Love Song," opens the door to past, present, and future alike by describing the kind of song the narrator is searching for (Burton Lane and Alan Jay Lerner, "It's Time for a Love Song," *Carmalina*, 1979). He never defines what will happen tomorrow, but as he searches the past to find what he needs, the lyric implies that rediscovering the right love song bodes well for the future. It sounds as if the song within the song might lift it to a sense of inevitability as the narrator discovers and explains what he's looking for. He insists, though quietly, that "it's time to remember / The songs that in days gone by / Could warm the sky in December." He seeks a song "filled with the fervor / Of a woman in love beyond reason" because such a song can remind us "how a world may forget / But the time for a love song is now."

Revenge is not the most common subject for a song. However, it does show up from time to time—a passion for vengeance mixed with the desire to gloat—as in Johnny Mercer and Sadie Vimmerstedt's "I Wanna Be Around" from 1959. Vimmerstedt was not a professional songwriter. A housewife, grandmother, and beautician from Youngstown, Ohio, she had sent Mercer an idea for a song two years earlier. She didn't know how to reach him so she addressed the envelope to "Johnny Mercer, Songwriter, New York, NY." The post office forwarded it to ASCAP and they sent it on to Mercer. He turned Vimmerstedt's amateurish version into a polished song and paid her one-third of the royalties. The line of hers that first caught his interest: "I wanna be around to pick up the pieces / When somebody breaks your heart" (Johnny Mercer and Sadie Vimmerstedt, "I Wanna Be Around," 1959).

No matter how intense a song might be, the songwriters of the Great American Songbook appeared never to break a sweat. They polished their work until it looked effortless, spontaneous, and inevitable. The best songs possess an artless quality, as if they spring into being each time you hear them because so much of the craft lies hidden beneath the emotionalism. With the illusion of simplicity, invisibility can create brilliance. Johnny Mercer was a lyricist who occasionally picked out a melody with a single finger because he could neither write music nor play it, but here he created a combination of a melancholy cry and a vaudeville number.

In the song's fourteen lines you find only two rhymes. "Let's see if the puzzle fits so fine" at the end of the second chorus rhymes with "like you broke mine" at the end of the third. At the end of the final chorus, "That's when I'll discover that revenge is sweet" rhymes with the next line, "As I sit there applaudin' from a front row seat." Mercer fills the rest of the song with the barely visible tricks of the lyricist's trade to lend it intensity when it needs it and make it inviting and satisfying to those who are listening. Assonance and alliteration are areas of strength for the English language and the Great American Songbook.

In addition to the few rhymes, Mercer relies on a wide range of techniques to make the song seamless. An assonant long "e" runs throughout the lyric to anticipate the rhyming words "sweet" and "seat." A lot of apparently insignificant words like "be," "me," and "he," but also some of the lyric's most important words: "pieces," "leave," "see," "sweet," and "seat." Internal rhyme appears several times, including "when he breaks your heart to bits / Let's see if the puzzle fits so fine," along with the repetition of "somebody" that contributes to the alliterative "s" that also recurs often.

These devices shape the narrator's eagerness to be around to watch. The song is quietly accusatory, a restrained cry, but he is itching to get back at her. The intensity begins to build with the word "smart" in the third line—"Somebody twice as smart as I"—and then builds again four lines later through a series of three accelerating "ee" sounds—"That mis'ry loves company, wait and see"—followed by continuing "ee" sounds into the next three lines and the rhymed lines in the final chorus.

Mercer has brilliantly matched words to music. In the final chorus the intensification erupts; the tempo increases and the rhythmic pattern becomes stronger. A straightforward song about bitterness becomes a high-energy vaudeville number that crows its way into the future.

This is exactly the kind of thing that the Great American Songbook made possible. An amateur songwriter sent a lyric to a highly skilled professional, who turned it into a song that feels inevitable. It wasn't personal; it was work. But its emotional underpinnings had to have reflected something Mercer grasped and then transformed by craft.

RECORDINGS

Louis Armstrong, "On the Sunny Side of the Street," 1957
Aileen Stanley, "All by Myself," 1921
Gertrude Lawrence, "Someone to Watch Over Me," 1921
Ruth Etting, "Nevertheless," 1931
Duke Ellington and His Orchestra, The Rhythm Boys, "Three Little Words," 1930
Frank Sinatra, "Get Happy," 1998
Ethel Merman, "I Get a Kick Out of You," 1934
Ella Fitzgerald and Louis Armstrong, "Let's Call the Whole Thing Off," 2022
Fred Astaire, "They Can't Take That Away from Me," 1937
Rosemary Clooney, "But Not for Me," 1981
The Foursome, "Bidin' My Time," 1930

Chris Sullivan, "Blah, Blah, Blah," 2012
Rebecca Luker, Philip Chaffin, "What Can You Say in a Love Song?" 2012
Ronny White, "A Rhyme for Angela," 1996
Maureen McGovern, "By Strauss," 2012
Bing Crosby, "Blue Skies," 1946
Frances Langford, "I'm in the Mood for Love," 1935
Tommy Dorsey and His Orchestra, "On the Sunny Side of the Street," 1945
Tommy Dorsey and His Orchestra, Frank Sinatra, "Polka Dots and Moonbeams," 1940
Dinah Shore, "I'll Walk Alone," 1944
Ink Spots, "Don't Get Around Much Anymore," 1942
Ginger Rogers, "Music Makes Me," 1933
Blossom Dearie, "I Hear Music," 1956
Ruth Etting, "The Song Is Ended (But the Melody Lingers On)," 1927
Fred Astaire, "Let's Face the Music and Dance," 1936
Frank Sinatra, "The Song Is You," 1943
Frank Sinatra, "As Long As There's Music," 1944
Tommy Dorsey and His Orchestra, Edythe Wright, "Music, Maestro, Please," 1938
Frank Sinatra, "The Music Stopped," 1943
Fred Waring's Pennsylvanians, "Soft Lights and Sweet Music," 1932
Tony Martin, "I Get Ideas," 1951
Johnny Desmond, "Dancing on a Dime," 2012
Ethel Merman, "Say It with Music," 1938
Karen Akers, "It's Time for a Love Song," 1997
Tony Bennett, "I Wanna Be Around," 1963

3

UNPREDICTABLE AND PREDICTABLE

Unpredictability is one thing, mischief another. Irving Berlin's "You'd Be Surprised" is a mischievous song that makes the case for unpredictability, especially in something as brief and as molded by convention as a popular song. In the 1920s and 1930s, such lyricists of the Great American Songbook as Berlin, Lorenz Hart, Ira Gershwin, Cole Porter, and E. Y. Harburg added spice to the brew. They longed to expand the limits of what they could do. Many of them loved to create surprise in their matching of syllable to note, words to melodies. They and their fellow lyricists mastered rhyme even though English has so few rhyming words compared to other Western languages.

Even so, they wrote lyrics with triple and quadruple rhymes and internal rhyme, and they invented rhymes when they had to. The best lyricists loved to rhyme. In fact, George and Ira Gershwin once wrote a song called, "I Love to Rhyme" (George Gershwin and Ira Gershwin, "I Love to Rhyme," 1937).

It starts simply enough before the rhyming threatens to overflow the limits of a single song. "I love to rhyme, / Mountaineers love to climb" sounds easy enough, but then the wordplay begins and the rhyming nearly overflows, from a third consecutive rhyme, "Criminals love to crime," to rhyming without end: "Capacity, veracity, audacity, / Did you ever know such fun?"

It feels almost as if Ira designed a tuneful lesson in rhyme for children set to George's inviting melody.[1]

The English comic novelist P. G. Wodehouse, who wrote American song lyrics with Jerome Kern in the 1910s and early 1920s, once told Ira Gershwin that his greatest challenge as a lyricist was finding three sets of triple rhymes for a single song. In "Shoes with Wings On," a song for Fred Astaire to perform in *The Barkley's of Broadway*, Gershwin faced just such a dilemma (Harry Warren and Ira Gershwin, "Shoes with Wings On," *The Barkleys of Broadway*, 1949).

He had already written "wing's on," "spring's on," and then repeated "wings on," as well as "glows up," "shows up," "close up" (which sings better than it reads). To solve his problem in the last chorus, he turned to a variation on something he'd already written, "wings on," "strings on," and "things on," followed by a final three lines that continue the short "i" sound: "And I go flying with 'em— / And the town is full of rhythm / And the world's in rhyme."

While there are probably hundreds of songs about music and melody, there are very few about rhyme. Maybe the lyricists don't want to give too much away. The lyricists Robert Wright and George Forrest set words to melodies by the Russian composer Alexander Borodin for the 1953 Broadway musical, *Kismet*. One of their songs, "Rhymes Have I," exceeds "A Rhyme for Angela" in its inventiveness (Robert Wright and George Forrest, "Rhymes Have I," *Kismet*, 1953).

A poet named Hajj sits in the marketplace in Mecca, trying to sell his rhymes. He explains, even boasts, about what he can do. He is, after all, a salesman. Wright and Forrest give full rein to the lyric's cleverness with language. Only this time, they're writing about language itself.

> An iota of iambic
> And a tittle of trochaic
> Added to a small amount of onomatopoeia.

Then Hajj shows off his "wares" in lines worthy of Gilbert and Sullivan's "Modern Major General":

> Sunny rhymes like virtue can hurt you,
> Learned rhymes, the camel's a mammal,
> And others very various on matters multifarious

The best lyricists prized wit; wordplay gave their songs a lift. No one loved to show off in rhyme more than Lorenz Hart. In 1925, the then-struggling Broadway production company the Theatre Guild asked him and his composing partner Richard Rodgers to write the songs for a revue designed to help raise money. The timing was serendipitous; after years of failure, Rodgers was just about ready to forsake music for a job as a salesman for a New Jersey underwear maker. The score that he and Hart wrote for what came to be called *Garrick Gaieties* included their first major song, "Manhattan." The next year, for a second edition of *Garrick Gaieties*, they wrote a sequel of sorts, "Mountain Greenery." Rodgers and Hart had arrived.

In "Manhattan," a young man shows the young woman he loves the wonders of New York, from the Battery to Coney Island, the Bronx Zoo to Delancey Street on the Lower East Side. In his lyric to "Mountain Greenery," about a newly married couple that leaves the city for the country (about which they know nothing), Hart invents a unique rhyme out of the blue, as if somebody dared him to do it (Richard Rodgers and Lorenz Hart, "Mountain Greenery," *Garrick Gaieties*, 1926). The result is funny, unpredictable, even dazzling. It's a city boy's way of saying how much he loves his new pastoral home: "Beans could get no keener re- / Ception in a beanery. / Bless our mountain greenery home!" I'm especially fond of the way that he extends the final line beyond the rhyme to land on the word "home" to remind the listener of what the song is really about.

Rodgers's music provides a setting for Hart's nonstop rhyming, but it contributes more than that. The composer and author Alec Wilder had a theory about what he called "the aggressiveness of repeated notes"[2]; he considers "Mountain Greenery" one of the best examples. The refrain's first four notes, "In our mountain . . ." are on the same pitch; it doesn't change until the end of the line. In the next line, the first words, "Where God paints the . . ." are also on the same pitch, but not the same pitch as the first line. In fact, they're a full octave apart. In other words, Rodgers achieves both consistency and variation at the same time. That sort of thing happens a lot in popular songs because it's a way to move a line along briskly while saving the emphasis for the rhyming words.

Overall, Rodgers keeps the melody simple because he knows that its effect will rest mainly on Hart's words and he doesn't want the melody to get in the way. The song's rhythm, however, is more complex and provides Hart with a way into the staccato lyric he matches to it. It starts with long notes that become shorter and shorter within a single line. It feels a little like a roller coaster that gains momentum until it slows to climb back up before gaining speed again. The opening line, "In our mountain greenery," moves from half notes to quarter to eighth before it slows to begin the second line and again accelerates: "Where God paints the scenery."

The lyric also shifts from momentary reflection in those two lines to a spontaneous bubbling up of delight: "Just two crazy people together."

The melody doesn't change tempo, but it feels as if it does. It feels free and spontaneous, bouncing lightly from measure to measure as a newlywed explodes with glee over where he finds himself with his bride. The song's inventiveness and youthful exuberance make it comic but also make room for emotion. In the end it is a celebratory love song that may require a listener to have been utterly in love to fully feel.

Lifelong New Yorkers born into comfortable families, Rodgers and Hart went to Columbia University mainly to write for the annual student-produced musicals. Once they began to work together in college and found their way professionally in the mid-twenties, Hart might set almost frenzied lyrics to Rodgers's lilting but bouncy romantic melodies. Although their Broadway scores were more sophisticated than such flapper songs of the day as "Ain't She Sweet" and "Five Foot Two," they helped to embody the joyful spirit of the age. It wasn't always easy. Both men drank heavily and Hart was a tortured gay man who believed that his work was worthless.

While they could write with amazing speed, Rodgers was contained and disciplined despite the drinking, while Hart would disappear on binges for days at a time. Aside from writing the music, Rodgers's main responsibility was getting the elusive Hart to settle down to work. At the start, though, they were young, their songs were youthful, and the books for their shows were frothy. For the next decade or two they turned out hit after hit, shows and songs alike, that conjure up again and again the frivolity of Flaming Youth that leads inevitably to a proposal of marriage.

Hart loved to see what he could get away with. A lot, it turned out. There was something antic about him, the large head atop his dwarf-like body. He stood only 4'10" tall. He gave off the aroma of a demon plagued by his own monsters, although there was also something sweet about him, a closeted gay man in a world that gave him no relief. His inner voice was bittersweet. It broke through from time in such love songs as "Falling in Love with Love" and "This Can't Be Love," both from *The Boys from Syracuse* in 1938.

Hart sets the lyrics of "Falling" to Rodgers's buoyant waltz, another example of a song in which words and music contrast ironically (Richard Rodgers and Lorenz Hart, "Falling in Love with Love," *The Boys from Syracuse*, 1938). Hart would sometimes set a lyric to one of Rodgers's soaring melodies to underscore the difference between what we expect from love and what we find. Present participles ("falling," "caring,"

Richard Rodgers and Lorenz Hart. New York Public Library. Public Domain.

"learning") set the song in the present, nod to the past, but also ease into the future. Some things never change. The music swirls as someone sings:

> Falling in love with love
> Is falling for make believe.

For this waltz, Rodgers composed an A section that keeps going over the same musical ground. The name for that kind of writing is strophic. He repeats a two-line musical phrase three different times, a step higher on the second use but then back to the initial pitch on the third. In something as familiar as a waltz, he creates both repetition and variety. At the same time, in the final line of the first A section, "Is playing the fool," Rodgers dips into a minor key: "Caring too much is such / A juvenile fancy." He moves back and forth between major and minor to play off an ebullient melody against a bittersweet lyric. A few lines farther into the song, "Learning to trust" begins in a minor key, returns to major with "just" and then back to the minor key for "school": "Learning to trust is just / For children in school."

Rhymes, near rhymes, assonance, and consonance mingle throughout Hart's lyric. The rhymes and internal rhymes pour out. Although "such" and "just" don't rhyme, "much" and "such" do, and all of them rely on the short "u" sound. The narrator sounds very blasé, very sophisticated. Only at the end does he admit that he's fallen in love with love itself, an everlasting love, "But love fell out with me." Then and only then does the music change to reflect the emotion in the lyric.

Rodgers never wants his melody to rest. He extends it as if it's one long melodic line divided into phrases, clauses, and sentences by Hart's lyric. Hart heard the unpredictability in Rodgers's airborne music and set to it a lyric that becomes ironic through contrast. Although the music came first, the song feels almost as if Rodgers somehow intuited Hart's words and designed a melody to parallel the unpredictability of love in the lyric. This unpredictable but perfect merging helps to understand Rodgers's ability to switch effortlessly when he worked with Oscar Hammerstein, who preferred to write the lyrics first.

In the second of the two songs, Hart borrows from the old courtly trope of love as an illness (Richard Rodgers and Lorenz Hart, "This Can't Be Love," *The Boys from Syracuse*, 1938). The lover loses his appetite, feels lethargic, and stops seeing his friends. He mopes about. Hart's lyric is a mock self-examination that uses love sickness to indicate the narrator's recovery. He's cured but he's also a romantic ready to fall again. That's what leads to the punch line:

> This can't be love,
> Because I feel so well—
> No sobs, No sorrows, No sighs.

In the last line, he finally confesses, "But still I love to look in your eyes."

Occasionally the inner Hart peeked through in his work, not with regret or bitterness, but with a level of wit and truth telling rare in a romantic ballad. This torch song written as a duet follows a lovers' quarrel. One of the lovers admits to being a fool:

> Very glad to be unhappy . . .
> Unrequited love's a bore,
> And I've got it pretty bad.
>
> (Richard Rodgers and Lorenz Hart, "Glad to
> Be Unhappy," *On Your Toes*, 1936)

The writing, rooted in talk, is clever enough: the paradoxical title followed by the headlong "fools rush in" and especially "unrequited love's a bore." You notice the line because it's showy but also creates character. Hart was capable of statements of compact wisdom that grew from a song's bittersweet context—something he learned about from his life and then applied to his songs. He didn't write about himself but he was in his lyrics. The character wallows in his own despair. It is a classic symptom of lovesickness.

At other times, the dark side of Hart erupted. The emotion is dark although the tone is ebullient. Like the narrator in "Glad to Be Unhappy," the character here admits that he's bored even though he's glad he's on his own (Richard Rodgers and Lorenz Hart, "I Wish I Were in Love Again," *Babes in Arms*, 1937). The surprise in the next to last line is worth the wait:

> The daily fights,
> The quick toboggan when you reach the heights—
> I miss the kisses and I miss the bites.

The second refrain is even darker, and has one extraordinary line whose barb digs deep as the lines play off against one another:

> The blackened eye,
> The words "I'll love you till the day I die,"
> The self-deception that believes the lie—

Rodgers, like Jerome Kern and Oscar Hammerstein, wanted to integrate the various parts of a musical into something knit tightly together with more complex characters who are, as a result, more believable. Kern had begun to move in that direction as early as his Princess Musicals in the late 1910s, but they remained loose jointed compared to what would come later, and the songs were often more interested in fun than feeling. As shows integrated more fully, songs created mood, deepened character, and advanced the story. Kern and Hammerstein had already achieved the goal in *Show Boat* in 1927, but they soon returned to the operetta-like musicals they had previously written. Rodgers and Hammerstein would continue the idea of the integrated musical with *Oklahoma!* in 1943 and their other shows through 1959, when Hammerstein died.

Hart, though, was content to write for the increasingly old-fashioned musical comedies, slap-dash affairs in which the songs added sparkle to the comedy. He was usually much more interested in making up rhymes rather than character or plot. Yet even in Rodgers and Hart's shows from the 1930s, they had begun to master the idea of character, one of the hallmarks of the Broadway musical during the time of the Great American Songbook. That was true even in songs not connected to a character in a show, but were Tin Pan Alley fare that had to stand on its own.

Songs had always had a character or narrator who "speaks" the lyric, but never more fully and emotionally defined than during the years of the Songbook. Because love is almost always the subject, point of view gives a song part of its distinctiveness. Consider the differences both musically and in the lyrics between "Glad to Be Unhappy" and "I Wish I Were in Love Again." Both characters are miserable but their worldviews could not be more different.

By 1940, Rodgers and Hart wanted to try something new. The world was tumbling into war and the national mood was darkening. When the novelist John O'Hara approached them about adapting his short novel *Pal Joey*, into a musical, they leaped at the idea. Even Hart seemed drawn to its darkness. They created in Joey the first antihero in a Broadway musical. Joey is a city boy, a con man, and a boor, but he's great in bed. When he begins an affair with Vera, a wealthy middle-aged woman, she knows exactly what she's getting: "He's a fool and don't I know it— / But a fool can have his charms." Those charms are entirely sexual. She adds later in the song, "Vexed again, / Perplexed

Gene Kelly and Vivienne Segal in Pal Joey. New York Public Library. Public Domain.

again, / Thank God I can be oversexed again—." It is one of the musical theater's great character soliloquies (Richard Rodgers and Lorenz Hart, "Bewitched, Bothered and Bewildered," *Pal Joey*, 1940). Yet Hart was mainly interested in internal rhymes, triple and quadruple rhymes, and in what he could get past the censors. If in the process he created a distinctive point of view, that was all to the good. On the other hand, in his inventiveness and his eagerness to show off, he sometimes undermined his own work.

Despite the show's relative darkness, Hart was not about to give up the sorts of things he loved to do. The challenge was to do them without losing a song's revelation of character. Hart often played the role of the cleverest kid in the room. He loved to show off, to scatter his attention-getting rhymes throughout his lyrics. His words were brilliant. Here's Hart at his best: the alliteration in the title "Bewitched, Bothered, and Bewildered" soon leads to more inventive wordplay—the triple rhyme, the internal rhyme, and the sudden change in mood to suggest that the final line is ironic and self-aware: "I'm wild again, / Beguiled again, / A simpering, whimpering child again." Rather than rhyming the final word in each line, he repeats it to suggest Vera's circumstance: a middle-aged woman involved with a younger man.

Hart rhymes the words that precede "again" with a particularly effective triple rhyme that underscores Vera's point of view ("wild," "beguiled," and "child") and then adds an internal rhyme ("simpering," "whimpering") to give even more emphasis to her knowing outlook. The shifts in tone continue through the song; Vera's sense of irony and her unwillingness to deceive herself come through clearly.

Hart could also crank out a generic love ballad whenever a plot line required it. Although the lyric to "Blue Moon" is a major standard, it's never been one of our favorites. Rodgers, though, believed in the melody—so much so that Hart wrote four different lyrics for it in the space of two years. His first try was for a 1933 movie in which Jean Harlow was supposed to sing it as her prayer to become a movie starlet. M.G.M. cut it from the final movie; they cut Harlow, too. Hart wrote the second lyric as the title number for the movie *Manhattan Melodrama* before its 1934 release. Next, the studio told Rodgers and Hart to write a nightclub number to the same melody for the same movie. Rodgers's work was finished but Hart came up with a torch ballad, "The Bad in Every Man." It, too, got snipped before release. Finally, Jack Robbins, the director of the studio's publishing company, decided that the song needed a more romantic lyric and a punchier title. And that led to "Blue Moon," the only Rodgers and

Hart song not introduced in a movie or show, and, ironically, their most successful song.

Yet aside from the image of the moon and a narrator who addresses the blue moon directly, the lyric is abstract and inflated (Richard Rodgers and Lorenz Hart, "Blue Moon," 1935). It is not the kind of song that shows Hart at his best, yet even here he pulled off a triple rhyme to try to add a little punch:

> You knew just what I was there for,
> You heard me saying a prayer for
> Someone I really could care for.

"Dancing on the Ceiling" is also a conventional AABA love ballad until the final shortened chorus, but Hart's lyric is more imaginative than "Blue Moon." Its verse does what verses are supposed to do: it establishes a character who has a reason to sing what's in the refrain. It provides dramatic context. A lonely young woman imagines her absent lover on the ceiling when she climbs into bed at night. She says she never sleeps but the boy "walks / Into my dreams and talks." The refrain that follows rests on the conceit that begins in the title and shapes the rest of the song. She tries to ward him off so she can sleep, but she's also "grateful to discover" that he's still on the ceiling that has become "a dancing floor / Just for / My love" (Richard Rodgers and Lorenz Hart, "Dancing on the Ceiling," *Evergreen*, 1931).

Aside from the twists and turns of the conceit, Hart relies on familiar patterns of rhyme and assonance. He seems to have been content to let the conceit do the work; otherwise, he wrote in a more restrained way than usual. Yet the first two lines, "He dances overhead / On the ceiling, near my bed," do create a sense of inevitability as long as Hart sustains the conceit.

No matter how predictable a song might be, something unpredictable gives the finished work greater vitality and even depth. Unpredictability contributes to how we hear it. A listener may not be able to explain how or why, but it adds to the pleasure.

We doubt that people think a lot about how craft combined with unpredictability can rise to the level of inevitability. You can evaluate the craft, but inevitability is the most subjective part of the response to a song. What we find inevitable may strike you as overwrought or self-important. But then you'll have your songs to substitute for ours. A sense of inevitability may work just under our awareness as listeners, but it does work. Sometimes it's essential to a song's success even if it means showing off just a little.

Ira Gershwin's fellow songwriters called him "The Jeweler" because he labored so meticulously over his lyrics, searching for just the right word, the right image, the right way to make an ordinary line distinctive. Like others of his kind, Ira loved words and their sounds, their ambiguities and suggestiveness, their precision. In "I've Got a Crush on You," a young woman speaks to her sweetheart, although it was a word Ira tried his best to avoid. It just didn't appeal to him. He had used "sweet" in several lyrics, but here he chose the juvenile-sounding "sweetie pie" (George Gershwin and Ira Gershwin, "I've Got a Crush on You," *Treasure Girl*, 1928). Today, some might see it as condescending—unless, of course, boy and girl are both very young and it's a private endearment. This is a case, circa 1928, of a girl chasing a boy. She persists until she gets him, so she sings in a state of youthful rapture. It's as if she's leaning in so nobody else can hear: "I've got a crush on you, / Sweetie Pie." She anticipates the "cottage we could share" as Ira sustains the feeling of youthful flirtation and sexiness through his word choices and his awareness of the tilt of "Sweetie Pie": "The world will pardon my mush / 'Cause I have got a crush, / My baby, on you."

The final line's insertion of "my baby" adds an insinuating touch as it completes the lyric's use of child-like language in a grown-up way. She's also not above a bit of showing off. Why wouldn't the young woman crow and show off too: "This isn't just a flirtation: / We're proving that there's predestination."

Ira creates an endearing mix of things to complete George's melody. It's also fascinating that both men might have misheard their own song. They intended it as an uptempo number and so it was until 1939 when Lee Wiley recorded it as a slow ballad.[3] When Ira heard it, he realized that it should have been sung that way right from the start—and as it has ever since.

Yet George's use of complex rhythms fits with their original intent to write an uptempo song. Ira's use of child-like language comes out of George's playful changes in rhythm: triplets, syncopation, and tied notes to shift the emphasis away from where you might expect it to be. In the title line, for example, George ties the note for "crush" to "on you." As a result, "on" starts a beat later. The delay helps to put more emphasis on "crush" and "you." Ira heard the words in the melody, the individual word to the specific note. That also helped him to hear the song differently from what he and George had originally written.

In a more significant word change by a different songwriter, Irving Berlin thought he had finished "All Alone," but he somehow felt he hadn't quite landed it (Irving Berlin, "All Alone," *The Music Box Revue of 1924*, 1924). Berlin believed that he would know when he had truly completed a song. He had originally begun the refrain, "All alone, / I am all alone." That's what was bothering him. He fretted over it for days before making a single change: "All alone, / I'm so all alone." That was all it took. He replaced repetition with a brief word that sustained the melancholy moan of "o" while intensifying the feeling. At the same time, he demonstrated his gift for simplicity and understatement. A less sure-handed songwriter might also have changed the notes in the new line to read (and sing), "I'm *so* all alone." Not Berlin. He understood that the key word in the line (and the song) is "alone," and the role of "so" is to deepen and anticipate it. The result was craft in the service of mastery.

Ira Gershwin, who thoroughly enjoyed his talent for wit and wordplay, decided to write a song for the 1927 musical *Funny Face* that would, in his words, "feature the sibilant sound effect by deleting the 'it' of 'it's' and slurring the leftover 's' with the first syllable of the following word"[4] (George Gershwin, Ira Gershwin, "'S Wonderful," *Funny Face*, 1927). That's why he wrote it even though it also had to suit two lovers in the midst of the flapper-dominated 1920s. Leading up to the writing, though, he was thinking about how to make the song distinctive. It's an exuberant love song, but he'd do anything to avoid coming out and saying, "I love you," something he hated to do.

> 'S Wonderful! 'S Marvelous!
> You should care for me!

Gershwin also dropped entire words and, in the process, created ambiguity. "You should care for me" begins with the dropping of the expected "that" as part of the narrator's wonder that she loves him. He appears to be telling her that he recognizes his good fortune: it's wonderful (that) "you should care for me." But with the word omitted, he's encouraging her to believe how wonderful it would be if she loved him. One is confident, the other hopeful, even eager, but also tentative.

He added to the effect by dropping letters and syllables. The result was romantic but light of touch, bordering on the silly, and—to coin a word—flapper-y, smack dab in the middle of the Roaring Twenties. Ira gave the duet's second verse to the woman, a flapper in full regalia, who immediately (and charmingly) starts by lopping off the beginnings and endings of words.

> When you said you care,
> 'Magine my emosh; . . .
> Permanent devosh.

Set to what Walter Rimler calls George Gershwin's natural, effortless melody,[5] it's hard to imagine it any other way. It feels spontaneous as if it were just waiting to be written down. Actually, George pulls it off through a lot of repetition, more than usual. In the release, though, the pitch leaps up when the narrator becomes more romantic. Ira, listening to what George wrote, hits the emphatic notes with "glamorous" and "amorous." In other words, inevitability, not as trickery but as an expression of a mutual sensibility in both men.

Nothing annoyed Ira Gershwin more than hearing someone sing, "It's wonderful! It's marvelous— / That you should care for me." He had reason to complain. He encountered the same problem in "That Certain Feeling," an appealing but lesser-known song that he and his brother wrote for *Tip-Toes* (George Gershwin and Ira Gershwin, "That Certain Feeling," *Tip-Toes*, 1925). The show opened only a few months after *Lady, Be Good*, their first Broadway collaboration. More than half a century later, he was still complaining about singers who miss what he called "the rhythmic point of the tune" by smoothing out the syncopation that starts a number of lines spread through George Gershwin's melody. Such lines as "the first time I met you," "I could not forget you," and "I've got what they call love," should be sung:

> (Beat) The first time I met you
> (Beat) I could not forget you.
> (Beat) I've got what they call love.

Anyone who's performed George Gershwin's melodies should have recognized that he placed syncopation at the heart of American music. America, he wrote, "is all colors and souls unified in the great melting pot of the world. Its dominant note is vibrant syncopation."[6]

If anybody equaled Ira Gershwin's linguistic mischief making, it was the impish E. Y. Harburg. He even looked impish. Born Isadore Hochberg, he eventually changed his name to Edgar Yipsel Harburg and soon acquired the nickname of Yip. That sort of name changing (and shape shifting) to sound more American was common among immigrants, especially Jews and Italians. Some explanations say that Yip came from Harburg's choice of Yipsel, Yiddish for squirrel, as his middle name. He was small and darted from place to place, both physically and intellectually. Others say that he borrowed it from the Yiddish acronym of the Young Men's Socialist League. He belonged when he was young, though he was never much of a joiner.

A political activist and left-wing romantic, Harburg grew up in a Yiddish-speaking family on Manhattan's Lower East Side, poorer even than the Gershwins. He and Ira met as students at Townsend Harris High School in Kips Bay on Manhattan's East Side. Years later, Harburg said that Ira "was the shyest, most diffident boy we had ever known. In a class of lower east side rapscallions, his soft-spoken gentleness and low-keyed personality made him a lovable incongruity. He spoke in murmurs, hiding behind a pair of steel-rimmed glasses. Ira had a kid brother who wore high stiff collars, shirts with cuffs and went out with girls."[7]

The two teenagers discovered a shared fondness for W. S. Gilbert's lyrics, worked on the school newspaper, and became lifelong friends. One day, Gershwin invited Harburg to his family's apartment so they could listen to recordings of Gilbert and Sullivan's songs. Harburg was dumbstruck. He had no idea that Gilbert had given his words to Arthur Sullivan to set to music. He and Gershwin would listen for hours.

During World War I, Harburg fled the country as a conscientious objector. The political climate was not good for those who believed in civil liberties. On his return, he and some friends opened an electrical appliance company that prospered before it folded early in the Depression. By the end of the twenties, Gershwin was a famous lyricist and Harburg was broke. But dating back to their high school years, both of them admired the popular light verse of the day and wrote it with some success. Harburg felt rootless, though. One day, Gershwin asked him if he owned a pencil, handed him a rhyming dictionary, and told him to get busy. Gershwin then introduced him to the composer Jay Gorney, who was writing songs for several Broadway revues.

In 1932, Gorney and Harburg collaborated on a flop called *Americana*, but the score included Harburg's first important song, "Brother, Can You Spare a Dime?" (Jay Gorney and E. Y. Harburg, "Brother, Can You Spare a Dime?" *Americana*, 1932). So important that you might even call it essential, especially during the Depression. Fifteen years later, for the successful musical *Bloomer Girl*, he and Harold Arlen wrote another strong anthem, this time for an African American slave: "We gotta be free / The eagle and me" (Burton Lane and E. Y. Harburg, "The Eagle and Me," *Bloomer Girl*, 1944). Harburg had the kind of range we expect from all the composers and lyricists of the Great American Songbook. Tell them what you need and they'll write it. Even without being told, there was no kind of song they wouldn't try and usually master.

After *Americana* closed, Harburg and Gorney moved to Hollywood where Harburg collaborated with a number of composers including Jerome Kern, Jule Styne, Vernon Duke, Burton Lane, and Harold Arlen. In the course of his career, he worked with forty-eight different composers, some for a one-night stand, others for years. He once explained his peripatetic career:

> I always liked trying on a new style . . . I'm a chameleon. I love putting myself into everyone else's shoes—and each composer lends me a pair.[8]

He and Arlen wrote the complete score to *The Wizard of Oz*, including the dazzlingly clever "If I Only Had a Brain," "If I Only Had a Heart," and "If I Only Had the Nerve" for the Scarecrow, Tin Woodsman, and Cowardly Lion, respectively. Arlen didn't know what Harburg would write because both men preferred that the music come first, but he did know the characters as well as the context within the movie. He recognized that he needed to provide a flexible melody that would fit each of the three of them and to which Harburg could set a comic lyric. He kept the harmony simple as he constructed a bouncy melody that skips up and down, with a few full octave jumps to add variety and drama, and to give Harburg more to work with. In the refrain the Scarecrow sings: "And my head I'd be scratchin' / While my thoughts were busy hatchin'," in which the melody jumps an octave between "head" and "I'd" and between "were" and "busy." The mood of the music is consistently upbeat even though the three characters are shaped by longing.

The standard AABA melody doesn't change from one character to the next, but Harburg adapts the lyric to fit the character who sings it. He gives each of them his own language of emotion by stretching and distorting words for the sake of comic rhyming, and to suggest that these three aren't quite human yet. There's a bit of Pinocchio in their need to find the wizard.

For the wobbly-legged, straw-brained Scarecrow (the eccentric dancer Ray Bolger), Harburg plays with language in a slightly addled way: "And perhaps I'd deserve you / And be even worthy erv you / If I only had a brain." For the gentle soul of the Tin Woodsman (Jack Haley), he invests sadness with an animating touch of wit: "When a man's an empty kettle / He should be on his mettle / And yet I'm torn apart." For the Lion (the irrepressible vaudeville comic Bert Lahr), Harburg lets the language fly: "But I could show my prowess, / Be a lion, not a mowess, / If I only had the nerve"—which Lahr insisted on pronouncing "noive." Harburg said of working on the score to *The Wizard of Oz*, "I loved the idea of having the freedom to do lyrics that were not just songs but scenes."[9]

Songs seem to have lost their sense of humor since the 1950s. If the sensibility is adolescent, and even the adult songwriters and singers have forgotten that love and sex can be both precious and ridiculous, it's no wonder that more recent songs take themselves so seriously. The songwriters of the Great American Songbook took their work seriously, but there was always room for inventiveness and a verbal prank.

Throughout his career, the cranky but impish side of Harburg's personality appeared and reappeared in his songs. He brought a different dimension to the Great American Songbook. Today, protest songs are a recognizable part of popular music. Not then. He was a committed social reformer and idealist who set out to write song lyrics about the causes he believed in: warfare, civil rights, women's rights. He learned quickly to combine his sense of purpose with audience appeal. Better to write lighthearted satire to try to persuade a packed house night after night than a polemic to reach fifty who already agreed with you. He learned to attack what he saw as injustice or puncture bloated egos with wit. For an overriding image of his ultimate optimism, he chose the rainbow. He created fantasy worlds where, one way or another, dreams might come true but staying true to the dream—following the rainbow—was essential.

Everybody knows "Over the Rainbow," but some may not know that Arlen and Harburg wrote it. Generations of Americans may also not know the circumstances of its composition or the need that it met—a song for Judy Garland in *The Wizard of Oz*, written almost as an afterthought—but we hold the song close. We recognize its melancholy but intuit its subtext of hope. More than eighty years later, few of us fail to recognize it. Most of us can sing it as well (Harold Arlen and E. Y. Harburg, "Over the Rainbow," *The Wizard of Oz*, 1939).

It is arguably the best-known and best-loved of all American songs in its empathy for a lonely child; its ability to create images that would feel at home in a story for children ("lemon drops," "chimney tops," and "happy little bluebirds"); its soaring but gently sad melody for a singer of power and vulnerability like Garland; and its reliance on Harburg's favorite image of the rainbow to insist on hope no matter how remote it may feel.

More than Berlin or Hart, certainly more than Porter, and even more than Hammerstein, Harburg could draw on the language of childhood without becoming insipid.

At first Arlen struggled to find a suitable melody. Frustrated, he took a drive with his wife to clear his head and suddenly heard in his inner ear a melancholy, questioning, yet somehow uplifting melody. He raced home to write it down before he lost it. Not unlike other songs by Arlen, it begins with an octave jump, this time in its very first word, from "some" to "where." The melody then emphasizes step-like movements to suggest Dorothy's mix of emotions and often shifts from major to minor keys to reflect her loneliness and doubt. The emotions are there but they become explicit only in Harburg's lyric.

Both men knew that Dorothy would sing this song in the farmyard after the adults have banished her because they are busy. Her mean, frozen-faced neighbor bicycles past to make things worse. Dorothy, lonely and fearful, retreats into a dream world accompanied by the three hired hands who appear to be her only friends. Only Auntie Em, her bedrock, remains behind; she is someone to come home to. The rest Dorothy redefines as part of the quest for Oz. They include the neighbor who becomes the Wicked Witch of the West and the peddler who becomes the wizard, a scoundrel and snake oil salesman in different garb. She has also entered a world where the way to triumph is to overcome fear. In this context Dorothy sings one of the great anthems of the Great Depression, a song of loneliness combined with the courage to dream of an uncertain but hopeful future.

Harburg continued to work in Hollywood but often returned to Broadway, where he wrote his most important show, *Finian's Rainbow*, with the composer Burton Lane, in 1947. He was blacklisted during the McCarthy years even though he was never a member of the Communist Party. He was inducted into the Songwriter's Hall of Fame in 1972.

When the early twentieth-century star Al Jolson sang the maudlin ballads that he loved, he would bite off his consonants, roll his Rs, and add a syllable to the end of many of his lines. By 1936, after Jolson's star had begun to dim, Harburg was ready to twit him in a song for the Jolson vehicle, *The Singing Kid*. Harburg relied largely on internal rhyme to make fun of Jolson's euphemistic nickname from early in his career. People called him a "mammy singer"; all those maudlin songs about Dixie:

> I love to wake up with the South-a in my mouth-a . . .
> With a cheer for Uncle Sammy and another for my mammy,
> I love to sing!
>
> (Harold Arlen and E. Y. Harburg,
> "I Love to Sing-a," *The Singing Kid*, 1936)

Harburg's joking at Jolson's expense continues with the added-on syllable ("sing-a") both on the same note to suggest not an Italian American dialect but an overly formal, by-then-hokey style of singing. Harburg sets all this to Arlen's music.

Just as Ira Gershwin loved to drop syllables at the beginnings and ends of words, so Harburg loved to add suffixes ("I Love to Sing-a") but most notably in a free-for-all about a free-for-all called "You're a Builder-Upper" (Harold Arlen, E. Y. Harburg, and Ira Gershwin, "You're a Builder-Upper," *Life Begins at 8:40*, 1934). One of the best Broadway revues of the Depression, *Life Begins at 8:40* had an unlikely beginning. The short-tempered Harburg and the even more irascible Vernon Duke had parted ways after clashing during their collaboration on *The Ziegfeld Follies of 1934*, after which Harburg invited Arlen to work with him on the new revue he'd been asked to write. Arlen, who'd been writing mainly for the Cotton Club's all-Black revues in Harlem, leaped at the chance to write a show for Broadway. Meanwhile, Ira Gershwin was largely idle because George was working with Dubose Hayward on *Porgy and Bess*. Harburg invited his old friend to join him as colyricist.

Gershwin and Harburg collaborated on the words, but this lyric's use of suffixes makes us think that Harburg did most of the work on it. It's one of the great lover's quarrels set to music. It's also a tribute to inconsistency as it indulges in a bit of comic masochism. Even so, the two people can't help loving one another. It starts with "you build me up and you break me down" and ends with "but I'm a stooge for your charms." The lovers even like the way they push one another around. Written as a duet, the song has one of them complain and then the other, but it all ends happily: "Sad but true, I love it I do, / Being broken by a builder-upper like you." From time to time, the song extends a line's final "you" over two notes so it's "you-oo." Even when Harburg doesn't add a suffix, he creates the same effect.

The lyric seems to stagger along, leading with a kind of logic to the use of alliteration and extended words ("Being broken by a builder-upper like yoo-oo"). That is, Harburg's jagged words probably derive from the uneven rhythms that Arlen had learned from jazz and the blues. Each time that Harburg adds "er" to a word—"You're a builder-upper, . . . / and I'm a giver-inner"—he takes advantage of the way the music bumps along rhythmically. It frequently moves back and forth between two notes, and Arlen's frequent use of dotted notes helped Harburg hear the extended words he relied on.

Most of the time, Harburg tacked his suffixes onto comic songs, but in *Finian's Rainbow*, he tried it with a romantic ballad (Burton Lane and E. Y. Harburg, "Something Sort of Grandish," *Finian's Rainbow*, 1947). He loved to shake songs out of their predictability even though this song's structure is the conventional AABA. His use of language could easily have sounded false, but he turned it into a comic ballad sung by Og the leprechaun. The other leprechauns have sent Og to America to find the gold that an Irishman named Finian stole from them and buried in the mythical state of Missitucky. After spending so much time around humans, Og finds that he's beginning to have feelings, including love and desire. He falls for Finian's daughter Sharon, the musical's main character. His song to her is sincere but he hasn't quite got everything straight yet, especially with the English language.

> Or we could be, oh so bride and groomish
> Skies could be so bluish blue.
> Life could be so love in bloomish

But he is, without a doubt, sincere, and Harburg turns his mistakes into a witty conclusion based in wordplay: "If my ishes could come true."

Burton Lane wrote some fine songs over the years, mainly in Hollywood, among them "Everything I Have Is Yours," "How About You," "It's Time for a Love Song," and "I Hear Music." His music reflected his own self-deprecating manner. It evoked emotion but it rarely showed off. In "Something Sort of Grandish," Lane is content to get out of the way once he provides a setting for Harburg's clever lyric. Everything about it is simple. It stays in major keys, and the rhythm is always on the beat. The melody skips occasionally, although it usually relies on the familiar first, third, and fifth notes of each chord. He seems to understand here and elsewhere what kind of melody he was written and what kind of lyric the music calls forth, especially in the context of a Broadway musical with a plot, a character, and a set of circumstances to consider.

The leprechaun Og realizes that he's becoming human when he's attracted to two different women at the same time. Like humans, he ponders his conundrum. If this is what it means to be human, he's all for it. Harburg doesn't use suffixes here but he does turn to his old trick of rearranging familiar words. He also brings on a new trick that he's especially fond of. It's an obscure figure of speech known as chiasmus, in which the writer repeats words, phrases, clauses, or sentences in reverse order. In Harburg's hands, it's an unvarnished delight that gives Og's song its title, structure, and wit: "When I'm not near the girl I love," he sings and then adds in the next line, "I love the girl I'm near." The wordplay doesn't stop there: "When I can't fondle the hand I'm fond of, / I fondle the hand at hand" (Burton Lane and E. Y. Harburg, "When I'm Not Near the Girl I Love," *Finian's Rainbow*, 1947). This is the complex playing with a word's sounds and its range of meanings that signifies the unique style of E. Y. Harburg.

Like Ira Gershwin, Harburg hated to come out and say, "I love you." It was the admission to himself that he had failed. He once observed, "I doubt that I can ever say 'I love you' head on. It's not the way I think. For me the task is never to say the thing directly, and yet to say it—to think in a curve, so to speak."[10] He could write conventional ballads though on his own terms. He used imagery of theatrical make believe in "Paper Moon"; well-known references for a love song to a city in "April in Paris" even though he'd never been there; and a touching bit of romantic time travel for what he and Arlen thought was their greatest song together, "Last Night When We Were Young."

In other words, they thought it was better than "Over the Rainbow," "It's Only a Paper Moon," and "Happiness Is Just a Thing Called Joe." For a song so laden with loss, the song is unusually straightforward with barely a metaphor to build on. One of the gifts of the Songbook's songwriters was their adaptability. The lyricists understood that their task was to complete what the composers had written, not only by fitting words to notes but by creating something to stand on its own emotionally, to connect the concreteness of language to the emotional suggestiveness of music.

In "Last Night When We Were Young," Harburg creates the song's paradox in the title and alludes to it throughout (Harold Arlen and E. Y. Harburg, "Last Night When We Were Young," 1935). Yet in a song so powerful yet delicate, he was wise enough not to rely on verbal gymnastics. He used some internal rhyme along with alliteration and assonance, but he also muted them. No razzle dazzle to call attention to itself but open vowels to shape the lyric and give it air: love as "a star" and "a song" that was "so real, so right" that it remains vivid for the narrator years later. Harburg's lyric feels like a natural extension of Arlen's music, as if both spring to life together.

Arlen sets up a distinctively complex rhythmic pattern, alternating dotted notes with triplets to give the melody an unsettled feeling. He also uses a false cadence that Harburg recognized as a way to emphasize his lyric's shifting sense of time to express the sense of what Harburg's biographers call "sudden, transformative loss."[11] At the end of the first two A sections, the listener expects the lines "life was so new, so real, so right, / Ages ago" to end each chorus. But Arlen extends the line by two notes as he did in "You're a Builder-Upper" and elsewhere. He gave Harburg room to add the words "last night," thereby circling back to the first words of the chorus and posing the central emotional paradox in a single line, "Ages ago last night." In something as brief as a popular song, that kind of minimal shift in the hands of masters can have a powerful emotional effect.

The song's sense of loss is palpable. It is inseparable from time both motionless and in motion at the same time. The narrator remembers the great love of his life so many years ago although it feels like no more than a moment. The two times interweave with one another as he remembers "last night / When we were young." The recurring paradox lies in the failure of love and the persistence of loss as the song moves through familiar images, the nature of time both actual and emotional, and the ever-fresh memories of what the narrator has lost. Yet Harburg's particular use of language instills present and past alike with immediacy: "Love was a star." A familiar enough reference, but it was also "a song unsung," filled with possibility. That double perspective—looking back now but also able to capture how it felt then—makes it "so real, so right." Time was nothing to fear although it has grown cold and the star has faded since "ages ago, / Last night." You won't realize it when you hear the song, but Harburg laid out the lines in ways that separate the two different times—always together but always apart:

> Life was so new,
> So real, so right,
> Ages ago,
> Last night.

The release that begins "to think" is the most dramatic of the four choruses, yet here the song also remains quiet, even constrained. Shaped by the closed vowel "i," it enables the narrator to reconsider the possibility he felt in his youth. He finds in it an image of spring and his continuing wonder at the fragility of all it represents. He imagines love's dependence on nothing more than a look or kiss, and the ease with which "something so splendid / Could slip away / In one little daybreak." The short, separated lines isolate "could slip away." The rhyme and assonance come close to being mute, yet the words woven to Arlen's heartrending melody render the song unforgettable. The look and kiss, destined to last forever, dissolve in nothing longer than a breath.

This song of memory resides in the present and the past but never considers the future. Perhaps the narrator is too caught up in the emotion of loss or too old to dream of tomorrow. He speaks to "you" and about "we" but never mentions himself. Especially in the final chorus, the twosome in "we" appears to be together; the song feels more like a dramatic monologue than a soliloquy. All that remains is to tell the story and remember the increasingly ardent "sighs and the kisses / The arms that clung."

Because Arlen so often departed from the conventional refrain of four choruses of equal length, Harburg had to be on his toes. Here, though, Arlen appears to play pretty much by the rules except for adding three final lines with an entirely different melody. That makes the song AABAC. Although Arlen's ending is hushed, Harburg's final rhyme ends with a reminder of the song's sense of time that passes—but doesn't.

Although he was masterful at the creation of heartbreak, Harburg much preferred to turn love on its ear in such songs as "Down with Love," "Buds Won't Bud," and "Poor You." He was the master of the turn of phrase and the tour de force. In "Poor You," he relies on cleverness to make the song memorable. He's always playing off against the unconventional within the conventional. Here he plays an engaging mirror game:

> When it is you I'm kissing, . . .
> You don't know what you're missing,
> For you're only kissing poor me.
>
> (Burton Lane and E. Y. Harburg, "Poor You," *Ship Ahoy*, 1942)

"Down with Love," Harburg's witty rejection of love, relies on the quickness of his phrases set to the tripping melody that Arlen gave him

(Harold Arlen and E. Y. Harburg, "Down with Love," *Hooray for What!*, 1937). He was also the master of the set-up, especially here where he writes a line that you expect, jostles you with a surprise, and then follows it up at breakneck speed until the end.

> Down with eyes romantic and stupid,
> Down with sighs,
> Down with Cupid.

You can barely keep up as the lyric races from a cliché to a whirlwind of wit. Every sentence ends with its own punch line:

> Brother, let's stuff that dove,
> Down with love!

Not only are the lines unpredictable in a musical world in which love is the highest goal, but they're set to Arlen's rollicking melody and embody the mastery of craft that we keep returning to.

Harburg was not an in-your-face lyricist like Lorenz Hart. They were both driven by their desire to turn the language topsy-turvy, but Harburg's lyrics were generally less intrusive because they were tied to character or circumstance. Somebody is talking to somebody in the cleverest sort of way. On the other hand, Hart wrote in the show-me-what-you've-got twenties while Harburg began his career a decade later.

Speaking of a tour de force from the twenties, it's hard to believe that anybody could top Harry Woods's 1926 sensation "When the Red, Red Robin Comes Bob, Bob, Bobbin' Along" (Harry Woods, "When the Red, Red Robin Comes Bob, Bob, Bobbin' Along," 1926). Its ebullience never slows, never releases its hold on the listener. The tune is bouncy and the rhymes and repetitions weave what sounds like nonsense into one of the most irresistible of all the pollyanna songs. The song couldn't be simpler, more engaging—or more unpredictable and complicated in how Woods pulls it off.

Right from the start, the combination of rhyme, alliteration, and repetition in the "red, red robin" that comes "bobbin' along" creates an immediate effect on mood: "There'll be no more sobbin' / When he starts throbbin'." Yet Woods is far from finished. He still has repetition, internal rhyme, alliteration, and two-word rhymes ("kid again" and "did again") up his sleeve, all of them set to a melody that never lets you sit still.

The melody, helped by the lyric, has a natural swing to it. The cheery tune, set to a moderately quick tempo, skillfully mixes steps, skips, and same notes to move things right along but always with a touch of pizzazz. As we've said many times, most songs have an AABA structure. Woods is obviously aware of it, but he manipulates it for his own ends. For example, he extends each of the first two lines of all five A sections. In the second line of the first A, he repeats the word "along" by using two notes that skip up the scale. The second A has a similar jump, as he rhymes "along" with "sweet song."

> When the red, red robin
> Comes bob, bob, bobbin' along, along

followed by

> There'll be no more sobbin'
> When he starts throbbin' his old, sweet song.

In addition to the along/song rhyme, he also adds some zip with an internal rhyme in the same lines, "robin" with "bobbin'" with "sobbin'" with "throbbin'." He then repeats the same pattern in the third and fourth A sections, beginning with a contracted "flow'rs" in the third so it rhymes with "hours" in the fourth.

The release that follows the second A reverses the rising sequences of the first two A sections. These A sections watch the robin with delight and anticipate its effect, but the release lets the robin speak for itself. Its lines pack their punch at the beginning—"Get up," "Wake up," "Cheer up"—and then descend to the robin's final bit of advice in a series of emphatic notes: "Live, love, laugh and be happy."

With the return to a third A, the outlook changes. Rather than talking about and then to the robin, the narrator speaks more personally. The encounter has changed his mood, perhaps permanently. That change extends through yet another A before the addition of a C takes him back to the innocence of boyhood that he sees as his way forward. Those lines are in a minor key to distinguish them from what precedes and follows. The song sounds as if it's finished, but Woods still has more to do. He adds an A to repeat a very slightly shorter version of the song's opening as the source of his new delight.

No one would call Woods a major songwriter, although he did give us songs that many people still remember, among them "Paddlin' Madeline

Home," "Side by Side," and "Try a Little Tenderness." He was also an accidental songwriter. Born with no fingers on his left hand, he managed to become a competent one-handed piano player. He passed the time at home and at Harvard by writing popular songs for his own entertainment. When "Red, Red Robin" suddenly became a hit, he decided to give up the life of a gentleman farmer to become a professional songwriter. He was one of the few from the time who usually wrote both words and music. As always, time shapes each of his hit songs. "Paddlin' Madeline Home" is about something that has been going on, is going on, and implicitly will continue (Harry Woods, "Paddlin' Madeline Home, 1925), "Side by Side," set in the present, looks forward to the future (Harry Woods, "Side by Side," 1927). "Try a Little Tenderness" offers good advice for what comes next and the best way to meet it (Harry Woods, Jimmy Campbell, and Reg Connelly, "Try a Little Tenderness," 1932).

Past, present, future, and the way a single song mixes them within its limits is an essential part of the story of the Great American Songbook. Circumstances may vary unpredictably, but time is inescapable because songs exist within time. More often than not, those in which it never stirs feel limited to the present. Yet all the people and parts—from the composer sitting down to write the first bars of music to the listener streaming on a smartphone—coalesce within the finished song to become newborn. The predictable is an essential part of every song, but so is the unpredictable. Songs bounce between the familiar and the surprising. Between them, they join song to listener in a way that comes alive—for at least three minutes at a time.

RECORDINGS

Bobby Short, "I Love to Rhyme," 1957
Fred Astaire, "Shoes with Wings On," 1949
Alfred Drake, "Rhymes Have I," 1953
Tony Bennett, "Manhattan," 1976
Susan Egan, Brian d'Arcy James, "Mountain Greenery," 1999
Rebecca Luker, "Falling in Love with Love," 1998
Jonathan Dokuchitz, Erin Dilly, "This Can't Be Love," 2002
Kay Coulter, Joshua Shelley, "Glad to Be Unhappy," 1954
Christopher Fitzgerald, Jessica Stone, "I Wish I Were in Love Again," 1990
Vivienne Segal, "Bewitched, Bothered and Bewildered," 1951

Ella Fitzgerald, "Blue Moon," 1994
Frank Sinatra, "Dancing on the Ceiling," 1998
Julie London, "I've Got a Crush on You," 1967
Chaim Tannenbaum, "All Alone," 2013
Peggy Lee, "'S Wonderful," 1949
Layton and Johnstone, "That Certain Feeling," 1926
Dooley Wilson, "The Eagle and Me," 1944
Ray Bolger, "If I Only Had a Brain," 1939
Jack Haley, "If I Only Had a Heart," 1939
Burt Lahr, "If I Only Had the Nerve," 1939
Judy Garland, "Over the Rainbow," 1939
Al Jolson, "I Love to Sing-a," 1936
Harold Arlen, "You're a Builder-Upper," 1934
David Wayne with Ella Logan, "Something Sort of Grandish," 1947
David Wayne, "When I'm Not Near the Girl I Love," 1947
Frank Sinatra, "Last Night When We Were Young," 2010
Frank Sinatra, Tommy Dorsey Orchestra, "Poor You," 1942
Audra McDonald, "Down with Love," 1998
Whispering Jack Smith, "When the Red, Red Robin Comes Bob, Bob, Bobbin' Along," 1926
Cliff Edwards, "Paddlin' Madeline Home," 1925
Nick Lucas, "Side by Side," 1944
Frank Sinatra, "Try a Little Tenderness," 1946

4

MEMORY AND ANTICIPATION

Yes of course Noel Coward is English and this is a book about American music, but a line from *Private Lives*, his most important play, is too good to ignore: "Strange," the character of Amanda says, "how potent cheap music is." By itself, it sounds much more negative than it actually is. The one-time lovers Amanda and Elyot run into one another several years after their affair ended. They loved each other deeply but their sharp tongues and fiery temperaments eventually drove them apart. Neither has been happy since, and they are now about thirty even though they've never quite grown up. They have just married other people and are on their honeymoons when they encounter one another on adjoining hotel balconies. It's one of those extravagantly artificial scenes that Coward wrote with such a sure comic touch that it carries its audience with it.

After the shock of the encounter subsides, Amanda and Elyot begin to chat. They take some easy swipes at one another's new spouses followed by awkward silences. The orchestra in the dining room below continues to play the same song throughout. Although the script doesn't call for it, most of the productions we've seen use Coward's aptly titled "Someday I'll Find You."

> Elyot: That orchestra has a remarkably small repertoire.
>
> Amanda: They don't seem to know anything but this, do they?
>
> Elyot: No.
>
> Amanda: Strange how potent cheap music is.[1]

The line is songwriter Coward's joke on himself, but Amanda is also right about popular music. A single song played just within their hearing is part of the mix that will renew their affair. Somehow or other, many popular songs are both maudlin and moving at the same time. A good song holds us, not because we're necessarily a mawkish lot, but because something genuine infuses it despite its easy sentimentality and flirtation with banality. Coward also observed, "In my early 20s and 30s it was from America that I gained my greatest impetus. In New York they have always taken light music seriously. There, it is, as it should be, saluted as a specialized form of creative art, and is secure in its own right."[2]

Irving Berlin wrote his first ballad of any consequence in 1912. In that same year, he had met and married a young woman named Dorothy Goetz. She was the sister of a friend and fellow songwriter named E. Ray Goetz, best known eventually (with Edgar Leslie) for the lyric to the 1917 standard "For Me and My Gal." Dorothy was going into show business and wanted to introduce a new song by Berlin, a year after he found wealth and fame with "Alexander's Ragtime Band." He offered her a song but also asked her for a date. Some months later they married. They honeymooned in Cuba, where she contracted typhoid fever. Six months after their wedding, she died.

Berlin was devastated. He could no longer write. If he could not produce hit songs, what would become of him? Would he still be Irving Berlin? Songwriting had freed him from the poverty and the social and emotional constraints of the Lower East Side. With "Alexander's Ragtime Band" already behind him, the immigrant from Tsarist Russia had become the all American boy by the time he was twenty-three. And then this.

His friend Ray Goetz took him to Europe to help him shake off his torpor. It didn't work. Finally, Berlin found his own way. It's not surprising that he found relief once he could channel his despair into a popular song. Although few of the songs from his long career were personal, weaving together notes and words was what he knew how to do. "When I Lost You" was his first significant ballad and one of his most personal songs. It also freed him to write again. He followed it immediately with one of his most successful ragtime songs, "When the Midnight Choo-Choo Leaves for Alabam'." Still grieving, how could he write such a cheery song? In the course of this book, that's one of the questions we've been trying to answer.

"When I Lost You" echoes what Amanda says about popular music: it's cheap and potent—mawkish and moving—at the same time. Berlin's short lament is the setting for a series of images that express the narrator's

Irving Berlin and Dorothy Goetz. Library of Congress. Public Domain.

sense of loss. They are familiar and simple, little more than a list of clichés, but Berlin was taking his first tentative steps toward mastering a songwriter's need to turn the familiar into something fresh and toward his own mastery of the simplicity that was at the heart of his work. In the long run he was the great master of believable emotionalism born of simplicity (Irving Berlin, "When I Lost You," 1912).

When a single individual writes both words and music, who knows which comes first, although we suspect that this song's emotion begins in the lyric. It feels like talk despite its slightly purple coloration. At the very start of his career, Berlin wrote only the words because he hadn't yet learned to play the piano, however minimally. The narrow range of the music feels as if it follows the rhythms of the talk. It rests not only on a slow tempo but Berlin's use of three-quarter time. To express his own sorrow, he returned to this singular moment in his recent past, and to waltz time, as the notes glide effortlessly along the scale. He laid out a mournful melody, slow of tempo, and so simple and straightforward that it feels as if he picked it out note by note using nothing more than an index finger.

The lyric consists largely of recognizable allusions, usually from memory and always in the service of grief. They are immediately familiar to everyone but they begin as Berlin's—or at least stand in for his, what the poet T. S. Eliot called the objective correlative. Every line begins, "I lost" to carry us loosely through the seasons, from "sunshine and roses" to "the whole winter through."

The allusions, a mix of the everyday and the elevated—sunshine, roses, heavens, and rainbow—become less observational and more personal toward the end when the speaker turns to the kind of sentimental hyperbole we expect in the most romantic lyrics: "I lost the angel who gave me / Summer the whole winter through." Ultimately, the song concludes with an internal rhyme that summarizes what has happened—"I lost the gladness that turned into sadness"—followed by the final line that joins place (sunshine, roses, et al.) to time, the present to the recent past.

In its brevity and its ability to make its final lines fulfill the lyric rather than merely end it, Berlin achieved something akin to the close of an English sonnet. The last two lines, despite their abstract language, are a brief dramatic culmination of what precedes. He would probably have seen the comparison as artsy-fartsy. Yet the lyric is an early example of Berlin's economy of line both verbal and musical that evokes something beyond mere statement. Everything turns on the single word, "When," a word about time. It follows the brief rhymed summary in the previous line and provides an incremental conclusion to the six preceding lines that begin, "I lost." "When" also allows him to give greater emphasis to "I," transforming it into a cry of grief. The sense of loss is no longer a recitation but a memory that the narrator cannot escape—"When I lost you." Ironic, though, that a song bemoaning immeasurable loss should free Berlin to begin to live again.

Twenty-five years later, the lyricist Eric Maschwitz wrote a similar kind of song, less "cheap" but more "potent." The writing is more skillful than Berlin's was in 1912. The references are appealing but also inventive and touching. Maschwitz was thirty-five when he wrote, Berlin only twenty-three, and popular songs in the thirties were generally more sophisticated than they had been two decades earlier. Maschwitz constructs a list of apparently random associations, from "a cigarette that bears a lipstick's traces" to "the 'Ile de France' with all the gulls around it" to "the smile of Garbo and the scent of roses." Some are ordinary—"A fairground's painted swings"—but most have a touch of elegance as in "a tinkling piano in the next apartment." Regardless, each of them is insignificant, but that's the point. They're all it takes to spring the memories (James Strachey, Harry Link, and Eric Maschwitz, "These Foolish Things," *Spread It Around*, 1936).

The lines are word paintings that float up in the narrator's mind. Although he remembers in the present, the fond memories continue to pain him because he can't escape them, a kind of insistent musing on what used to be, made more vivid by the use of tense. Yet most of the memories consist of phrases; they have no verbs. They are still and persistent as he remembers them. Nothing about them ever changes. They exist beyond time.

The song's reinvention of the familiar is compelling: the playing off of opposites to suggest how things were then and how they are now. The narrator remembers a cigarette that "bears" traces of lipstick with its suggestion of weight and endurance; the weightless gulls swoop and dip around the great ocean liner as if in tribute, their grace sufficient to suggest both pleasure then and sadness now; the surprising joining of mutually ambiguous and untranslatable mysteries: "Garbo's smile and the scent of roses." But the cigarette, ocean liner, smile, and scent do not change. The character in the song lists them because he's unable to forget them. They are frozen in time; he is frozen in emotion.

As usual in catalogue songs, they come in no particular order; they are his binding memories of someone he loved and lost. The lyricist's skill eventually transforms the random to the purposeful in the closing lines of the refrain. Everything in the song is recognizable, yet the surprises abound. The commonplace "winds of March" make the narrator's heart dance. More than that, though; the line transforms him. In his heart he becomes "a dancer"; it embodies the joy of a moment turned to sorrow now that she is gone for good.

> A telephone that rings, but who's to answer?
> Oh, how the ghost of you clings.
> These foolish things remind me of you.

There's no escaping them: "those little things remain, / That bring me happiness or pain." The emotional shift intensifies the relationship between experience and memory that lies at the heart of the song.

There then follows a simple statement of a fact—a ringing telephone—that the lyric transforms into a poignant question: "who's to answer?" The line's most important word—"who's"—lands on the most emphatic note. The emotional gap between the start and finish of the line captures the song's intent in miniature.

Maybe the most striking word in the refrain sits in the middle of the next to last line: "Oh! How the ghost of you clings." Emotion and memory combine in a singular way: evanescent yet present, given substance and intensity. This is a ghost that clings. The music creates movement: a series of tripping notes that culminates in the leap to the emphatic "clings."

The final surprise occurs in the final lines of each chorus. The closing rhyme appears at the end of the second and third lines and includes the line that restates the title: "Oh, how the ghost of you clings! / These foolish things." That sets up a final unrhymed line, a way to create quiet clarity at the end: "Remind me of you." It's what the song is about. It's also an example of apostrophe, a literary device in which someone speaks to someone else who's absent or dead. Like Berlin before him, Maschwitz relies on it for the song's emotional authority.

Maschwitz's skill lay in finding an apt complement to James Strachey and Harry Link's melody—both verbal and emotional. The melody in the chorus steps along briskly but not rapidly until it reaches a key word to emphasize. I've added the emphasis:

> A *cig*arette that bears a lipstick's traces,
> An airline ticket to ro*man*tic places,
> And still my *heart* has wings.

The melody leaps up at those moments but then returns to its narrow range of notes. Strachey and Link also vary the key from major ("cig") to minor ("bears a lip-") and back to major ("... stick's traces"). The song is melancholy and the narrator finds no escape, but he's able to remember wonderful times. They gave him more than he had ever had before but he cannot shake loose.

The best thing about the music, though, lies in its use of syncopation to make each memory feel spontaneous. The narrator begins on the second beat of the measure: (Beat) "A cigarette," (Beat) "An airline," (Beat) "And still." Is it the briefest pause to entice the memory? The taking of a quick breath to be able to face it? Or a small way to move the line forward? The rest of the lines consist of quick notes to give them a feeling of talking in the moment. The use of monosyllables increases the effect. The line has momentum but not speed. It's about motion rather than tempo; accelerating the tempo would undermine the song.

The release drops the syncopation. The essential word "you" begins the first line on the first beat and then repeats it three more times in the next line and a half. It feels almost accusatory in its inevitability. Then it quiets before returning to the final A section: "I knew somehow this had to be." Overall, the release is the most dramatic part of the song; an element of resignation eases but does not replace the intensity of his emotions.

In a stylistically different but equally affecting catalogue song on a similar theme, "Thanks for the Memory" has a more unusual backstory.

Bob Hope and Shirley Ross sing "Thanks for the Memory." Screenshot.

Bob Hope, a vaudeville hoofer and comic who had fought his way to success in Broadway musicals, was about to make his first movie at the age of thirty-five. Costarring with the singer Shirley Ross in *Big Broadcast of 1938*, Hope played a radio emcee who broadcasts from one of the ocean liners in a transatlantic race. He also owes alimony to three ex-wives (including Ross) who have pursued him on board to collect. Late in the movie, Buzz (played by Hope) and Cleo (played by Ross) encounter one another in a dimly lit Art Deco bar in a quiet corner of the ship. A bar is a good place for stepping outside of time. The plot stops for a few minutes in this congenial setting for hiding or confessing truths. They talk for a few minutes and then begin to sing. They're still in love with one another although they're having trouble admitting it (Ralph Rainger and Leo Robin, "Thanks for the Memory," *The Big Broadcast of 1938*, 1937).

It sounds ready-made for a song; place, circumstance, and emotions feel aligned. But the director Mitchell Leisen had gone to the composer Ralph Rainger and the lyricist Leo Robin to ask them to help him solve a problem: "I want to show that they are still in love, but they dare not say it." Then he applied the kicker. "Hope will sing it," he explained. "While it's a serious song, a guy like that has got to get laughs."[3] He left the collaborators with no idea of where to go or how to get there. "When I Lost You" is about the death of a beloved and "These Foolish Things" about a long-gone love affair, but "Thanks for the Memory" had to be both wistful and comic about divorce in the 1930s.

Hope and Ross give a warm but sophisticated performance as twentieth-century urbanites whose debonair veneer masks deeper feelings. Rainger's music could not be less dramatic, but it provides a lovely setting for the drama of the two people, their memories, and their abiding if unstated affection. Set to Rainger's gentle melody, Robin's lyric lays out a series of contrasting memories from their marriage, from the elegant to the everyday, romantic to comic—castles on the River Rhine to the Hudson River Line, Cuban rum to hash at Dinty Moore's. Hope's character is pensive and wry through much of the song; Ross's is in good humor, although she soon finds herself in tears. They give one another shoulders to cry on as the song ends with a touchingly ironic understatement: "No tears, no fuss, / Hooray for us." When Rainger and Robin first performed it for the studio heads, they found to their astonishment that these tough businessmen were sobbing.

It's understandable. The song is funny and irreverent on one hand, touching and sad on the other. Listening (and watching a clip of the scene), you hope against hope that they'll find their way to one another. Rest assured; they do. The happy ending is about ten minutes away. In its original dramatic context, the song is filled with possibility but also anxiety. Will affectionate memory be enough to draw them back together? Rainger and Robin juggle the characters' range of reactions adroitly: laughter, sweet memories, sadness, and regret. The lyrics are sophisticated and bittersweet, as are the people who sing them.

The refrain's first line, "Thanks for the memory," emphasizes the first word, as it should. These people had it good together for a while and still recognize that they care for one another. The line then moves downward to suggest the sadness of memory. The next three lines, a list of memories, provide a musical sequence that moves upward with each successive line. Each line begins on a higher pitch than its preceding line: "Of candlelight and wine, / Castles on the Rhine, / the Parthenon and moments on the Hudson River line." The memories set to music remind the two characters in a song written as a duet that they had happy times before whatever caused their divorce. The notes in the chorus's last line, "How lovely it was," move down to suggest that what was happy is over and gone. Robin's skill at following Rainger's gently sad melody line by line, musical phrase by musical phrase, and note by note is a lesson in lyric writing in a collaboration.

Other catalogue songs—most of them, in fact—have little interest in character or situation. Each is a tour de force, a bit of clever showing off by whoever writes the lyrics. The melody provides little more than a musical setting for the lyric writer's inventiveness. No one was better at this exercise in wit than Cole Porter because his mind worked that way and, perhaps, because he wrote both music and words and could thus adapt the one to suit the other. The list doesn't need to make much sense as long as each part of it connects to the song's overall theme: here, an older woman lists off the many ways in which she explains why she's happier than she used to be. The stanzas grow progressively naughtier. Even as late as 1950, after more than a quarter-century of writing such songs, Porter had lost none of his youthful cheekiness:

> When I was dreamier,
> I slept with an old French premiere,
> I sleep easier now.
>
> (Cole Porter, "I Sleep Easier Now," *Out of This World*, 1950)

Porter wrote more of these catalogues than any other songwriter: witty lists that never run out of steam. They date back to "Let's Do It" from *Paris*, his first hit, in which he piled on the wit and wordplay to rescue the song from vulgarity even though everybody knows what "do it" really means:

> In shallow shoals, English soles do it,
> Goldfish in the privacy of bowls do it.
> Let's do it, let's fall in love.
>
> (Cole Porter, "Let's Do It," *Paris*, 1928)

By the time he wrote his first major show, *Anything Goes*, in 1934, the listing became almost surreal. Typical of catalogue songs, nothing had anything to do with anything except for the title line. Add to that Porter's ranging imagination and a sense that he was setting challenges for himself so that no matter how broadly he wandered, he always returned to the title line and the witty, unpredictable, even far-fetched connections that he made. Watch where the romantic image of a rose takes us. Porter begins conventionally, "You're a rose," but soon suggests that he's got something else up his sleeve: "You're Inferno's Dante." Then and only does he spring the surprise and leap to the punchline: "You're the nose / On the great Durante" (Cole Porter, "You're the Top," *Anything Goes*, 1934).

100   CHAPTER 4

People are intrigued by what goes on behind the scenes. How else to explain all those backstage musicals produced by Hollywood studios for decades. Audiences ask writers, "Where do you get your ideas?" It's an unanswerable question, but sometimes there's a story. In this case, it led to a song that's content to live in the present. By the late 1930s, Hoagy Carmichael was an established composer in Hollywood but his collaborator, the lyricist Frank Loesser, was a newcomer. One night, Carmichael and his wife invited the Loessers to dinner. Afterward, the two men went to the piano to try to come up with a song. Hours later, they had accomplished nothing. Eventually, the foursome stood at the door saying their good nights when Lynn Loesser remarked, "Look at us, four sleepy people." The two men raced back to the piano and within an hour had finished "Two Sleepy People."

Considering how quickly Carmichael wrote the melody, its sophistication and unconventionality are striking. The rhythm skips along unevenly, suitable for a meandering conversation just before dawn. To do this, Carmichael combines eighth notes and triplets to keep the song tripping along in a playful, bouncy way. The refrain begins with a leap up and then down ("Here we are") followed by a sequence of rising step-like passages:

> . . . out of cigarettes,
> Holding hands and yawning
> See how late it gets.
>
> (Hoagy Carmichael and Frank Loesser, "Two Sleepy People," *Thanks for the Memory*, 1938)

Then it's on to lines that move down to end the A section: "Two sleepy people by dawn's early light, / And too much in love to say goodnight." Notes that rise and notes that fall: very much in love but also very tired. Loesser has attuned his lyric to the music's suggestive emotions. He heard the words in the music.

The most distinctive part of Carmichael's melody lies in his use of harmony. Almost every chord goes beyond the familiar first, third, and fifth notes of the scale. Instead he chooses sixth, seventh, and ninth chords to provide a rich harmonic structure for the song's easy, loving conversation.

The lyric and its approach to time reflect the world in which Carmichael and Loesser wrote. The song's setting—dawn after a night spent together—is a moment in a larger story with a before and perhaps an afterward as well. The sleepy young couple in the lyric sits up all night because they can't bear to part. They're madly in love but it's all quite innocent. Even so, because

Carmichael and Loesser were writing the song for a movie, the Motion Picture Production Code would never have allowed it. Loesser solved the problem by making sure the couple is married. That might have made it more respectable, but it also makes it sexier and funnier.

As they sit close together in a "cozy chair," she asks if he remembers why they married. He answers, "To rent this little nest, / and get a bit of rest." Between "bit of" and "rest," Hope pauses ever so slightly; make of it what you will. They're obviously passionate about one another, but we wonder if Loesser is signaling indirectly that they were having sex before they married. The implications are clear before and after the ceremony, but what comes across from their remembering is the pleasure they take in one another. As the sun begins to rise, she notices how messy they look. He adds that he has lipstick on his collar and she has wrinkles on her dress.

As was often the case, the lyricist who had to react to the Code's objections often outwitted the bearers of the blue pencils. If the couple was courting, they had spent some time necking and petting. But because they had to be married, the lyric feels like postcoital bliss for two people who know that marriage is imperfect but who revel in its sexual and romantic delights: "Two sleepy people by dawn's early light / And too much in love to say goodnight."

Nobody wrote better verses than Ira Gershwin. They feel like an essential part of the song even if they have their own tone, direction, and language. The verse here is irreverent, assertive, pushing back. The writing is filled with exclamation points. Initially, the character in the lyric demands the attention of "Old Man Sunshine." He refuses to buy what Mr. Sunshine is selling:

> Never tell me dreams come true!
> Just try it—
> And I'll start a riot.
>
> (George Gershwin and Ira Gershwin,
> "But Not for Me," *Girl Crazy*, 1930)

Gershwin sustains the attitude for the remaining ten lines, witty and half dismissive. In the end he rhymes "Pollyannas" with the final line, "It's all bananas!"

From that laugh line, clever and cynical, the song glides into a sad, introspective ballad. Rather than baying at the moon, the narrator looks within to reveal the emotions beneath the yapping, but the refrain would have been weaker without the verse, the song less dramatic, the surprise less telling. The song moves from defiance to regret: "They're writing songs of love, / But not for me."

Just maybe, the verse to "Love Is Here to Stay" is even better (George Gershwin and Ira Gershwin, "Love Is Here to Stay," *Goldwyn Follies*, 1937). It's an exercise in indirection that eventually takes you where the narrator wants you to be. The man who speaks is clearly an adult. He reads the newspaper and, in 1937, finds the state of the world confusing. Between the Depression at home and the rearming of Nazi Germany in Europe, who can blame him. He admits to not knowing how things will turn out, but then the point of view shifts. "Nothing seems to be lasting," he admits, "But that isn't our affair." That's because what he and his love have is permanent: "I mean, in the way we care." We especially like the way the lines turn on the ambiguous "affair."

"I mean" may very well be filler. If it is, it's an effective way to use up two beats. It reasserts the conversational nature of the language; softens the larger "something permanent" from the previous line; and suggests that the narrator is thinking out loud, sorting things out as he goes along. The verse settles him in a comfortable chair and identifies him as a man who raises questions and is aware of the ambiguities of the world. Now he can bring his devotion and wit to what he believes as he makes distinctions between the transitory and the permanent. The combination of wit and romantic hyperbole intermingle throughout the refrain, but it springs from the verse.

A poor verse weakens the rest of the song, but a good verse enhances it. It makes the song's first claim on the listener's attention because it precedes the refrain, the part of the song where the narrator's emotions are on show. But the verse reveals what motivates the narrator, what set of emotions or circumstances compel him to burst into song. In other words, it gives the song its sense of theatricality.

It's not uncommon for verse and refrain to seem as if they're coming from different directions. The shift can be dramatic. The narrator in this four-line verse by Cole Porter sounds as if he sees falling in love as the romantic equivalent of a business deal: "After watching your appeal from ev'ry angle, / There's a big romantic deal I've got to wangle" (Cole Porter, "All of You," *Silk Stockings*, 1954). Then Porter gives him a bit of clever wordplay to end. It has no sign of the eroticism to follow. The only indication might come in the third line: "For I've fallen for a certain luscious lass"—but even that seems perfunctory (except for "luscious").

Yet "All of You" might just be Cole Porter's most erotic lyric: "The eyes, the arms, the mouth of you, / The east, west, north, and the south of you."

A lesser-known song called "Sand in My Shoes" has a Porter-like tropical feel and a level of eroticism in both the music and lyric (Victor Schertzinger and Frank Loesser, "Sand in My Shoes," *Kiss the Boys Good-Bye*, 1941). It is languorous yet somehow energized. The verse begins with a melodramatic cliché: "Out of sight, out of mind." In fact, the entire verse is nothing but clichés about the narrator's decision to leave her lover behind. Now, though, she wants to hold him again. Predictable, even perfunctory lyric writing, but its purpose is to provide a setting for the dramatic surprise and seductive tropical allure with which the refrain opens. Although we know where the song takes place, the image seems to come from nowhere. It's a winning line. She puts on that particular pair of shoes one morning and finds that they still have sand in them ("Sand in my shoes"). That's all it takes to draw her back:

> Sand from Havana,
> Calling me back to that ever so heavenly shore,
> Calling me back to you once more.

The language of the refrain offers little beyond familiar references to soft guitars, tropic seas, and moonlight. The striking lines—the image of sand in her shoes—begins and ends the refrain and lends the song its distinctiveness. A fitting image for a tropical paradise to which the narrator longs to return. She can't forget him despite the time spent apart: "All that is real is the feel / Of the sand in my shoes!"

Was this a one-night encounter? It's hard to know. The narrator never removes her shoes to, say, walk on the beach. She's an outsider who probably arrived on a cruise ship, although now "my life's an endless cruise." Despite her recognition of an empty future, the song pulsates with desire and has a strong rhythmic tempo, and the key line, "Sand in my shoes," is irresistible.

On the other hand, the verse and refrain in Milton Ager and Jack Yellen's "Ain't She Sweet" are cut from the same emotional cloth. Both are playful, youthful, and high energy. In the verse, the narrator is speaking to someone, pointing out his girl. He's obviously smitten; he boils over with delight. She's smashing and he's smashed so he asks his friend to tell him the truth. The refrain is a series of questions that begins and ends with the title line (Milton Ager and Jack Yellen, "Ain't She Sweet?" 1927). He keeps repeating himself because he's so lucky—or is it because he's not sure if she returns the same feeling. While he and a friend are casting an eye on this flapper, she's standing off somewhere else.

In a fair number of flapper songs, the boys pursue the girls with more ardor than the flappers seem to return. They use the language of praise so common in romantic songs for so many years, but the songs have come a long way from allusions to perfect beauty and eternal love. Now they're more about "turned-up nose, turned down hose, / Flapper? Yes sir!, one of those" (Ray Henderson, Sam M. Lewis, and Joe Young, "Five Foot Two, Eyes of Blue (Has Anybody Seen My Girl?)," 1925). The verse creates what will amount to a third character, an observer who watches a young man "wild and tearing his hair" because he can't find his girl.

The refrain consists of what the frantic lothario has to say. He's desperate because he knows what he's missing and because of his underlying fear that she might be sharing "It" girl with somebody else. This is, after all, the age of Clara Bow, the "It Girl": "But could she love, could she woo? / . . . / Has anybody seen my girl." As always (when it works), the verse sets up the refrain by providing a dramatic context. Here it creates a wildly youthful moment that the refrain sustains.

The refrain's motivation comes from the verse. The verse may speak to us but the refrain may speak to a beloved in a soliloquy, a dramatic monologue, or even in a duet. We may learn something about the place of time in the song. A song may be simple or complex, it may skim the surface or delve into a lover's heart, or it may be 1920s jaunty or 1930s/1940s heartsore.

Because the songs of the Great American Songbook are not personal expressions of how "I" feel or what "I" remember or regret, they can build on a more complex set of emotions and the way people express them or respond to them. Although many of them are about young love, very few ache with adolescent angst. There, once again, is where craft intersects with authenticity (see chapter 1).

All those memories; lists of them. Are they accurate? We know what memory does to what we remember. It edits, distorts, shifts emphasis, forgets, and invents. "Are you sure you weren't there?" we ask. In songs, though, it gets it right. The memories in "These Foolish Things," "Thanks for the Memory," and dozens more are reliable. The narrators remember what they saw and what happened. The trace of lipstick had to have been there and so did the gulls whirling and wheeling in New York harbor. They are essential to the emotion that Maschwitz sustains through "These Foolish Things."

We have exceptions, of course. Between them, the songs of the Great American Songbook touch nearly every outlook on love. We have a lot of songs about remembering, some about forgetting, but almost none about faulty memories, in part because they must be duets for one person to remember and the other to correct. The composer Frederick Loewe and the lyricist Alan Jay Lerner collaborated on the best of them, although Lerner had written a less effective version of "I Remember It Well" with the composer Kurt Weill for their show *Love Life* in 1948. Such a song is most likely to occur in a show or movie where the audience already knows the characters. The song comes as a slight digression at a particular point in the plot. It feels authentic, even inevitable, because it's personal for no one except the characters who sing it (Frederick Loewe and Alan Jay Lerner, "I Remember It Well," *Gigi*, 1959).

A man and a woman in late middle age (to be kind) encounter one another after many years. Now an aging boulevardier, he had cut a dashing figure when he was young, always with a beautiful woman on his arm. She had been one of them and she remembers. He tries to remember, summoning all that remains of his charm:

> He: That dazzling April moon!
> She: There was none that night.
> And the month was June.

She mocks him just a little but she is also kind because her accurate memories are as warm as his faulty ones. He asks if he's getting old. She replies by calling him "a prince of love."

He basks in the memory that she has restored to him. He believes her entirely, as does the listener, but this is one of those songs where certainty and uncertainty mix. The feelings are true even if some of the facts are suspect. The cloudiness of memory; the mix of emotions; the delicacy and wit; the humor; the strong sense of character; the lyric laid out in snatches of conversation, short sentence by short sentence; and a lyric that combines with the melody in a moment of musical conversation to brighten a day for two people beyond their prime.

Loewe helps to shape the conversational duet by giving Lerner a melody that perfectly reflects the patterns of everyday speech. The range of notes is narrow, with much more of the lyric spoken rather than sung as the two former lovers played originally by Maurice Chevalier and Hermione Gingold complete the song through their blended performance. The trick of completeness comes from the way in which Gingold's lines echo

Chevalier's musically as they dispute one another verbally. The emotions range from confidence to confusion, dismay to delight. Lerner's lyric finds its form in Loewe's complex structure. Because the song is a conversational duet with short musical lines full of interruptions, it is much longer than the usual thirty-two bars. The overall shape is AABACAABA, a rondo in which Loewe composes two complete popular song structures (AABA) separated by an additional release C that begins:

> He: How often I've thought of that Friday—
> She: —Monday
> He: . . . night.

Aside from the single one-word interruption, this is the song's longest sequence. The sprightly melody gives way to questioning through the use of minor chords to create a setting for a romantic reminiscence. Meanwhile, the two B sections beginning "that dazzling April moon!" and "you wore a crown of gold" use identical chords for emphasis, especially on "dazzling April moon" and "crown of gold," before returning to a third A section. The characters again echo one another in a series of brief musical phrases that lets Lerner play out the exchange of memories, corrections, and then a final recognition that characterize the duet until the end.

Michael grew up on a lot of the songs from the Great American Songbook because his parents sang and danced to them. It's hard to believe that the earliest of them are a century old. That's because they are standards, songs that have outlived their initial popularity to become a permanent part of America's music. On the other hand, the Songbook's dates are more or less arbitrary. Some of the songs written in the first twenty years of the century and others from the sixties and seventies and even beyond also belong in the Songbook. Stephen Sondheim is a latter-day part of the Songbook; Bob Dylan is not. It focuses on the songs of Tin Pan Alley and Broadway; Dylan's approach is a world away from Cole Porter's.

Ragtime, jazz, and the blues helped to define these songs, as did syncopation, especially the African American use of syncopation that dates back to work songs and field hollers and anticipates so much of the American music yet to come. Eventually, it got us moving, dancing, and even walking in new ways, mainly off the beat, always in motion. We might have named it the American strut.

During the two decades leading up to World War I, Blacks and whites alike strolled onto the dance floor to move to an insinuating but propulsive music helped along by the lyrics' combination of romance and sex. Many of these syncopated songs were self-referential. Their lyrics sang about ragtime, syncopation, dancing to ragtime, and holding your honey close while you danced. This ragtime "coon song" lyric by Irving Berlin is relatively benign, but you feel its sexuality in the hot tune and suggestive lyric:

> Hug up close to your baby,
> Throw your shoulders toward the ceilin',
> Lawdy, lawdy, what a feelin'.
>
> (George Botsford and Irving Berlin, "Grizzly Bear," 1910)

The farther back the Songbook reached, the closer it came to ragtime. We heard those infectious ragtime songs and we started to hum and scamper to the syncopation. Music and dancing were raucous and sexual, and in some big city neighborhoods the races mixed freely on the dance floor. Many of these songs were also overtly racist. Not all ragtime songs were "coon songs," but nearly all "coon songs" were ragtime songs. As odious as these ragtime "coon songs" are, they, along with their white composers and lyricists, recognize the origins of ragtime in African American music. They help to make ragtime and especially syncopation an essential part of the Great American Songbook soon to arrive.

What was going on musically beneath the veneer of Victorian society in America was astounding. At a time of increasingly proper middle-class behavior designed to parallel the rigid social norms of the Gilded Age, disreputable saloons encouraged the mixing of the races, even when the prostitutes were white and their male partners were Black. At worst, they danced together in newly named places called dives. The word came into use during the nineteenth century's last years because to find these places you had to go down a flight of stairs—you metaphorically had to dive—and then often made your way down a long dark hall until you came to a dimly lit room with a bar along one wall, a few musicians squeezed into a corner playing wild music, and a waxed floor for the sexually charged dancing.

The author Dale Cockrell writes, "The music they fashioned—exhilarating rhythms, a brass sound, the thumping bass, and sinuous melodies—came out of an improvised, oral tradition, a music-of-the-air that was not published or written down."[4] As the dancing became more boisterous, the prostitutes and even the men might start shedding clothes and grinding their hips together. A lot of these places also had cribs nearby, so the women could take their partners to finish what they'd started on the dance floor. Respectable people began to attend to watch the goings-on. Some found the decadence reprehensible, others found it seductive.[5]

Not all dives allowed the races to mix. Those that did soon became known as "Black and Tans," places that "welcomed patrons both black and white, that enabled music enjoyed by both races, and that encouraged the sharing of bodies, both through dance and through sex."[6]

In Black and Tans, dancing to ragtime found its first home. The music had grown up in saloons and whorehouses in and around St. Louis before it spread quickly across the country. Its ragged melodies required a different way of moving that led often to a casting off of restraints. It wasn't respectable but it was irresistible. Through much of the nineteenth century, minstrel songs along with sentimental and parlor ballads shaped America's taste, but dives were also flourishing, especially in New York City. Every attempt by the forces of reform to shut them down led to closings, but the owners simply moved to another block and reopened. This jubilant sinning seemed to have had a life of its own. Moral reformers in New York City and elsewhere found no difficulty connecting licentious behavior to ragtime.[7]

Despite the wackiness of flappers, their beaux, and the wild Charleston they did, romance returned to popular music in the twenties and continued into the thirties and forties. True love flourishes in these songs as does its loss. Many feel as fresh today as when they were new. Each of them, a miniature in the service of love, is definitive in its own way. Along love's nearly endless line, each song is a single tick along the way.

Cole Porter's "After You, Who?" is not one of his best-known ballads (Cole Porter, "After You, Who?" *The Gay Divorce*, 1932). It has little in common with the torrid Latin exoticism that characterizes many of his most famous love songs—"Begin the Beguine," "Night and Day"—but it, too, is definitive in its expression of emotion. Porter's ballads are best known for their barely concealed eroticism, but in "After You, Who?" recognition and need replace passion. Things may be wonderful, the narrator thinks, but how long can they last. His affirmation of his love comes with an element of pleading. He understands how badly he needs her, how essential his reliance on her love is.

The narrator feels the need to look to the future despite his understanding that he and his beloved are true to one another. Because songs trade in intensity, they often feel moored in the present. Here we are now, and that is everything because our feelings will never change. This song isn't like that. The narrator knows what he has and cherishes it. What enriches the song's emotionalism is his underlying fear that he may lose it. That tension creates the song's understated sense of time.

Confident enough of his feelings to say them aloud face to face, the narrator raises questions to show how tentative such a love can be despite its strength and to underscore his need. The lyric consists of questions, in a virtually invisible merging of music and lyric:

> Hold my hand and swear
> You'll never cease to care,
> For without you there what would I do?

The song is reflective but not deeply introspective. It lives in a state of "what if." It continues:

> I would search years
> But who else could change my tears
> Into laughter after you?

It is not a torch song. Its moderate tempo and rhythmic melody move in a musical arc that rises and falls line by line. But the arcs vary in length and in how high the notes rise. The rhythm also alternates short and long notes to emphasize the movement in each line. In the six lines just above, "Hold my hand and swear" and "you'll never cease to care" rise from beginning to end, then tail off to the troubled question as it rises to "there" and then drops off again at the question he needs to ask but can barely manage.

Creating simplicity that's effective can be daunting, yet Porter's mastery of his craft makes the result feel spontaneous. His skillful rhyming underscores the narrator's point of view. "Swear," preceded by the assonant "hand," goes on to rhyme with "care" and, in line three, rhymes internally with "there." The end of the third line, "what would I do," feels exempt from rhyming, at least for now. Those extra descending four notes, four words, carry the depth of his need and his underlying fear. The rest of the chorus tries to answer that question in another series of questions. Porter's buoys up the clarity of the emotion with complexity in both music and lyrics.

The final three lines begin with an ordinary rhyme of "years" and "tears" followed by the barely noticed internal rhyme "who" that links "what would I do" to the refrain's final word. Once again, that last line has an internal rhyme, "laughter after," followed by "you." What might seem to be an extra word completes the rhyme with "what would I do." Two add-on rhymes, but here those words put the focus on his emotion and the subject of his love.

Written as the opening number for Fred Astaire to sing in the 1932 Broadway musical *The Gay Divorce*, the song did not survive the show's adaptation into an Astaire–Ginger Rogers movie musical two years later. Hollywood, sensitive to the ever-more-insistent demands of the Hays Office, changed the title to *The Gay Divorcee*. Apparently, in the eyes of the often-obtuse guardians of public morality, it was okay for a divorcee to have a good time as long as the divorce wasn't enjoyable.

Originally a sprightly fox trot, "After You, Who?" has been performed more recently by such jazz-inflected singers as Helen Merrill and Sylvia Syms at a much slower tempo to underscore its mix of affirmation and potential sadness. We would argue that Porter's moderate tempo is much closer to the spirit of the song. It is a seamless blending of words and music that feels as if it says everything in a single breath. The elegance of alliteration and rhyme wedded as they are to sentiment make this a distinctive Cole Porter song and lift it to the level of inevitability.

We've all been there. Whatever we hear in a good popular song often conjures up an emotional moment that somehow reflects our own lives. It connects to us, we to it, close enough so we recognize it. It will be simplified, clarified, and idealized, made perfect in ways that ordinary emotion rarely is. Yet in the most accessible of ways, it can speak to us and for us. We find pleasure, even satisfaction, in the hyperbole, the language of praise and despair, joy and grief, in equal measure from song to song. The song expresses our emotion for us.

Most of the time, love is a song's lingua franca, the singular but always changing experience in all its variety, emotional highs and lows, and claims on our daily lives, dreams, and memories. Even if it doesn't parallel our lives today, it feeds on memory both personal and communal because memory is inescapable. It has its own insistence.

Memory lives by its own timing. It helps to explain why a couple will possess "our song" until it becomes a subtext to their lives together. Something so temporary borders on permanence. They know it the way they know their own skin. Who knows the history of the song or how they attached themselves to it or they to it? It stays alive in their hearts because it stays alive in their memories and their sustaining closeness to one another. It can also help to fill the void if love should come to an end.

For years, whenever Michael's wife and he would hear the World War II ballad "You'll Never Know," she would take his hand and squeeze it. It required nothing more. Sometimes they'd wonder why they settled on a song written when they were seven years old.

Our guess is that every generation claims that its songs make up a great American songbook. But the songs we're writing about are largely apolitical, shaped by the hyperbole of romantic love, deepened by wit, and suggestive in content rather than blunt. They're also inventive within their limits of subject matter and length. Eventually, the songwriters (and the best singers) learned ways to propel a slow ballad, to give it thrust, rhythm, and drama without speeding up the tempo. We have a hunch a certain amount was intuitive, but George Gershwin usually started a melody on the offbeat. He began the habit in the 1920s when a lot of his songs had short, percussive melodic lines. You can almost hear him banging on the piano to get them out, to keep them moving, a kind of jazzy staccato drive that embodied the new music. Lines with no more than four or five beats that Ira somehow bent words to.

"Embraceable You" appears to be a relatively simple song but is actually a small masterpiece in which George Gershwin uses a number of his familiar techniques. First and foremost, his use of syncopation. The chorus begins with an example in each in the first two lines: (Beat) "Embrace me, / (Beat) My sweet embraceable you," and then repeats the same pattern in the next two lines (George Gershwin and Ira Gershwin, "Embraceable You," *Girl Crazy*, 1930).

George's melodic lines lengthened and became more lyrical in the 1930s, but he never lost his delight in syncopation or his ability to propel a tune. In the song's second line, Ira sets the words "my sweet embraceable you" to notes that move quickly—short, short, short, leap, short, short, short. The rhyme word, "embraceable," consists of four beats—short, long, short, short—followed by the short of "you." The pattern repeats in the next line, "You irreplaceable you." Ira's words have found the rhythmic flow of George's music.

The verse relies on memory as an explanation to bring a young man and the woman he's fallen for into the present. He's previously fled from the women who pursued him. He hasn't had anywhere near the love life he might have had. At first, the lines have an undertone of humor, but then they turn more serious when we realize that he's trying to convince someone played on the Broadway stage by a pre-Hollywood Ginger Rogers: "My intuition told me / You'd come on the scene." The verse then opens to an unconventional AABAAC song. George's music invents, not by tossing away the expected but by altering and extending it. Each of the first two A sections is only four bars long while the release is the predictable eight. Instead of a single eight-bar third A to complete the song, George again writes two brief A sections, beginning "I love all" and "above all." Then the coup de grace, George's major innovation here, an eight-bar C section to end the song: "Don't be a naughty baby." The result: AABAAC. George also frequently uses a particular pattern of notes: long, short, long, long, as in "braceable you," "tipsy in me," and "gypsy in me." He uses the same pattern eight times in this one song and elsewhere throughout his other melodies. His weave of notes sings.

Ira's lyric sets most of the A sections in the present, but at the release the mood of George's music changes. Ira translates it into a shift in perspective. At the release's opening, Ira's lyric creates a deeper sense of time. The music leaps briefly into the past, from the plea to "embrace me" now to "just one look at you—my heart grew tipsy in me." A change in perception in the lyric and intensity in the music reveals something previously hidden. Rather than a flirtation or a seduction by a confident young man, the chorus is a moment of recognition and an urge to act.

Similarly, Irving Berlin used triplets to help thrust the emotional narrative forward (even though their quickness can make them hard to set lyrics to). Surprise helps. When he visited England in the 1920s, people praised Berlin's new song, which they called, "What Shall I Do?" When they heard him perform it, they praised it but wondered aloud what a "wattle" is. But he was moving the song forward through triplets and contractions: In the title line, "What'll I do," "What'll I" makes all the difference.

It felt almost natural for songwriters to take from one another, partly because the songs were tightly structured, narrow in subject matter, and insistently conventional. When somebody invented something new within those constraints, other songwriters listened and then raced to the piano to tease out permutation upon permutation in the service of writing a hit. It wasn't a matter of influence directly, more like an awareness and appropriation of what worked. Songwriters carried popular music's familiar tropes with them, along with the history of the music that preceded them. It was at their fingertips waiting to be used and extended.

One very hot day in July 1945, the composer Jule Styne and the lyricist Sammy Cahn were driving around Los Angles in Styne's convertible. They had already collaborated on such major wartime hits as "Guess I'll Hang My Tears Out to Dry," "I Fall in Love Too Easily," "I've Heard That Song Before," and "I'll Walk Alone." Styne said, "Let's go to the beach." Cahn replied, "Let's write a Christmas song." They drove to the nearby

William Rogers Agency that represented both of them, found a piano and typewriter, and by the end of the day had written, not a Christmas song, but a song for the winter that we still sing and hear on the radio every December, "Let It Snow, Let It Snow, Let It Snow."

The setting resembles other winter songs intended for the Christmas market. As early as 1938, Irving Berlin had written "I've Got My Love to Keep Me Warm," followed by Cole Porter's "You'd Be So Nice to Come Home To" in 1943 and Frank Loesser's now controversial "Baby, It's Cold Outside" in 1949. In each of them, the storm is outside, the fireplace inside, and seduction proceeds. They rely on sexual implications, although Porter's is the most directly erotic while Loesser combines the comic with the seductive. Styne and Cahn's "Let It Snow" stays well within the accepted bounds of suggestiveness. Outside the weather is "frightful." After an evening with the lights down low, he lingers (and lingers) to avoid having to go back out into the storm.

> The fire is slowly dying
> And, my dear, we'll still goodbye-ing.
> But as long as you love me so

The final lines make it clear that despite what might be going on, they truly do love another: "Let it snow! Let it snow! Let it snow!" (Jule Styne and Sammy Cahn, "Let It Snow! Let It Snow! Let It Snow!" 1945). We wonder if the young man ever does return home in this song defined by the here and now.

Every now and then, things escalate. There are only so many possible combinations of notes, and somebody accuses somebody else of plagiarism. Most of the time those who sue are unknown songwriters who feel aggrieved or are trying to cash in on somebody else's success. Soon after Jerry Herman had his first great success with *Hello, Dolly!*, an unknown songwriter claimed that the title song's opening notes matched something he had written. The songwriter never brought suit, but the issue troubled Herman: "This was some hillbilly tune. . . . It had been published and it had been recorded but it was hardly being sung in nightclubs in Manhattan." He said during a deposition, "The only notes that stay in my brain are from songs that I love and admire, and I would never, ever fall in love with a song about the joys of being born and raised in Kansas."[8] There's that New York sensibility at work, an important part of the way the Great American Songbook viewed the world.[9]

Perhaps the most egregious example of a good songwriter's stealing from a better one occurred in 1952 during the shooting of the movie musical *Singin' in the Rain*, starring Gene Kelly, Debbie Reynolds, and Donald O'Connor. This was one of several musicals produced by Arthur Freed, a former song lyricist himself. He had overseen several musicals featuring songs by famous songwriters.

They included what *Time Magazine* liked to call "biopix," highly fictionalized versions of the lives of famous songwriters—*Till the Clouds Roll By* about Jerome Kern (1946) and *Words and Music* about Rodgers and Hart (1948)—as well as original stories that featured mostly familiar songs by one songwriter or songwriting team—*Easter Parade* with songs by Irving Berlin (1948), *An American in Paris* with songs by the Gershwins (1951), and *Singin' in the Rain* (1952) with songs by Freed and his major collaborator Nacio Herb Brown.

Reviving Brown and Freed's songs from the 1920s and 1930s, *Singin' in the Rain* told the comic tale of two silent movie screen lovers who can't stand each other in real life but who must adapt to the arrival of career-threatening talkies. Fitting Brown and Freed's songs to the script and characters proved easy, but during shooting, codirector (with the movie's star Gene Kelly) Stanley Donen realized that O'Connor needed a better number than the one they'd given him. He could find nothing suitable in Freed's catalogue but suggested that Brown and Freed write a new song using Cole Porter's knockabout "Be a Clown" as their model.

Porter had written the song as part of his 1948 score for *The Pirate*, also starring Kelly and also produced by Freed. It was a tour de force of wit and invention: "Why be a great composer with your rent in arrears, / Why be a major poet and you'll owe it for years, / When crowds'll pay to giggle if you wiggle your ears?" (Cole Porter, "Be a Clown," *The Pirate*, 1947). Freed had first become an associate producer on *The Wizard of Oz* in 1939 and since then had largely given up songwriting.

Freed and Brown loved the idea of writing a new song and, in Donen's words, "They certainly did that!" Some online sources say that Betty Comden and Adolph Green, who wrote the *Singin' in the Rain* screenplay, also wrote the song after they got Porter's permission to use his melody. No matter who wrote it, the new song, "Make 'Em Laugh," was brilliant in its lyric and in O'Connor's performance: "You can study Shakespeare and be quite elite, / You could charm the critics and have nothing to eat, / Just slip on a banana peel, the world's at your feet" (Nacio Herb Brown and Arthur Freed, "Make 'Em Laugh," *Singin' in the Rain*, 1952). But there was too much noise about it for any explanation to be entirely believable. The new song was much too similar in melody and words for comfort. People raised questions about whether or not Brown and Freed or Comden and Green had committed plagiarism. Donen noted that "Cole Porter, to the day he died, never said a word to Arthur."[10]

Porter never pursued the matter, perhaps because he was still grateful to Freed for hiring him for *The Pirate* right after he'd had two Broadway flops in a row. Donen called "Make 'Em Laugh" "100% plagiarism"[11] and, when Porter's good friend Irving Berlin visited the set and heard it, he was livid. He might have been that angry in part because in the first half of his career, he was often accused of plagiarism because he was not a skilled musician. From the very beginning, people accused him of having a "pickaninny" stashed away in Harlem to write his successful ragtime songs. That sort of thing infuriated the insecure Berlin.

Interviewed by William Baer in 2002, Comden and Green confirmed that Brown and Freed wrote the song. Apparently, everyone liked Freed, but they were all embarrassed by the song. As Betty Comden said, "We just looked at each other, raised our eyebrows, and moved on." When Berlin heard the song, he turned to Freed to ask, "Who wrote that song?" Suddenly Arthur was flustered and pulled Berlin away, as if he had just realized what he had done. No one ever understood how Brown and Freed could have written the song and not realized what they were doing, but that was the general consensus.[12]

Quantity matters. Not as much as quality, but it's hard to be a major songwriter if you haven't written more than a dozen songs, no matter how good they are. But consider the quality of what the men and women of the Great American Songbook wrote, the standards many of us still recognize, can sing, and, more importantly, hold close. They matter to us.

Stephen Foster preceded the Songbook and John Lennon, Bob Dylan, and Bruce Springsteen came after. But the riches that came from such people as Jerome Kern, Irving Berlin, the Gershwins, Cole Porter, Harold Arlen, Thomas "Fats" Waller, Richard Rodgers, Lorenz Hart, Oscar Hammerstein, Harry Warren, Dorothy Fields, Duke Ellington, Johnny Mercer, Harry Warren, and E. Y. Harburg, among many others, are unequaled in our musical history. By the time Kern, the oldest of them, died in 1946, Mercer, the youngest of them, had already written such standards as "I Thought About You," "Skylark," "Blues in the Night," "Laura," and "Too Marvelous for Words." They turned out the work.

The Great American Songbook relies on the durability of memory. Its songs attach themselves to us; if they last long enough, they ease their way permanently into our memories. We conjure them up at suitable moments or they arrive unbidden but rarely unwelcome. We find ourselves humming something from who knows how long ago. Yet even though a song may record only a moment, it lives in time. It floats in an ether of past, present, and future. We remember, we act, we despair, we hope.

Exactly a century before we wrote this paragraph, Irving Berlin had come to the conclusion that the craze for ragtime, ragtime songs, and ragtime dancing was finally winding down. It had started before the turn of the century. He had made his reputation by writing ragtime songs, and his first major hit, "Alexander's Ragtime Band," had extended their lifespan by nearly a decade. Now he feared the craze was coming to an end; he would have to find something new.

Berlin had written several ballads, only one of any importance: "When I Lost You," when Dorothy Goetz, his first wife, died. He tried again but hedged his bets. It was that old struggle between the familiar and the fresh. His first stab at it—"All by Myself"—was innovative and career changing (Irving Berlin, "All By Myself," 1921). He wrote a mournful lyric but wed it to music with a moderate tempo, strongly rhythmic and made jaunty by his use of syncopation carried over from ragtime. He called it a "rhythm ballad."

> I want to rest my weary head
> On somebody's shoulder,
> I hate to grow older,
> All by myself.

The success of "All by Myself" persuaded Berlin to write more romantic ballads. It was the 1920s, though, the time of the flapper, bathtub gin, and jazz. Berlin persisted. In the first half of the decade, he wrote three major ballads, "What'll I Do," "Remember," and "All Alone." While Flaming Youth was out dancing the Charleston, he was writing melancholy slow waltzes that moved his career and America's tastes in new directions. Each was a success and freed him from the limitations of ragtime songs.

As the blues also became a national music and found a white audience during these same years, it makes sense to consider Berlin's sad waltzes along with the blues as the harbingers of the torch ballads that appeared and became so important before the end of the decade. They were the antidote to all that was frivolous during the twenties. Critics infrequently think of Berlin as a great innovator, but, in his own quiet way, he was exactly that. He wasn't especially interested in originality for its own sake. He once said that a song is good or bad regardless of whether or not it is original. These songs in their own time were both good and innovative—for him and for American music.

Berlin's "How About Me" from 1928 is not as well known as his slow ballads from the early years of the decade, but we find it equally affecting (Irving Berlin, "How About Me?" 1928). As usual, it deepens emotion through simplicity, Berlin's stock in trade. He sets the song in the aftermath of a love gone wrong. The narrator can't bear the present and can only look to the future with despair. The opening words in the refrain's first two choruses make it feel as if the lovers, probably married, have separated very recently. You hear it in the immediacy of the melancholy but syncopated opening words, "[Beat] It's over/ [Beat] All over." It's as if the narrator is sighing in the face of his loss.

Berlin's melody moves in steps, up or down, across a narrow range of notes. In a song meant to be introspective, he creates a narrator who appears to be speaking to the loved one he has recently lost. We would argue, though, for seeing the song as elliptical—speaking to someone absent as if present—a soliloquy rather than a dramatic monologue. Berlin wisely avoids vocal histrionics to create a speaker who seems to speak outwardly but whose point of view is inward.

The song is a frozen moment in a larger narrative—they fell in love, she fell out of love, and she left—but time is standing still. The song's narrator says over and over again, "It's over," as if he can't quite believe it. At the same time, bereft of the lover who may very well have been his wife, he cannot keep from imagining a painful future in which he plays no part. A new "someone" makes a fuss over her and talks about her to his friends. It's a way to make the narrator believe what he cannot bear. But the sense of hopelessness comes through most inescapably in the repeated title line. Bound by the present, he grieves for a future he can imagine but will never have.

He envisions these things happening in the world in the near future, but he always turns back to himself, "But how about me?" Like so many love songs, "How About Me?" has two characters at its center, "I" and "you." The lines that rhyme focus on "I"; those that don't focus on "you." The song is about his feelings, but it keeps going back to her. The other two characters—figments of his raw imagination?—only deepen his sorrow. They are a new lover and, most unbearable of all, the baby they never had. Speaking to his lost love, the narrator bemoans the fact that baby

Will climb upon your knee
And puts its arms about you
But how about me?

Is he regretting that she will never put her arms about him, or that he will never hold their baby? Both add depths of poignance to the song. Even so, a song about two lovers who have lost one another is hardly unusual, but the reference to the baby comes out of the blue. It is a touching moment, made more so by placing "and maybe / A baby" where "it's over, / All over" sit in the previous A choruses. The lines' artless emotionalism finds expression in the chorus' one-syllable words, its touching familiarity, its asking of the final question, and its descent into despair—the child they never had.

About twenty-five years ago, Michael provided some guidance for a student over a period of three or four years. Just before he graduated, his mother came to see him for a friendly chat about Matt's time in the school. At one point he asked her if she had anything she wanted to ask him. She said, "I hate the music he listens to." That wasn't exactly what Michael expected to hear on a lovely day in May, but he said, "Why not ask him to turn it down?" All was well, but then he stuck his foot well into his mouth: "Besides," he said, "how different is it from what you listened to?" She stood up, all 5'2" of her, and stared him down, "Please," she said, "I'm Springsteen!" He knew that he had been chastised.

What Matt's mother taught him that day was something about the way songs function in a culture. In his youth, they still bridged the generations; since the advent of rock and roll, they've defined each generation. The gain is in a sense of identity and connection within a generation, the loss is in history and a connection between the generations. There's something satisfying for a little girl or boy, sitting on Grandma's knee, as they sing a song together.

The standards of the Great American Songbook bridged the generations and, in a diminished way nearly a century later, still do. What they sing about is always timely. The capacity of love to confuse and clarify, sow despair and reap ecstasy: love for the first time and the last, the refusal to fall again, and the readiness, the emotions of an eager adolescent and a wary adult. Running through all of it is a song's capacity to make us believe if only for five or ten minutes at a time. Perhaps it's more "believe in" than believe. We choose to believe, perhaps because a song sees itself in us just as we see ourselves in it. It is an umbrella of emotion spread wide, an act of exchange that rises in our hearts to conviction.

An act of exchange includes implications of commerce. Songwriters during those years were determined to reach the broadest possible audience. They owned their own publishing companies to rake in the results of their successes. They understood the need for songs that were accessible and shaped the response of the listener through the melding of words and music into a song, a new third thing equal to more than the sum of its parts. The songwriters merged melody with language as they mastered syncopation along with jazzy harmonies and rhythms; then they turned to the elevated language of romantic speech or the earthy wit of wordplay.

A few pages back, we wrote that many songwriters create emotion through their use of the familiar and the simple. Few songs could be simpler yet more touching than Irving Berlin's "Say It Isn't So" from 1932. He was at the height of his powers; at about the same time, he also wrote "Let Me Sing (and I'm Happy)," "Let's Have Another Cup of Coffee," "Easter Parade," "Supper Time," "Soft Lights and Sweet Music," and "How Deep Is the Ocean?"

In that same year of 1932, other songwriters wrote "I Gotta Right to Sing the Blues," "It's Only a Paper Moon," "Alone Together," "It Don't Mean a Thing If It Ain't Got That Swing," "I've Told Ev'ry Little Star," "The Song Is You," "April in Paris," "Isn't It Romantic," "Lover," "I've Got the World on a String," "Night and Day," "Keepin' Out of Mischief Now," "Where the Blue of the Night Meets the Gold of the Day," "I'm Getting Sentimental Over You," "Try a Little Tenderness," "Love Me Tonight," and "Brother, Can You Spare a Dime?" All these and more in a single year to reflect the diversity and quality of the Great American Songbook at its best. We could have made the same point from almost any of its thirty years.

"Say It Isn't So" demonstrates Berlin's mastery of simplicity as the songwriter creates the narrator's fearfulness and need for reassurance (Irving Berlin, "Say It Isn't So," 1932). The verse typically establishes a dramatic situation, in this case the ease with which gossip spreads and the hurt it causes. The narrator speaks directly to the one he loves and fears he has lost: "I know that they're mistaken, / Still I want to hear it from you." What starts as gossip and a last tremor of hope in the verse rises in the chorus to pleading and eventual heartbreak.

Because songs are so brief, repetition can be wasteful. How much of what you've already said do you need to say again—and again? But here the repetition expands and deepens the tolling of his despair. In seventy-six words, the chorus repeats the title line (or a variation on it) seven times. Its sibilant monosyllables coupled with the imperative "say" mark off each of the song's emotional stages. He doesn't ask for all that much—"Say that ev'rything is still okay"—but hears only silence. A present time never moves.

RECORDINGS

Tony Bennett, "When I Lost You," 1987
Ella Fitzgerald, "These Foolish Things," 1957
Bob Hope and Shirley Ross, "Thanks for the Memory," 1938
Charlotte Greenwood, "I Sleep Easier Now," 1950
Sutton Foster, "Let's Do It," 2011
Bob Hope and Shirley Ross, "Two Sleepy People," 1938
Judy Garland, "But Not for Me," 1943
Rosemary Clooney, "Love Is Here to Stay," 1988
Fred Astaire, "All of You," 1957
Bobby Short, "Sand in My Shoes," 1955
Gene Austin, "Ain't She Sweet," 1927
Gene Austin, "Five Foot Two, Eyes of Blue," 1926
Maurice Chevalier, Hermione Gingold, "I Remember It Well," 1958
Max Morath, "The Grizzly Bear," 1963
Fred Astaire, "After You, Who?" 1932
Ella Fitzgerald, "Embraceable You," 1959
Rosemary Clooney, "What'll I Do," 1984
Connie Boswell, "Let It Snow! Let It Snow! Let It Snow!" 1946
Judy Garland and Gene Kelly, "Be a Clown," 1948
Donald O'Connor, "Make 'Em Laugh," 1952
Martha Wainwright, "All By Myself," 2011
Rosemary Clooney, "How About Me?" 1990
Annette Hanshaw, "Say It Isn't So," 1932

5

A MATTER OF TIME

Penelope Green wrote in the *New York Times*, "The distance between past, present, and future is only an illusion, however persistent."[1] The melancholy "Autumn Leaves" interweaves its allusions to time so deftly that the listener is barely aware of the movement. They make the song feel as if time barely moves: "Since you went away the days grow long. / And soon I'll hear old winter's song" (Joseph Kosma, Jacques Prevert, and Johnny Mercer, "Autumn Leaves," 1950).

Music starts, somebody sings, and time stands still as lovers dance. They hold one another close to the music without seeming to move or even breathe. They are locked in an embrace within a song. Yet time is always present because the songwriters of the Great American Songbook relied on it to firm up the emotions they chose to express. They mastered the manipulation of time in something as brief as a song. It takes nothing more than a few words for the rustling of leaves to shift barely perceptively from time to time. Yet that bit of movement that takes no more than a few words is essential. These songs shimmer in time as if they're timeless. They live in the present for the narrator and probably for the listener as well. They may record no more than a moment of emotion, but they occur in time, often looking to the past or projecting into the future. Songs remember and hope, however briefly. Without hope, they see a bleak tomorrow.

Living in Paris as the early great Modernist painters were first emerging at the turn of the twentieth century, Gertrude Stein wrote, "Time . . . makes identity."[2] Unlike young Picasso and Matisse who lived and worked in a revolutionary, avant-garde world, songwriters were out to write good songs that sold a lot of copies. Even so, Stein's line resonates. The narrator in each song lives in time, as we all do, but time shaped and directed by the emotional point of view designed by a composer and a lyricist. The well-crafted approach to time is essential to the narrator's identity within a song.

The song has ended, one song tells us, but somehow the melody lingers on. "Lingers" is the word to rely on (Irving Berlin, "The Song Is Ended (but the Melody Lingers On)," 1927). Memory takes the narrator back to a "moment of bliss" as lovers sang and danced "to our heart's content." An example of carpe diem, the song tells you, if you didn't already know, that "summer will pass away / Take your happiness while you may." The love lasts only as long as the lovers can see the descending moon. All that remains in the present is a lingering melody one of them cannot forget. The tension between present and past creates the sense of time, although neither present nor past can move. The memory is set and the narrator cannot escape it. The inability to escape the emotions of loss and loneliness when a love affair ends creates a narrator who is anchored in the present yet beset by memory.

Elsewhere as well, the seasons seem to stand still. In this song it's more a delay than a halt, something tentative rather than permanent (Frank Loesser, "Spring Will Be a Little Late This Year," *Christmas Holiday*, 1943). But loss remains until spring finally arrives. The delay is a matter of emotion rather than weather. It's frightening but "time heals all things, / So I needn't cling to this fear." As the overblown verse says, the narrator lived through January and February "tragic'lly" as if "I'm dying" because he has had to live without her. Its final line, though, turns to the refrain for another way to make the point. Its opening is resonant but quietly insistent. For as long as he endures a persistent winter, the passing of time will slow:

> Spring will be a little late this year,
> A little late arriving
> In my lonely world over here.

The loneliness defines a space. With her gone, he is "over here," isolated with only the sense of loss and the recognition of the way time seems not to pass.

Spring is obviously not only a season but a common image of hope and restoration. It's a healing image, although it's slow to revive "the music it made in my heart" when he and she were together. Loesser was still a young songwriter in 1943, capable of wonderful songs but also of lapses. This is one of the first songs for which he wrote both words and music, but he included the line, "Yes, time heals all things," a cliché merely repeated rather than reanimated. It's the weakest line in the song but also a sign of the narrator's passivity or, perhaps, helplessness. At the same time, it lets him anticipate the future. Because time does heal, he needn't fear. The melodramatic statement of loss gives way to calm about the future. It's "merely" that spring will be delayed only by "a little" and for this year only. The song is melancholy, but the lyric promises a way through if only he can be patient.

Stanislaus Fodorski, a Hungarian immigrant, comes to the United States to teach engineering at the Southern Baptist Institute of Technology. Even Dean Elizabeth Hawkes-Bullock admits that it's not an impressive college. Fodorski is surprised to learn that the dean is a woman and that he will be boarding with her. He eventually adapts to his new life as a teacher and becomes a student favorite at the same time that his relationship with the dean warms. Sitting on the porch together one night, they reminisce about past romances:

> Once upon a time
> A girl with moonlight in her eyes
> Put her hand in mine . . .
>
> (Charles Strouse and Lee Adams,
> "Once Upon a Time," *All-American*, 1962)

The song is hushed and elegiac as memory idealizes their youthful experiences. It feels almost like a dream because everything happened so long ago. The title line, "Once upon a time," suggests that time has transformed it into something as vivid yet distant as a fairy tale, perhaps because what they have lost is irretrievable.

The song is from the Broadway musical *All-American* with a score by Charles Strouse and Lee Adams, and starring Ray Bolger and Eileen Herlie. It's an excellent example of how deftly the Great American Songbook handles time. A song set in the present as part of the developing relationship between two people devotes itself to memories until, at the end, it looks sadly to the future. The song ends with a touching sense of loss that feels permanent: "But somehow once upon a time / Never comes again."

Songs invite many of us to swoon over romance in images of heaven and forever, and first kisses that seem never to end, but all of us know that reacting to a first kiss or a love described as eternal takes place in time. We've sometimes described songs as one-act plays or paintings—brief moments in a larger narrative that suggest a world beyond the stage, the frame or the thirty-two bars of a song. Deena Rosenberg writes of George and Ira Gershwin (although it's true of many of the best songs of the Great American Songbook) that their songs are tiny one-act plays that take "a character on a journey from one point, often stated in the title, to another, usually encapsulated in the last line."[3] Although there's something implied beyond them, they are also complete despite their brevity. They come from somewhere and they have somewhere else to go. It's not always easy to know where either is. Time races by so quickly that they haven't done half the things they want to. Perhaps ambiguity played off against desire is the point:

> Oh, well—
> We'll catch up
> Some other time.
>
> (Leonard Bernstein, Betty Comden, and Adolph Green, "Some Other Time," *On the Town*, 1944)

Songs give us moments frozen in time. The drama usually has two characters—you and me—in either a soliloquy or dramatic monologue:

> With time on my hands
> And you in my arms
> And love in my heart . . .
>
> (Vincent Youmans, Harold Adamson, and Mack Gordon, "Time on My Hands," *Smiles*, 1930)

The song has little drama. Its tone of quiet contentment suggests post-coital bliss. Love flourishes but quietly, because nothing else claims the narrator's attention. Time floats, or perhaps it would be better to say that the lovers float together in time. Whatever moments the speaker has are "all for you."

Memory shapes song after song, usually when a love affair has ended and the narrator can't get the one he loves out of his mind. But songwriters are very good at working the permutations. The love is secure; the lovers' only regret is that they didn't find one another sooner. The song is early

Jerome Kern; he had not begun to write the rich romantic melodies for which he became so well known. The tone is light and P. G. Wodehouse's lyric amusing as the lovers enjoy one another (Jerome Kern and P. G. Wodehouse, "You Never Knew About Me," *Oh, Boy!*, 1917). The melody has a tone of melancholy (faux melancholy?), but rather than bemoaning their past without one another, they go all the way back to childhood and sigh amusingly:

> Life might have been Heaven,
> If I, then age seven,
> Had but met you when you were three . . .
> But I never knew about you,
> (Ah! What we might have been.)
> And you never knew about me.

One of the most dramatic of duets, though, reveals the normal hesitation of people who meet and feel drawn to one another in a romantic but more realistic way. Early in the first act of Richard Rodgers and Oscar Hammerstein II's *Carousel*, Billy Bigelow and Julie Jordan begin to talk to one another. He is worldly, cynical, and roughhewn; she is innocent and open-hearted. Both are lonely and unsettled. They are intrigued but also frightened. Billy suddenly turns to her, "You! You tryin' to get me to marry you?" Julie can only answer, "No." They bring their pasts with them, but they spend their time sorting out the present moment and daring to consider the future. They advance and retreat; he bullies but she has some gumption; it surprises him. Time stops as honest feeling confronts the unknown.

Julie and Billy sing the soaring "If I Loved You," not because they're in love or even want to fall in love with one another, but they cannot ignore the newness, fear, and allure: "Longin' to tell you, but afraid and shy, / I'd let my golden chances pass me by" (Richard Rodgers and Oscar Hammerstein II, "If I Loved You," *Carousel*, 1945). Hammerstein's weave of dialogue and song makes this one of the cherished scenes in Broadway musical history. If Julie and Billy follow where it leads, their encounter will change their lives. The lyric's repetition of "if" underscores how tentative they feel as if to disguise what they've begun. They imagine and sing with increasing conviction yet are still unwilling to act on a dream, separated by their past but eager to discover a future together.

The drama in a song often comes from the way the verse sets up a situation to make the refrain necessary: in the narrator's need to speak but also in the relationship between music and words. The requirements of music, so abstract at its best, and the requirements of words, so concrete at their best, suggest an incompatibility. Whichever comes second, words or music, has the primary task of creating reconciliation. Imagine a songwriter like Irving Berlin or Cole Porter whose writing consisted in part of finding a way—the way—to fit notes and words together. One then the other? Or back and forth? Like a great puzzle with success or failure in the wind, and always the songwriter's need to be an honest broker with each song's emotionalism.

"Always," one of Berlin's most famous and most popular songs, has an unusual history. It's also one of Berlin's simplest songs—on the surface. It's an exercise in the complexity behind simplicity. A young woman named Mona, the fiancée of Berlin's musical secretary, asked him to write a song for her. Berlin spontaneously hummed a melody and sang, "I'll be loving you, Mona." Later, he went to work on it when he and the playwright George S. Kaufman were also working on *The Cocoanuts* for the Marx Brothers (although it never appeared in the show). He changed "Mona" to "always" and completed the song. Kaufman, always a cynic about anything romantic, told Berlin that he ought to have changed the line to "I'll be loving you Thursday."

At about the same time, Berlin began to court Ellin Mackay, the daughter of one of New York's wealthiest and most prominent Roman Catholic families. Her father Clarence was known for, among other things, his rabid anti-Semitism; he disinherited his daughter and referred to his new son-in-law as "that show-business Jew." Berlin published the song, gave it to Ellin as a wedding gift, and assigned all its royalties to her. That one song earned her in excess of three million dollars, and that started with 1920s dollars.

Berlin found the song difficult to complete to his satisfaction (Irving Berlin, "Always," 1925). Its structure is unusual. Rather than AABA, in this simplest of songs, Berlin creates an ABAC pattern. He also had a terrible time finding the closing lines, but after a long struggle, suddenly wrote:

> Not for just an hour,
> Not for just a day,
> Not for just a year,
> But always.

Again, what could be simpler? The composer and author Alec Wilder, with his interest in innovation in popular songs, calls "Always" a "straightforward pop tune and, for me, a contrivance."[4] Berlin was furious. He once referred to Wilder as a "fucking longhair." Philip Furia, who wrote the first essential work about popular lyricists, called the song "mawkish."[5] We understand why they disliked it. Its abstract sentiments barely move because they lack grounding in experience or imagery. The song starts nowhere and goes nowhere. Or so it seems.

Despite its flaws, this is a masterful creation of time and its emotional effect. Its simplicity creates a sense of inevitability. In the 1920s, when Berlin was writing some of his greatest mournful ballads—"What'll I Do," "All Alone," "Remember"—he wrote "Always," at least one song to affirm the depth of a sustained love. But it's more complicated than that. As the verse makes clear, the narrator has endured loss. He knows what it feels like to be blue. Might this be Berlin's brief hearkening back to the death of his first wife, Dorothy, dead after six months of marriage, and a recognition of what Ellin means to him? The verse begins by looking to the past ("Ev'rything went wrong"), but by the end he has come into the present because he has found a new love ("Now that I've found you at last").

The refrain, though, is entirely about the future. The narrator in the present moment affirms what he sees ahead with complete confidence ("I'll be loving you, / Always."). The love won't be perfect. He tells her that when she needs "a helping hand, / I will understand, / Always, always." That singular repetition of the title word makes clear that his understanding and adaptability make these few lines the song's most important. The love will survive even the tough times.

Ultimately, this isn't a song about loving somebody "always" but what losing love and then finding it again can mean, along with the need to sustain it despite everyday imperfections. The title word is a useful hyperbole beneath which a deeper truth lies. Written as a waltz, the most romantic of song forms, it is an idealized reflection in very romantic terms of what a love affair or a marriage is like. These popular songs with their simplicity and sentimentality can still tell truths. Beneath the obvious, there lies some wisdom.

Most songwriters said little about the alchemy that turns base metal to musical gold, but Deena Rosenberg, explaining why the Gershwins's songs were inherently dramatic, wrote that they combined "a rhythmic drive and complexity and the ambivalence of the blue note"—a legacy of Black and Jewish music that George brought into the theater—merged with the wit and emotion of Ira's lyrics.[6]

The emergence of Jewish songwriters in Tin Pan Alley and then Broadway in the 1910s and 1920s changed the nature of American popular song. They had been listening to ragtime, jazz, and the blues in the streets; it had become part of America's and their musical DNA. They got it. They were also driven to succeed, so they took the sounds of African American music and then borrowed, stole, and adapted what they heard until it spread from coast to coast. Their timing could not have been better. Here was a new generation of composers and lyricists ready to stake their claim to Tin Pan Alley and Broadway.

Of the first-tier songwriters who established themselves before 1930, only Cole Porter, Harry Warren, Duke Ellington, Hoagy Carmichael, Johnny Mercer, and Thomas "Fats" Waller were not Jewish. The melancholy and joy of African American and Jewish music created an unlikely new American sound, both raffish and romantic, that Americans embraced then and that still helps to shape American popular music. The beat is different, the lyrics are different, the sound is different, but what set the Great American Songbook in motion continues to shape American song.

Nothing does more to create a song's theatricality than its sense of time and place. Time helps to ground a song in human experience despite the hyperbole of romantic love. Even when a song suspends time, it still takes place in time. The mastery of time and its manipulation are part of the craft (and craftiness) of the songwriters of the Great American Songbook. They construct songs that speak believably and individually to large numbers of people. When imagination touches craft and craft touches desire, songs become believable. The men and women who wrote them always had tricks of music and language up their sleeves designed to draw us in, especially because we were eager to be drawn.

Place helps to ground a song. It might be a crowded street, a country lane, daytime or night. It might be a town, a hilltop, a metropolis—a place you know and long to return to ("Take Me Back to Manhattan") or are new to ("A New Town Is a Blue Town"). A character in a song might be riding in a taxicab or sitting in an easy chair. He may stroll through the fog or dance in the sunshine. Sometimes the sense of place is clear, sometimes suggestive, but it is often essential to the substance of the song, and time is always lingering somewhere nearby.

A couple argues; they part angrily. Unable to sleep, the narrator telephones in the morning to see how she is and, by extension, apologize. It's more need than choice. The implied setting, easy to imagine, is a dark apartment and a bed with the blankets tossed every which way because he never slept. He never had "my favorite dream, / The one in which I hold you tight." Now, though, "I had to call you up this morning / 'Cause I couldn't sleep a wink last night" (Jimmy McHugh and Harold Adamson, "I Couldn't Sleep a Wink Last Night," *Higher and Higher*, 1943).

A decade earlier, deep in the Great Depression, Johnny Green and Edward Heyman wrote an unadorned ballad of deep longing (Johnny Green and Edward Heyman, "I Cover the Waterfront," 1933). A desolate woman stands alone by the docks deep into the night. She looks out over what she calls "the great unknown" as she wonders when or if her lover will return. She "covers" the waterfront in a constant, continuing present as she longs for his return and the sky "covers" her in turn. This is no comforting image of a blanket but rather the weight of a dark sky. Each image of place reflects her isolation and despair. "I'm covered," she says, "by / A starless sky above."

Most songs have a similar subtext, consciously or not. Writing about the unlikely Miracle Mets that won the World Series in 1969, the journalist Devin Gordon observed, "It's only a miracle if you tell it . . . unstuck from time. . . . If you move the period, you change the sentence, and you change the story. Move it far enough into the future and every tale of triumph becomes a story about loss."[7] It's true of baseball and it's true of love songs. The Rockies may crumble and Gibraltar may tumble because they're only made of clay, Ira Gershwin wrote, "But our love is here to stay" (George Gershwin and Ira Gershwin, "Love Is Here to Stay," *The Goldwyn Follies*, 1937). It's a witty and reassuring hyperbole, but we also know that it's true only as far forward as we can hope and imagine, and sometimes tonight is good enough.

The song is a willful assertion of order and permanence in a world about to go mad. It grows out of desperation as much as confidence. Confused by what he reads in the daily newspaper, a reader reacts to what he sees all around him: "The less I comprehend / The world and all its capers / And how it all will end." The dramatic context in the verse—a person reading the newspaper—and Ira's wit throughout save the song from sentimentality. When you come right down to it, a love that will last forever isn't much of an idea. For the song's three or four minutes, the Gershwins knew where to put the period.

Actually, George died before he and Ira had finished the song. No one is entirely sure how much help the composer Vernon Duke gave. Probably less than originally thought. Duke was a friend, but he was also an irascible man. One suggestion he did take: Ira thought that adding dotted notes in the ninth and tenth bars on the word "and" was a good idea—"The radio and the telephone and the movies that we know."[8]

Many good songs know where to put the period even though they approach love and time in different ways. Unlike the ultimate confidence of "Love Is Here to Stay," in this song the lyricist and occasional composer Johnny Mercer created a musical setting for a character who dashes headlong into the future (Johnny Mercer, "Something's Gotta Give," *Daddy Long Legs*, 1954). The lovers are stuck, but for only so long. Everything changes; everything is about to explode. The narrator pushes forward. They aren't young, but the narrator's passion sweeps him into the future. He is humorous, boastful, and unstoppable. He starts out talking to her, trying to overwhelm her with his own determination as the song recasts itself as seduction:

> When an irresistible force such as you
> Meets an old immovable object like me, . . .
> Something's gotta give . . .

Before long, though, his determination wraps itself around both of them:

> We'll find out as sure as we live,
> Something's gotta give.

In a "restless world," someone else approaches the question of love tentatively. The song is wistful and dreamy, its rhythm gentle and flowing (Victor Young and Edward Heyman, "When I Fall in Love," *One Minute to Zero*, 1952). The narrator is no youngster. He knows that too often "love is ended before it's begun." He prefers not to give his heart until he can give it completely and forever to someone who's receptive; then he'll fall. It's a lot to ask. Meanwhile he contemplates and waits.

Yet the same lyricist also wrote, "I wanna be loved with inspiration, / I wanna be loved starting tonight." One song is reflective, the other assertive. From the beginning, the music is insistent, even demanding. The first five notes of the refrain set a tone, a motif, for the entire song. In each of the four-line A sections, Green repeats those same notes in three different lines. Predictably, the rhythm is strong and driving. Although the narrator wants a love that's strong yet tender, "I only ask for the chance, ..." (Johnny Green, Edward Heyman, and Billy Rose, "I Wanna Be Loved,"

1933). Heyman heard something different in the music, something reflective in Victor Young's melody for "When I Fall in Love," something strident, even needy, in Johnny Green's "I Wanna Be Loved." Yet both lyrics trade in hyperbole. It's essential to the ways in which popular ballads often speak.

"I Wanna Be Loved" uses a conventional AABA structure. Within those limits, a narrator tells someone what he wants: "I wanna be loved starting tonight." The burden is the other person's: "I want your eyes to shine in my direction. Make me care!" "When I Fall in Love" also starts with AABA but then adds an additional C at the end to complete the song's ruminative mood. That final chorus also reveals that the narrator is singing to a specific person. Desire and need find someone worthy of loving even though it hasn't quite happened yet. The song's shaping word is "when": "When I fall in love with you."

When we suggested to a friend who's an authority on theater music from opera to Broadway that you can think about songs as either one-act plays or paintings, he said that some theater songs are exempt from time. He argued especially for story songs in which somebody tells a story about somebody else, especially in a Broadway musical. He's right; everything freezes. The plot stops while we listen to the song. In *Brigadoon*, just before a wedding, a comic character remembers her mother's wedding day. That's the joke. The song is funny but it has nothing to do with the characters or their stories. Time stops while somebody tells a story, but that doesn't mean it isn't memory. The past contains it only as long as we can keep it in mind. I remember the day, the narrator says, I remember and I laugh.

Songwriters count on the sentiment and the word itself. Irving Berlin and Stephen Sondheim both wrote songs they called "Remember," just as the Gershwins and Kurt Weill and Maxwell Anderson wrote songs called "Will You Remember Me?" We found well over a hundred songs with "remember" or "memory" in the title, some standards and many forgotten. And that's only in the title. The two words capture one of the essential viewpoints of popular lyrics. Yet for every song about loss or "forever," we also have songs about falling in love "again." The long list includes such titles as "I'll Never Say 'Never Again' Again," "I'm in Love Again," "Again" ("This couldn't happen again"), "Ready to Begin Again," and "Taking a Chance on Love" ("Here I go again"), in which the word "again" appears two dozen times.

Songs in which time plays an important if sometimes subtle role range from the direct and intense to reassuring observation. They appear to stand still but maybe they don't; they appear to be in motion but maybe they aren't. It can get surprisingly complicated in only a few bars and a few words. The great romantic ballad "As Time Goes By" approaches time in a complex way, but it feels impersonal because lovers never speak to one another. It's a song about advice, abstract but also deeply rooted in memory and experience (Herman Hupfeld, "As Time Goes By," *Everybody's Welcome*, 1931; *Casablanca*, 1942).

We learn very little about the narrator, but he feels to us as if someone older and more knowing tells someone younger what he has learned over the years. Despite the flux all around us, some things never change. The present persists until the last few lines, but it draws upon the past to keep the present alive. Although time passes, "the fundamental things apply." "A kiss," he says, "is still a kiss." Time doesn't stop but the most important things, no matter how simple, remain, perhaps beyond time, perhaps in all times. That's for physics to sort out.

The refrain is dramatic because someone from one generation guides someone from another. A sympathetic voice speaks to someone younger, more innocent, perhaps anxious. Like "Love Is Here to Stay," the song plays off the transitory against the permanent. The advice starts in the verse where the narrator accepts the world as it is. He tries to reassure his listener. Although they live in an unsettled time, he argues for relaxation because the "simple facts of life" do not change. The refrain plays out as an offering of reassurance in the face of anxiety. The permanence of love stands against the passing of time—time, itself, which measures change but which also veers and adapts ever so slightly although we perceive it as fixed. No matter what, a kiss is still a kiss.

The songwriter Herman Hupfeld in only four lines plays with Albert Einstein and, of all things, the theory of relativity:

> Yet, we get a trifle weary
> With Mr. Einstein's the'ry,

The lyric introduces a personal note in these lines and urges the listener to replace the conceptual with the actual:

> So we must get down to earth,
> At times relax, relieve the tension.

Time may be relative, but to find a love that lasts, you have to recognize that you remain earthbound while everything around you changes. Then, only in the last two lines, the lyric nods toward the future: "The world will always welcome lovers." Words like "always" and "forever" are the kind of hyperbole that songs often rely on while, at the same time, remaining earthbound: an older person has offered advice from experience.

In the 1932 musical *Take a Chance*, two small-time gamblers seek their fortunes on Broadway. In the course of the show's ramshackle plot, they meet a tough nightclub singer played by Ethel Merman. The composer Richard A. Whiting and the lyricist B. G. DeSylva wrote Merman a performance number about a prostitute named Eadie. Its uptempo drive and bluesy, bawdy lyrics were well suited to her and her character.

The song sets up a memory. In fact, it has three different layers of time. Merman sings about two middle-aged women she knew, probably hookers, who sit talking about the past. Mabel, "sporty, fat and over forty," remembers a now-dead pal named Eadie who had a shady past but also "class, with a capital K" (Richard A. Whiting and B. G. DeSylva, "Eadie Was a Lady," *Take a Chance*, 1932). From Merman's character to the woman in the song to Eadie, the song layers time. Because it's a performance number, when Merman sings it, ironically, the show comes to a halt until she finishes.

More than three decades later, in the composer John Kander and the lyricist Fred Ebb's *Cabaret*, Sally Bowles, a singer in a seedy Berlin nightclub, has a chance to escape what's happening in 1930s Germany. Instead she chooses to live in carefree ignorance of what's coming. She remembers Elsie, a former roommate who "rented by the hour." When Elsie died, the neighbors came to gloat, but Sally sees something different, even enviable, in her. Because she lived on her own terms, "She was the happiest corpse / I'd ever seen." Sally not only remembers Elsie, she uses her to affirm her own choice to remain in the present as if nothing will change because, after all, "Life is a Cabaret, old chum" (John Kander and Fred Ebb, "Cabaret," *Cabaret*, 1966).

More often than not, love songs with a sunny outlook find themselves content to live in the present. The sentiments are simple, I love you and you love me, but then comes the kicker—and that will never change. It doesn't matter if it's love at first sight, a new love after the loss of love, or a love that survived a bouncy ride. It's here and it's now—for now.

The director Mike Nichols's first movie, *The Graduate*, ends on a note of uncertainty. Benjamin has rescued Elaine from her wedding and they have fled to a crowded bus. He's wearing a windbreaker and sneakers, she a wedding gown. They sit next to one another in the back row, facing slightly away from one another. She glances at him but he doesn't look back. Their faces are expressionless. In the aftermath of audiences' widespread romantic response to their escape, Nichols said, "I think ten minutes after the bus leaves, the girl will say to him, 'My God, I have no clothes.' At least they're out of the terrible world they lived in, but they're not to be envied."[9] The movie's previous hour and forty-five minutes held viewers so intensely in the present that it was hard to reconcile the rest of it with what happens on the bus as it pulls away into whatever future Benjamin and Elaine have.

Songs don't usually end that ambiguously, but they do often live intensely in the present before suddenly turning to the future. The play of time and its capacity to surprise, upend, or reassure is a defining quality in the songs of the Great American Songbook. The songwriters were especially good at manipulating present, past, and future for emotional effect, especially within the constraints of so many popular songs. The way they handle time helps to shape the emotions in song after song—not only time but the way it provides a setting for dozens of emotions, sometimes fixed, sometimes changing even within such a minimal context. Sometimes we see the change coming, sometimes it surprises. Either way, if the song's any good, it satisfies.

In a cheery song from the Great Depression, "I Found a Million Dollar Baby (In a Five and Ten Cent Store)," a young man tells a sweet comic tale in which he finds true love (Harry Warren, Mort Dixon, and Billy Rose, "I Found a Million Dollar Baby [In a Five and Ten Cent Store]," *Crazy Quilt*, 1931). He's telling his story to someone; the lyric is a dramatic monologue and he's the story's punchline. There he was, walking down the street on a weekday in spring when it started to rain. The implication is that he is out of work, although it doesn't dampen his mood. In fact, he calls the April shower "lucky." He darts into a nearby five and ten to wait out the storm. Intending to stay for an hour, he stays for "three or four" because he notices a young woman selling china. When the people standing around notice his interest, he becomes self-conscious:

> And when she made those eyes,
> I kept buying china
> Until the crowd got wise.

He may be broke, but he's not that broke. The song has nothing to say about how they introduce themselves or agree to have a cup of coffee. The courtship never appears in the song. Suddenly, though, the song jumps to the present in what seems in retrospect like an inevitable transition, a single word dropped perfectly onto the music as he brings the person he's talking to up to date. "Incident'ly," he says, as he gives the story its happy ending. If the person he's speaking to should happen to "run into a shower" just as he did:

> Just step inside my cottage door,
> And meet the million-dollar baby
> From the five and ten cent store!

Life isn't a freeze frame. Neither is a single kiss nor an isolating memory. The songwriters of the Great American Songbook knew that as well as anybody, but they also knew how to pull off three to five minutes of idealizing and imagining to make us believe in what they wrote. If the song became a hit, listeners believed in it again and again for a month or two. Then, tired of the repetition on the radio or the 78 rpm recording they'd bought, they sought out something new. Those few minutes of music and words achieved something unbelievable in their own small way. They stopped time even though it never stopped moving.

That's the paradox at the center of so many songs from these years. At first glance everything sounds conventional and predictable, but the hidden complexity is essential to what makes many great songs unusual. The songs that manage the feat range from something lighthearted and sweet to something impassioned. It's the writing, the craft, rather than the emotion, that makes the day. Without the craft, there would be only "blah, blah, blah, moon."

No one manipulated time with greater complexity and nuance than Cole Porter, one of the few of his time who wrote both words and music. Night is the natural setting for his love songs, a time of mystery, the shedding of restraints, and the rise of romance and the erotic. His ballads vary from quiet to intense, eager to sad to buoyant, but all of them swim in the passion that accompanies desire, desire unrequited, desire fulfilled, desire remembered. Lorenz Hart's insouciant line, "Unrequited love's a bore," feels as if it belongs to Porter. Yet for a surprising number of these songs, the sexuality comes from the music while the language is romantic, even elevated. Porter's lovers are not people who sneak off to make love in the back seat of a 1930s Plymouth; they are worldly and sophisticated but no less besotted.

Raised in wealth by a doting mother, Porter was born in Peru, Indiana, but he absorbed East Coast upper-class style as if he'd been born to it. Despite his struggles to establish himself on Broadway and the terrible pain he endured from a crushed leg that eventually had to be amputated, he made everything look effortless. He had started to write songs seriously as an undergraduate at Yale. When his early shows flopped, he licked his wounds in Paris and on the Riviera. As one of the few non-Jews in the top tiers of songwriters during the Great American Songbook, he once told Richard Rodgers that he was the most Jewish composer of all. Rodgers, startled, asked why. Because, Porter explained, I do more writing in the minor keys. He understood that the kind of songs he was most suited to write would benefit from the undertone of melancholy the minor keys gave him.

Ironically, one of his best friends was Irving Berlin, who grew up in poverty on the Lower East Side. Unlike Berlin, whose extraordinary range gave him access to the entirety of the American people, Porter was usually content to write the kinds of songs he knew he was good at. In songs that were among his finest work, he gave a style and voice to the kind of people he might have partied with at country houses in Newport or on Long Island's Gold Coast. In addition to the elegance and sophistication of his writing (which enchanted the American public for decades), the layers of time invest his songs with point of view, mood, and a rich sense of character.

Isolation and separation play an essential role in some of these songs, especially the quieter ones. For "In the Still of the Night," it's hard to tell if the narrator is alone, but he feels separate from the one he loves. Yet the beloved might be asleep beside him (Cole Porter, "In the Still of the Night," *Rosalie*, 1937). Have they made love but he's unable to sleep? The Latin beat of the music invests the quiet with a background of smoldering passion, however understated. Maybe he's watching her as he begins to think and then to wonder. The hour is late, the room dark. Except for the light of the moon.

Time passes largely unnoticed until questions creep into his mind to dominate the second half of the song. Time creates motion because his mood changes. What began as "the still of the night" becomes "in the chill, / Still / Of the night." Do you love me, he wonders, will you continue to love me, or will my dream of our future "fade out of sight / Like the moon / Growing dim"? What starts as a reverie in the deepest hours of night now hinges on the ambiguous word "still" as the moon sets. "Still" here is one of those words that demonstrates Porter's mastery of a form as short as a song. It could mean the quiet in the room as it and the emotions turn chilly. Isolated as it is on its own line, it could also suggest an even deeper stillness brought on by doubt. The story remains unfinished.

That sense of questioning and emotional incompleteness also appears implicitly in Porter's frequent shifting between major and minor keys. Although the song follows a conventional AABA pattern, Porter never quite repeats the A sections exactly. It's as if he's written variations on A. The result is a series of surprises that recurs throughout the melody. In the opening few words of the refrain, "In the still," the first two words consist of two steps in a major key, but "still" takes only a half-step as it shifts from major to minor. It gives unusual emphasis to the most important word in the lyric. Often songwriters use minor keys to suggest melancholy or loss. Porter, however, uses it to create a haunting effect, intensified by the unusual chords that change as often as his shifts in key. It's as if the use of key doesn't matter; the shifts suggest a melodic and chordal fluidity that create a haunting sound characteristic of Porter's ballads. In a lyric that moves quickly from certainty to questioning, melody and harmony suggest the narrator's emotional state.

For those songwriters who were not collaborators, especially Porter and Irving Berlin, it would be fascinating to know if they wrote the melody or lyric first, or if they worked back and forth between them. In his own way, Porter here moves toward a kind of musical modernism, more like Cezanne than Pollack. Cezanne never reaches abstraction while Pollack clearly does. In the same way, Porter never moves to atonal music. His complexity and unpredictably separate him here from the standard structure of many popular songs. Unlike Berlin, who constantly innovated and could apparently write any kind of song if he was willing, in his words, to sweat over it for hours, Porter usually worked back and forth between witty catalogue songs and heated ballads. Yet within those kinds of songs that he wrote again and again, he constantly innovated.

Another Porter ballad, just as quiet, ruminates on parting. A lover speaks to his beloved to remind her of how her departure makes him feel (Cole Porter, "Ev'rytime We Say Good-Bye," *Seven Lively Arts*, 1944). Time stops because with her gone the present keeps repeating itself. Life without her is so empty that it stands outside time. Only when she's near does spring arrive and time resume. When she leaves again, the chords change from major to minor, a sure sign of sadness. Porter's strength lies in his ability to weave eroticism, sadness, stillness, and romance in a single song. The narrator hears a lark begin to sing. He affirms that no love song is finer but, he says, the results are strange when they part:

> But how strange
> The change
> From major to minor
> Ev'ry time we say good-bye.

Over the course of these songs, the tempo may increase and the eroticism intensify, but the introspection continues. A catch phrase like "I've Got You Under My Skin" takes on sexual implications borne out in the lyric (Cole Porter, "I've Got You Under My Skin," *Born to Dance*, 1936). They're necessarily indirect in a song written for a 1936 movie, but they are also unmistakable: "I've got you deep in the heart of me, / So deep in my heart, you're really a part of me." The way Porter repeats the words "deep" and "heart" by varying their use in these two lines intensifies the passion while underscoring both the apparent permanence but also the possible change in the affair.

The song also feels too immediate to think that the narrator is alone. His emotions keep shifting as he responds to her because the song, told in the present, is a history of their affair. He had tried to resist because he knew that "this affair never will go so well." Having succumbed, he'll do anything to keep her near despite the warning that keeps him up at night: "Don't you know, little fool, you never can win, / Use your mentality, / Wake up to reality." The song's one constant, the unchanging beat against which the affair plays itself out past, present, and future, lies in the repeated title line, "I've Got You Under My Skin."

Frank Sinatra recorded a superb, sexy, but swinging version of the song in 1956, but it diminishes the song's emotional complexity and leads audiences to think that Porter wrote it as an uptempo number. In 1936, the original movie performance by Virginia Bruce expresses everything that Porter wrote and suggested even though the singing is stiff.

"Night and Day" is among the most erotic and insinuating of Porter's songs (Cole Porter, "Night and Day," *The Gay Divorce*, 1932). It's startling to realize that the song's verse repeats the same note thirty-five times. Porter used the drumming sound to create "the beat-beat-beat of the tom-tom" and to anticipate by contrast the lushness and density to follow: "Night and day you are the one, / Only you beneath the moon and under the sun." Actually, Porter's use of time is simple here. The narrator imagines his beloved through contrast that keeps her always in his mind:

near and far, in daytime and darkness, and "in the roaring traffic's boom, / In the silence of my lonely room." Porter sets the song in what appears to be a permanent present; only the narrator's mood changes. It depends entirely on her, especially at the end when his misery boils over:

> There's an, oh, such a hungry yearning burning inside of me,
> And its torment won't be through
> Till you let me spend my life making love to you

At that moment, dissatisfied with the world he lives in, he dares to dream about a possible future but with little confidence. He loves her profoundly, but his sexual desire leads him forward. For the most part, though, he feels lost in the present.

At the other end of Porter's emotional range come the songs about casual sex, either an affair or a one-night stand. The songs don't lack emotion or a sense of time, but everything is temporary and giddily transactional, and that suits the lovers just fine. Porter replaces longing or the fear of loss with insouciance, not a quality you find in many other songwriters' work (Cole Porter, "Just One of Those Things," *Jubilee*, 1935).

The lyric here feels off-handed though not unkind; the affair was lovely but now it's over. It was never made of anything stronger than gossamer. As it ends, he retraces its delights, from the irresponsible relish of "just one of those crazy flings" to the indirect sexuality of "a trip to the moon on gossamer wings." However long it lasted was one present moment sustained by the lovers' sexual delight in one another. Only at the end, with the most casual tip of his hat, does he offer a gentle farewell in the same spirit they they've recognized right from the start. It's nothing more than a friendly nod to the future:

> Here's hoping we meet now and then.
> It was great fun,
> But it was just one of those things.

Some years later, Porter wrote "It's All Right with Me," also about the end of a love affair, although here someone is trying to recover from it when a new possibility arises (Cole Porter, "It's All Right with Me," *Can-Can*, 1953). He's met someone; he likes her; now what? He's not over the last one. As he puts it, "It's not her face but such a charming face." That word "but" means everything. The next line gives the game away, "That it's all right with me." The song is an encounter in which the past looms over the present, although a small step toward the future might just be possible. It's about spending a night, not starting an affair, but who knows. And then he realizes that he might not be quite ready. He also doesn't want to send her away with nothing. Porter performs a nicely balanced dance of memory, regret, desire, and anticipation. The man is gentle but also eager yet perhaps not quite ready to take the step. Or is he?

> They're not her lips but they're such tempting lips
> That if some night you're free, . . .
> It's all right with me.

"Night and Day" borders on obsession, but it's not the only song to do so. Porter and his contemporaries learned to do a great deal in something as small as a song. They could carry emotion to its most extreme in a wide variety of ways. Their approach was highly skilled but impersonal; that somehow gave them unequalled range in the portrayal of emotion and the establishing of tone and point of view. As always, the mastery of craft was at the heart of it.

Drugs were not a major problem from the twenties through the forties, but addiction appeared in songs. Early in the century, songs set in Chinatown mention opium as "pipe dreams vanish ev'ry care" (Jean Schwartz and William Jerome, "Chinatown, My Chinatown," 1906). Farther uptown, during the Harlem Renaissance, Cab Calloway was crooning and crowing about "Minnie the Moocher," who "messed around with a bloke named Smokey / She loved him though he was cokey" (Clarence Gaskill, Cab Calloway, and Irving Mills, "Minnie the Moocher," 1931). But these songs are set in out of the way places, dim or wild places, like Chinatown or Harlem.

In a song they wrote in 1932, Harry Warren and Al Dubin also used the idea of addiction to describe love, but the tone was markedly different (Harry Warren and Al Dubin, "You're Getting to Be a Habit with Me," *42nd Street*, 1932). What started as fun has turned serious, but the narrator hasn't lost her sense of humor. She sees what's happening, but rather than breaking it off, she can't get enough of it:

> Let me stay in your arms I'm addicted to your charms
> You're getting to be a habit with me.

The use of the present participle "getting" means that what begins in the present continues into the future. The addiction to love will last.

Some of these songs work by creating a sense of urgency in which nothing but love and the loved one matters. This one begins with no more than a casual glance that turns into love at first sight (Richard Rodgers and Lorenz Hart, "My Heart Stood Still," *One Dam Thing After Another*, 1927). What happens suggests necessity and permanence. Lovers sing to one another in the present because the moment is so compelling:

> I took one look at you,
> That's all I meant to do,
> And then my heart stood still.

Love at first sight may not be especially believable, but we can still wish it was. In a dramatic context, it's one of those things that we're willing to believe at least until the movie, play, or song ends. The surprise, the unpredictability, the swiftness, and the arrival from nowhere give the lyricist an appealing way to idealize love—one of the enduring tasks of the Great American Songbook. Typically, the tone changes from song to song although all of them have one thing in common: the sudden falling, whether it's quiet, contemplative, or dramatic.

For the musical *Pipe Dream*, Rodgers and Hammerstein wrote a quiet first act finale for the male lead to sing to the woman with whom he will eventually fall in love (Richard Rodgers and Oscar Hammerstein II, "All at Once," *Pipe Dream*, 1955). It takes only the smallest moment to suggest its inevitability: "You start to light her cigarette / And all at once you love her." Rodgers set a restrained but sweet melody to Hammerstein's straightforward lyric, adorned only with occasional internal rhyme and assonance. To underscore the immediacy of falling at first sight, Hammerstein wrote in the present tense.

Another song with the same title but written a decade earlier, Kurt Weill and Ira Gershwin's "All at Once" has a more complex perspective. Even in such a restrained song, Gershwin can't avoid being inventive. The lyric is about love at first sight, although, typical of Gershwin, it never mentions love—"All at once, I knew I'd met my one for all" (Kurt Weill and Ira Gershwin, "All at Once," *Where Do We Go from Here?* 1945).

Gershwin's lyric plays off against the use of a number in the title. In the song's second half, "all at once" becomes "once or twice" because the narrator thought that he had found his "one for all" before. He soon found out "that someone never would do." He feared he would never fall when "all at once, my one for all was you." He also adds a nice allusion to a telephone call to demonstrate how the narrator has finally fallen in love at first sight: "For I found when I heard you hello-ing / That my heart somehow was answering your call."

In two very good but very different songs, concentration is the key to obsession. No matter what happens—skies turn gray, trouble brews, people say they're through—the narrator relies on concentration to see himself through: "Whenever the blues become my only songs / I concentrate on you" (Cole Porter, "I Concentrate on You," *Broadway Melody of 1940*, 1940). Everything can change—weather, seasons, the reactions of others—but concentration, the sign of his love, persists. Whatever comes and goes in the passage of time, their love is always alive in the present.

The song also draws its emotional power from a secondary theme of seduction that merges with concentration on "the light in your eyes when you surrender / And once again our arms intertwine." That's one of those euphemisms that the songs of the day had to rely on; fortunately, they are pretty easy to spot. Porter's melody has the brooding sexuality that he mastered early, but the narrator is apparently young—the one element in the song that's hard to fathom. Adolescent hormones have apparently given way to uncommon wisdom:

> To prove that even wise men can be wrong,
> I concentrate on you.

In Thomas "Fats" Waller's sprightly, jazz-inflected melody and Andy Razaf's jaunty conversational lyric, "Concentratin' on You" treats the same set of circumstances in a very different way (Thomas Waller and Andy Razaf, "Concentratin' on You," 1931). The narrator makes fun of himself because he's busy being in love. No matter what goes on in the course of a day, he's got "a one-track mind." "Concentratin'" has got him addled; he loves being giddy:

> I can't figure two and two.
> Got crazy ways, I'm in a daze,
> Concentratin' on you!

Finally, another song in the present, this one uptempo but downbeat, as the narrator dwells hyperbolically on his own sanity. The verse is about loss and what it's done to him:

Thomas "Fats" Waller. Library of Congress.

I'll never be the same, dear,
I'll always place the blame, dear,
On nobody but you.

>(Walter Donaldson, "You're Driving Me Crazy
>[What Did I Do]," *Smiles*, 1930)

It's routine stuff until the refrain takes off. He still bemoans the loss but also describes what it does to him. The mix of loneliness and blame in a driving melody makes the song distinctive. In a song in which he seems to be facing reality, he has no idea why he left but he knows where to place the blame: "What did I do / To you?"

Defined by time no matter what they have to say about love, these songs demonstrate again and again how well the alchemy of collaboration works despite its unlikeliness. There's a deep connection that defines many collaborations—some where the two partners are faithful to one another for decades—the Gershwins, Rodgers and Hart, Rodgers and Hammerstein—and others where they bounce from partner to partner. Despite E. Y. Harburg's friendship with Harold Arlen and the great songs they wrote together, Harburg worked with several dozen composers in the course of his career. How they pulled off their collaborations is an essential part of the story of the Great American Songbook. Part of it was professionalism, but part was also adaptability, reliance on craft, and ease with language. All the things we've been writing about. The impersonality of it. The inauthenticity of it. Until craft plus intuition lend a song the authenticity that listeners seek.

RECORDINGS

Nat King Cole, "Autumn Leaves," 1955
Ruth Etting, "The Song Is Ended (But the Melody Lingers On)," 1928
Sarah Vaughan, "Spring Will Be a Little Late This Year," 1953
Ray Bolger, "Once Upon a Time," 1962
Betty Comden, "Some Other Time," 1960
Lee Wiley, Leo Reisman Orchestra, "Time on My Hands," 1931
Cy Young, Barbara Cook, "You Never Knew About Me," 1965
John Raitt, Jan Clayton, "If I Loved You," 1945
Maude Maggart, "Always," 2005
Frank Sinatra, "I Couldn't Sleep a Wink Last Night," 1944
Annette Hanshaw, "I Cover the Waterfront," 1933
Michael Feinstein, "Love Is Here to Stay," 1998
Eydie Gorme, Steve Lawrence, "Something's Gotta Give," 2018
McGuire Sisters, "When I Fall in Love," 1955
Dinah Washington, "I Wanna Be Loved," 1962
Dooley Wilson, "As Time Goes By," 1943
Ethel Merman, "Eadie Was a Lady," 1947
Jill Haworth, "Cabaret," 1966

Bing Crosby, "I Found a Million Dollar Baby (In a Five and Ten Cent Store)," 1932
Ella Fitzgerald, "In the Still of the Night," 1956
Sarah Vaughan, "Ev'rytime We Say Good-Bye," 1961
Diana Krall, "I've Got You Under My Skin," 1998
Fred Astaire, "Night and Day," 1933
Rosemary Clooney, "Just One of Those Things," 1982
Michael Feinstein, "It's All Right with Me," 2008
Bing Crosby, "You're Getting to Be a Habit with Me," 1933
Jessie Matthews, "My Heart Stood Still," 1933
Perry Como, "All at Once," 1972 (Rodgers and Hammerstein)
Taylor Dorsey, "All at Once," 2014 (Weill and Gershwin)
Carmen McRae, "I Concentrate on You," 1986
Connie Boswell, "Concentratin' on You," 1931
Nick Lucas, "You're Driving Me Crazy (What Did I Do?)," 1930

6

YOUR WORDS AND MY MUSIC

Somebody once asked Cole Porter who wrote "Some Enchanted Evening." He replied, "Rodgers and Hammerstein, if you can imagine that it takes two people to write a song." Yet during the three decades and more of the Great American Songbook, nearly everyone who wrote songs was a collaborator. Collaboration was essential to the way that most professionals worked. Even Irving Berlin, early in his career before he learned to pick out his own tunes on the black keys, collaborated with a composer named Ted Snyder. Their songs included "Wild Cherry Rag" (1909), "Oh. How That German Could Cook" (1909), and "Take a Little Tip from Father" (1911). Strictly speaking, collaborators weren't songwriters at all; they were composers or lyricists. They needed someone else to work with before they could complete a song.

Somebody once approached Eva Kern, the composer's wife, at a party shortly after the opening of *Show Boat*, to praise the show and single out "Ol' Man River" as the greatest song ever written. He went on and on, growing more and more enthusiastic. When he finally paused for a breath, she said, "You're very kind but I'm afraid my husband didn't write 'Ol' Man River.'" The man apologized as profusely as he had praised. Ms. Kern interrupted, "No, no. It's all right. You see, my husband wrote dum-dum-dum-dum. Oscar Hammerstein wrote 'Ol' Man River.'" Irving Berlin was a songwriter and so was Cole Porter along with a few others like Harry Woods ("Try a Little Tenderness") and Herman Hupfeld ("As Time Goes By"). The rest were specialists. Hoagy Carmichael wrote some lyrics and Johnny Mercer an occasional melody, but Carmichael was mainly a composer and Mercer a lyricist.

Robert Frost wrote that "poetry is when an emotion has found its thought and the thought has found words." We've tried unsuccessfully to track down the citation in his writings; numerous online sources quote it without attribution. No luck, but it's adaptable to songwriting. Perhaps a song from the Great American Songbook, when so many songs were the result of collaboration, is the moment when an emotion finds its music and then the words in somebody else's hands also find the music and thus the emotion, too.

Audiences have long been intrigued by what goes on in show business. How do writers, directors, designers, and performers create the illusion? It helps to explain the long-term popularity of backstage musicals on both stage and screen. The fascination persists. How else to explain the YouTube links to rehearsals and recording sessions of Broadway musicals? We recently came upon a link to a Tony Awards ceremony in which we could watch Kelli O'Hara as Anna Leonowens in a revival of *The King and I* do a costume change in forty seconds while another cast member sings on stage.

The interest extends to songwriters, not because those from the Great American Songbook were writing about themselves but because two people could work together to create a new song. It may just be possible that collaboration was so effective during the decades of the Songbook when songs were the result of craft and professionalism rather than personal testimony. On Broadway or in a movie, though, the process became personal and dramatic because the collaborators were writing for specific characters at specific moments in their lives. The act of writing is not usually dramatic. Writers sit at their desks until they finish and then they stand up. That's why stories about songwriters often romanticize the relationship between the collaborators.

In some ways, the relationship between a composer and a lyricist might resemble a love affair or a marriage. It made sense that the songwriters are also the lovers in at least a couple of musicals. In 1978, the professional relationship between the composer Marvin Hamlisch and the lyricist Carole Bayer Sager evolved into something romantic and provided the basis for their successful musical *They're Playing Our Song*. The romantic relationship ended in the early eighties but they continued to work together.

Lady, Be Good! was the Gershwin brothers' first Broadway show together. The MGM adaptation from 1941 dropped the punctuation in the title, replaced all the songs from the 1924 original except the title number and "Fascinating Rhythm," and concocted a new plot. Composer Eddie Crane and lyricist Dixie Donegan are still in love after their second divorce from one another. The plot combines their need to collaborate with their reluctance to get back together again. Nacio Herb Brown and Arthur Freed wrote one of the replacement songs, a love ballad about songwriting called "Your Words and My Music" (Nacio Herb Brown and Arthur Freed, "Your Words and My Music," *Lady Be Good*, 1941). Brown and Freed's workmanlike song weaves together Dixie and Eddie's collaboration with their feelings for one another. They try to fight them off but this kind of movie requires a happy ending: "With your words and my music / A wonderful love song / Is born."

In a similar set of circumstances, Aaron and Georgia, the main characters in the 2007 stage musical *Curtains*, are a divorced songwriting team who have to work together. The John Kander and Fred Ebb show is a send-up of backstage murder mysteries. The police detective assigned to the case would love to be in musical theater. Toward the end of the first act, he and Aaron get talking about writing songs. Aaron guides him about the way a song happens:

> It can start with a note.
> Which can become a phrase.
> And then you try handing words off each branch.
>
> (John Kander, "I Miss the Music," *Curtains*, 2007)

He also cautions him about talking about love:

> Or you'll have to say "fits like a glove"
> or "As certain as push comes to shove."
> You will pine for the woman you're constantly thinking of.

He further cautions him about the word "life" because it leads to such clichés as "cuts like a knife" and "heartbreak and strife," and that leads into the song as Aaron says, "When you find you're missing your . . ." The obvious word is "wife." Aaron knows that he's still in love with Georgia but he won't admit to it. The closest he can come is to put it into a song:

> I miss the song.
> Since she's not with me
> It comes out wrong.

The lyric explains how songwriting has changed for him since they no longer write together:

> But when you're writing a song
> Without a partner,
> That's a completely different matter.

He concludes, "I love the music / I made with her." Kander and the lyricist Fred Ebb were also partners. Ebb died during the writing of the score; some have suggested that "I Miss the Music" is Kander's love song to Ebb.

Collaborators spent a lot of time with one another, but they also had different tasks. They might have become close friends or the relationship might have been entirely professional. They were supposed to complement one another, but a composer might have heard one thing in his music and a lyricist something else. Even the Gershwins, as devoted as they were to one another, sometimes quarreled. They were usually working in the same room, George at the piano and Ira at a nearby desk or bridge table, though sometimes they would sit together at the piano bench.

The composer Frederick Loewe and the lyricist Alan Jay Lerner would sometimes separate because their quarrels were so intense, but they always got back together eventually. Loewe, born in Germany, would usually return to Europe to live the elegant high life of Paris or Berlin, while Lerner, much more determined to keep working, would collaborate with other composers—Kurt Weill, Burton Lane, and Andre Previn—while he waited for Loewe to return.

Some composers wrote the music and had it delivered by messenger to the lyricist; they didn't work in the same room. In other words, it doesn't matter how they collaborated as long as they turned out the songs.

Songwriters in New York found their own collaborators because they hung out in bars where songwriters gathered or because a mutual friend introduced them. The composer John Kander and the lyricist Fred Ebb met in 1962 when Tommy Valando, their music publisher, introduced them. They met at Ebb's apartment soon after that to write a song to see if they were compatible. They first came up with a mock title song for *Take Her, She's Mine*, a musical then running on Broadway, but Kander suggested that they write a ballad. That night they finished "My Coloring Book," which became a hit recording for Barbra Streisand and began their collaboration. They then wrote a complete score for an unproduced musical, *Golden Gate*, which the producer and director Harold Prince described as "a test to see if the collaboration was any good."[1]

They went on to write eighteen Broadway musicals between 1965 and 2015, including *Zorba, Cabaret, Chicago,* and *Kiss of the Spider Woman*. Kander and Ebb's critic and biographer James Leve wrote, "What best defines their voice is the contradictory nature of their collaboration: the composer and lyricist have strikingly different artistic temperaments, the former demonstrably sentimental, the latter campy and cynical."[2]

Hollywood worked differently. Studios would hire a number of songwriters, nearly all of whom had started in New York but who were lured West by the combination of sunshine and money. Not all of them loved it. They were, in effect, signing away their independence. The studios assigned composers and lyricists to one another willy-nilly. Because they were skillful and relied on their craft, they usually adapted quickly to the new way of doing things. Some did the work, took the money, and grabbed the next train back. Ira Gershwin and Harold Arlen loved California; Berlin, Porter, and George Gershwin were always ready to return to Manhattan. Some of the time, Rodgers and Hart did their work in New York and mailed it to California. Berlin, as eager as he was to return to his family in New York, hung around for the shooting to make sure they handled his songs properly.

Even so, the studios often treated their songs with disrespect. They were just one more piece of the movie to be manipulated. Like screen writers, songwriters were usually not taken seriously. The filmmakers offered big money and then did as they pleased with the results. The lyrics might disappear because a director turned a song into a dance number or, even worse, background music for a scene of dialogue. A producer might also tell the songwriters that they were going to write new songs for a movie version of a hit musical from Broadway. Out went the songs of Cole Porter or Rodgers and Hart, and suddenly lesser songwriters in California were writing replacements for fellow composers and lyricists whose songs they admired.

The lyricist Gene Lees once said that setting words to music was the better way to write because beginning with the words made a song feel forced. Somehow, he said, the concreteness of language is more resilient than the music. It's hard to explain why, but so many songs start with the music that it might be so. Beginning with the words feels counterintuitive. Music is abstract and suggestive; that should make it more flexible than language. Words are concrete, grounded in experience. They express the song's emotions directly or metaphorically, and they have their own music. The lyric connects love to the listener's experience. In the unnumbered foreword to his collection of lyrics, Ira Gershwin said that he wrote "by fitting words mosaically to music already composed."[3]

Putting a song together in the first half of the twentieth century resembled an assembly line, the industrial model of the day. Two different people wrote the music and lyrics while others wrote an arrangement, published the song, hired a conductor and musicians, and then hired a singer to perform in a movie or on the stage before recording it. More songs began with the music than the other way around, but a good number of songs also began with the words. The Gershwins, Arlen and Mercer, and Arlen and E. Y. Harburg began with the music. So did Harry Warren and Al Dubin almost all the time, although "Lullaby of Broadway" was an exception. Dubin wrote the words in a Mexican whorehouse and read them to Warren over the telephone because he knew how much Warren missed New York. Like so many other lyricists, Harburg wanted the music to come first because "a great song requires a great melody that comes right out of the heart and brain of the composer without any constriction imposed by a lyric . . . a great composer brings out the best in a lyricist: the melody acts as a discipline on his wit and invention."[4]

Jerome Kern insisted on writing the music first. The songwriters who came of age in the twenties and thirties called him "the Dean." Despite his shyness, he was very emotional and could be intimidating, even imperious. He made a point of collaborating only with people he liked. Dorothy Fields was nineteen years younger than he and irreverent. He had been raised in upper-middle-class comfort, she in show business, but he came to be very fond of her and loved her lyrics. She called him Junior and he let her get away with it. In 1936, he and Fields were collaborating on the Astaire-Rogers movie *Swing Time*. Fields said of the sumptuously romantic "The Way You Look Tonight," "The first time Jerry played that melody for me I had to leave the room because I started to cry"[5] (Jerome Kern and Dorothy Fields, "The Way You Look Tonight," *Swing Time*, 1936). She soon came up with the idea for a lyric that would play the abstract "someday" and the concrete "tonight" against one another:

> I will a feel a glow just thinking of you
> And the way you look tonight.

The single sentence's inherent music and natural rhythm make the song feel as if both words and music emerged whole in a single moment.

Fields had a gift for lifting everyday language to the level of melody, never more so than here.

Kern rarely made an exception to his determination to write the music first. In 1940, when Paris fell to the Nazis, Oscar Hammerstein was heartbroken. He loved Paris more than any other city and poured his feelings into a lyric. Kern understood the depth of Hammerstein's distress and willingly set it to music. "The Last Time I Saw Paris" was their only song together not written for a show, although they did place it in the movie *Lady Be Good* (Jerome Kern and Oscar Hammerstein II, "The Last Time I Saw Paris," *Lady Be Good*, 1940).

When Richard Rodgers wrote with Lorenz Hart, he wrote the music first, but Hammerstein, his second major collaborator, preferred to write the lyrics first. Rodgers adapted effortlessly to Hammerstein and also began to write more melodiously than he had with Hart. In other words, there are no rules. It's up to the individual songwriters. Hammerstein was a slow worker. He could spend as long as three weeks on a single lyric even though he usually wrote very simply. Beginning with *Oklahoma!*, when he gave Rodgers a finished lyric, he noticed that "it takes him an hour or two and his work is done. He responds remarkably to words, and when he likes them, they immediately suggest tunes to him."[6] Rodgers's explanation paralleled Hammerstein's: "When the lyrics are right, it's easier to write a tune than to bend over and tie your shoe laces. Notes come more spontaneously than words."[7]

Johnny Mercer would usually be in the same room with the composer, but he would zone out as he listened so intently to the music and to what he was trying to write that he rarely replied to anything the composer said. He worked for half a day at a time, but when he returned the next morning, he'd reenter the zone for as long as it took. A notoriously slow worker, he might need several weeks to finish a lyric. This story involves Mercer and either Arlen or Warren. The composer asked Mercer in passing how his wife was. He got no answer so he went to lunch. When he got back an hour and a half later, Mercer was still lying there. Without opening his eyes, he said, "She's fine."

Once Mercer had finished a lyric, he'd come back to earth. In one instance he and composer Harold Arlen loved what they had written, but both felt that the opening was weak. Finally, Arlen said, "Why not move this section to the top." The frustrated Mercer agreed. And so "Blues in the Night" begins, "My mama done tol' me / When I was in knee pants" (Harold Arlen, Johnny Mercer, "Blues in the Night," *Blues in the Night*, 1941).

When the composer Kurt Weill fled the Nazis, first to France and then to the United States, he already knew about jazz and liked it. Yet he wanted to work, not with lyricists, but with literary figures, especially Maxwell Anderson and Langston Hughes. Weill insisted on setting his music to a finished lyric, but he found that he was spending enormous amounts of time teaching a playwright and a poet how to write a lyric. Anderson had to learn that it wasn't dialogue and Hughes that it wasn't a poem. At that point, Weill turned to working with lyricists, particularly Ira Gershwin and Alan Jay Lerner, although he did continue to work with Anderson.

Weill and Gershwin had a problem, though. Weill was used to writing music once he received a lyric; Ira Gershwin was used to setting lyrics to music. They worked out a compromise: they agreed that Gershwin would send Weill eight bars' worth of lyrics. Weill sent back the eight bars of music to fit Ira's words plus another eight bars of music. Ira set words to the new eight bars and then wrote eight more bars of lyrics. It drove them crazy, as did the fact that Weill was in New York and Gershwin was in Hollywood. Weill moved to California.

Yet there was more to it than geography because making a song is a tricky business. Just how do you cobble together music and words to make the result seem effortless and spontaneous when it's anything but, especially when two sets of hands are doing the work? The lyricist E. Y. Harburg had an intuitive understanding of what happened when composer and lyricist pulled it off because he also understood a great deal about the reconciliation of opposites. He'd been writing songs for a long time when he observed, "The words give destination and meaning to the music, and the music gives wings to the words. Together as a song they go places you've never been before. . . . The composer is merely luckier; he works in a medium in which the appeal is directly to the emotions. The lyric writer must hurdle the mind to reach the heart."[8]

Even so, composers could be very possessive about their work. Jerome Kern, trained in operetta, did not like jazz because musicians changed what he'd written. In the 1930s, he struggled to write in the new swing time. For the movie *Swing Time*, Fred Astaire wanted to dance with Ginger Rogers to the new up-to-date rhythms. Kern was not especially happy with the idea but he was game—except he couldn't make it work. He, the arranger Robert Russell Bennett, and Astaire spent an entire afternoon together. Astaire would dance while Kern tried to set music to the beat of his movements. It took hours but he finally got it. To thank Astaire, he wrote a dance number for him titled "The Waltz in Swing Time."

Richard Rodgers was appalled when he heard Peggy Lee's highly stylized recording of "Lover." He had written it as a waltz in 1932; Lee recorded it with a frenetic Latin-tinged arrangement in 1952. He told someone that she should have left it alone: "I don't know why Peggy picked on me when she could have fucked up 'Silent Night.'"[9] Then he found out what the recording was earning him in royalties and stopped complaining (Richard Rodgers and Lorenz Hart, "Lover," *Love Me Tonight*, 1932). Almost predictably, in 1939 he and Hart had written a song called "I Like to Recognize the Tune": "I want to savvy what the band is playing. / I keep saying, must you bury the tune?" (Richard Rodgers and Lorenz Hart, "I Like to Recognize the Tune," *Too Many Girls*, 1939).

Many composers and lyricists loved to perform their new songs for their fellow songwriters. It was a way to test what they'd written. They could be very tough critics as well as enthusiastic admirers, but they were all professionals and prided themselves on their honesty with one another. During the thirties, they'd gather in the Gershwin brothers' large Manhattan brownstone to play their new songs for one another. E. Y. Harburg, who was a regular at these sessions, said:

> You wouldn't dare write a bad rhyme or a cliched phrase or an unoriginal or remotely plagiarized tune, because you were afraid of being ripped apart by your peers. The continuous give-and-take added to the creative impulse. It worked as an incentive, opened up new ideas, made it necessary to keep working and evolving.[10]

Jerome Kern hosted similar gatherings one Monday evening a month at his home in Hollywood. A mutual friend called Kern to say he ought to invite Jule Styne after the newly arrived Styne had written his first hits. Kern said that he'd been wanting to meet him. A few nights later, Styne found himself in the company of Kern, Ira Gershwin, Harry Warren, Hoagy Carmichael, Johnny Mercer, and Harold Arlen. Styne recalled, "If anyone had written a new song, it might be played that night." Kern said to him, "You've got a No. 1 song now. Please play it for us." When he finished playing "It's Been a Long, Long Time," he and Kern talked about it. All Styne could think was, "Good God, I'm actually talking to the Jerome Kern."[11]

The next day, Kern called Styne to invite him to breakfast. Styne got no sleep at all, wondering if Kern had recommended him for a movie or if he'd written a new melody and wanted Styne's reaction. After breakfast, in the library, Kern opened a drawer. Styne thought he'd be taking out a script. It was a daily racing form; Styne was known throughout Hollywood as a knowledgeable gambler. Kern, who loved to play the horses, said, "I hear you're the greatest handicapper in town. Ira Gershwin told me."[12]

Kern developed a different kind of relationship with Johnny Mercer when they wrote the songs for the Fred Astaire/Rita Hayworth musical *You Were Never Lovelier*. Kern was fifty-seven, painfully shy, and revered by his fellow composers as the greatest of them all. Mercer was only thirty-three and outgoing, but he wrote:

> We hit it off right away. I was in such awe of him, I think he must have sensed that. He was very kind to me, treated me more like a son than a collaborator. And when he thought I had a great lyric he said, "Eva, Eva, come down here" and kissed me on the cheek and he said, "Eva, I want you to hear this lyric." Well, of course I was thrilled that he liked it that much.[13]

"I'm Old-Fashioned" is the song that moved Kern to act so impulsively (Jerome Kern and Johnny Mercer, "I'm Old-Fashioned," *You Were Never Lovelier*, 1942). He had written one of his soaring melodies, but Mercer brought it down to earth through a series of familiar old-fashioned references from the "sound of rain / Upon a windowpane," to "the starry song that April sings." Each of the allusions lasts only a line but each of them also points to the song's closing in which the narrator affirms his desire to remain old fashioned as long as the one he loves returns that love. Avoiding the hyperbole and wit of a song like the Gershwins's "Love Is Here to Stay," Mercer keeps the language simple and devoid of a great deal of drama except in the release where the narrator follows Kern's ascending, increasingly dramatic music to assert the possibility of love's permanence against the transitory nature of everything else: "But sighing sighs, holding hands, / These my heart understands."

Beyond that, Kern composed a melody that feels old fashioned without a trace of syncopation. Usually a stickler for well-constructed, perfectly formed songs, he discarded the standard AABA form. The first chorus establishes a melody in three lines, ending "I love the old-fashioned things." Rather than repeating it for a second A, Kern writes a new three-line melody in a release that gives Mercer the chance to expand on the things that someone old-fashioned embraces even though they come and go, particularly the rain and April.

It is by far the most dramatic part of the song. That's not surprising; it's a good place for a song's climax. But Kern gives Mercer a series of short phrases, each a measure long, the start of each phrase set one note above the last: from "sighing sighs" to "understands." Kern then returns briefly to A for two lines ("I'm old-fashioned, / But I don't mind it") before inventing a new C section to end the song. Mercer's lyric takes advantage of the innovative ending to have the narrator turn directly to the one he loves to say that he wants to be old-fashioned "as long as you agree / To stay old-fashioned with me." At the end, a song about personal pleasures becomes a love song. Kern has written an unusual ABAC with which Mercer matches an open-hearted lyric that matches emotional directness to melodic innovation, illustrating yet again the complexity behind simplicity.

Mercer was lucky. Any collaboration comes with its own perils. A true collaborator becomes something more than someone who completes a task and walks away. When Arlen and Harburg were finishing their score for *The Wizard of Oz*, it suddenly dawned on them that they had no song for Judy Garland. They needed something that would suit a child of twelve as well as an eighteen year old with a big voice, something sad but with a glimmer of hope. "Over the Rainbow" turned out to be a major challenge. Arlen could not come up with a melody that satisfied him. He and his wife went for a drive one night so he could clear his head. As he passed Schwab's Drug Store in Hollywood, a soaring melody suddenly swept through his mind. He raced home to write it down. He said years later, "It was as if God had said, 'Okay, you've got your melody. Now stop whining.'"

Arlen called Harburg the next morning. When Harburg arrived, Arlen played the tune for him. His piano style was elaborate and ornamental. Harburg couldn't find the melody in it. He said, "Harold, I can't write a song to that. Play it again." He did, but Harburg could still find nothing in the song to connect to. The two men weren't angry but they were upset. They were highly professional and had had great success; they were also good friends. Finally, Harburg suggested that they try again tomorrow. When he got home, he called his friend Ira Gershwin and invited him to come with him the next day. Arlen played the melody for both of them. Gershwin was as puzzled as Harburg. Then he had a brainstorm: "Harold, play it with one finger." When Harburg heard the unadorned melody, he said, "Oh, that I can write to!"

That doesn't mean it was easy. The word "rainbow" never appears in L. Frank Baum's original book. Harburg put it in the song and thus in the film to counter Baum's description of Kansas as an arid place of browns and tans. But the struggle to write the lyric provides a lesson in the fragility of a lyric even though it may feel inevitable, and also the tentativeness of the process. Harburg began with a dummy title: "Over the Rainbow Is Where I Want to Fly." "A title," he said, "has to ring a bell, has to blow a couple of candles off." What he found most daunting were those first two notes an octave apart. He tried a number of titles: "I had difficulty coming to the idea of "Somewhere." For a while I thought I would just leave those first two notes out. It was a long time before I came to "Somewhere over the rainbow."[14]

Jule Styne was a songwriting machine. He wrote the music for such World War II hits as "I Don't Want to Walk Without You," "I'll Walk Alone," and "It's Been a Long, Long Time" before moving to Broadway, where his successful scores included *Bells Are Ringing*, *Funny Girl*, and *Gypsy*. A scrap of an idea and he'd start writing tunes, often finishing something in just a few minutes but then calling the next morning to announce (without saying hello), "Listen, it won't work." "What won't work, darling?" "The thing, yesterday, the thing."[15]

That Tin Pan Alley mindset made him suspect when he began to write for Broadway. The colyricists Betty Comden and Adolph Green, with whom he eventually wrote several successful shows, at first saw him as "a pop songwriter, a peacockish, movie-jaded tunesmith, not necessarily a composer and certainly not one of Broadway quality."[16] But Styne felt ready for the Big Apple.

He was a musical bumblebee, flitting here and there and everywhere, and in the process turning out some memorable melodies. He always hoped that at least one song from each of his scores would become a hit. Yet he had learned to write for Broadway in Hollywood. The film composer Walter Scharf said of him:

> If you think about it, Republic [Studios] was where Jule got his start in theatrical training. . . . He was always so careful that the music would fall in with the lyrics. He developed a great knack of being cognizant of the lyrics at Republic. When the high notes came, the right vowel would be on them. He'd never have a high note on a closed vowel. . . . He married the music to the words.[17]

When he was still writing for the movies, Styne's most successful songs resulted from his collaboration with the lyricist Sammy Cahn. Styne would drive them both to work in the morning. Cahn, who was given to late-night carousing, rarely spoke, but as they drove, he'd hand Styne a list of possible titles or partial lyrics. When they sat down to work, they usually started from a title or dummy lyric. They wrote and rewrote separately, often in Styne's house. Jule would sit at a desk, scribbling notes before trying out what he had at the piano, while Sammy hunted and pecked at a typewriter in another room. When they finally came together to finish the song, Cahn would ask Styne to play the new melody over and over again, as slowly as he could. "Play it again," he'd say, "but slower." He was absorbing the tune, the rhythms, and the emphases so he could add or change words.

Harburg, who was more thoughtful than most about the writing of songs and the results, observed that "the words give destination and meaning to the music and the music gives wings to the words. Together as a song they go places you've never been before." It was the result of their composer's and lyricist's mastery of craft. Harburg was also one of several lyricists who loved to talk about rhyme. He relished digging down into the details of lyric making. It was his craft and he was proud of it. A song like "Happiness Is Just a Thing Called Joe" is a fine example of his work but also underscores the possibilities that arise when a composer and lyricist like, trust, and respect one another. In this case, the composer was Harold Arlen.

In 1940, the composer Vernon Duke and the lyricist John Latouche had written the score for the all-Black Broadway show *Cabin in the Sky*. Among their songs were the title number and "Taking a Chance on Love." Ironically, Duke had asked Harburg to collaborate on the score, but Harburg turned him down because he felt that Duke's elegant melodies didn't fit the characters or their situations—poor African Americans living in the rural South during the Great Depression. Duke was furious at him.

Three years later, as the M.G.M. producer Arthur Freed was overseeing the show's adaptation into a movie, he asked Harburg to write some additional songs, what Freed called "Southern songs." Harburg understood that he was to write songs for African Americans to sing. He also understood that there could be no better person to write the music than Harold Arlen. The composer had a passion for the blues and had been raised on the melancholy of Jewish liturgical music. As the jazz critic John

W. Wilson wrote, Arlen belongs "alongside Duke Ellington rather than Richard Rodgers or Jerome Kern or Irving Berlin."[18]

Arlen, who understood clearly what he had achieved but retained his natural modesty, once told an interviewer:

> I have been able to capture the feeling, and only the feeling of the black experience in my music.... "Happiness Is Just a Thing Called Joe" is wistful and poignant but it's not the blues.... There are a number of blues strains in my songs.... There's a rapport there ... but technically you can't really call that the blues either.[19]

Harburg, who collaborated with dozens of composers, saw in Arlen a mix of African American musical sensibility and a grounding in Hebraic melodies that gave Harburg "a fresh chemical reaction."[20] The collaborators did not replace any of Duke and Latouche's songs but added five new songs, including "Happiness Is Just a Thing Called Joe." Arlen initially took a melody from his trunk but decided that it was too ordinary to serve as the story's major love song intended for the singer Ethel Waters. Harburg tried to change the composer's mind; he loved what Arlen had written. Insisting that the composer play it one more time, Harburg suddenly blurted, "Happiness is just a thing called Joe." The best lyricists have a gift for hearing words in the music. Yip Harburg was no exception. He said later, "Harold had a lot of tunes that he threw away that I would love to resuscitate."[21]

Arlen, who usually wrote complicated melodies, here writes something much simpler (Harold Arlen and E. Y. Harburg, "Happiness Is Just a Thing Called Joe," *Cabin in the Sky*, 1943). The smooth legato rhythm relies on a series of quarter notes followed by a long note at the end of each line: "He's got a way that makes the angels heave a sigh." The melody moves stepwise in 4/4 time, with an occasional skip for a touch of variety. Arlen is in complete control as Harburg will be when he adds the lyric. Perhaps the most complicated part of the song lies in the way Arlen constructs an unusual ABACA pattern, but the changes from section to section are subtle. Although the B section changes key, beginning with "he's got a way that makes angels have a sigh / When they know little Joe's / Passing by," both melody and rhythm are the same as in A. The only strong contrast comes in the three lines of C ("Troubles fly away an' life is easy go. / Does he love me good, / That's all I need to know") where both melody and rhythm rise climatically to "easy go" before Arlen soon returns to a third A at the end.

Although the song is a love ballad, Harburg was very much aware that he was writing for a distinct character: a religious, middle-aged Black woman who loves her conniving husband but tries to reform him. The lyric contrasts images of poverty ("The cabin's gloomy and the table's bare") with images of hope ("He's got a way that makes the angels heave a sigh"), but Harburg also emphasized rhyme as a way to propel the song. He said, "You want to rhyme as many places as you can without the average ear spotting it as merely mechanical."[22]

His biographers point out some of the best examples in the song. They include rhyme, internal rhyme, and assonance. They're the lines we'd have chosen too: "He's got a smile that makes the lilacs wanna grow" and more subtly, "Sometimes the cabin's gloomy an' the table bare." Harburg could flaunt his rhyming in bright colors, but he was also capable of small telling touches to engage the ear of listeners without their ever knowing it.

It's hard to believe, but hearing words in the music and suddenly blurting out a title is something some lyricists are very good at, none more so than Sammy Cahn. When he began his collaboration with Jule Styne early in World War II, Styne brought him a completed melody. Cahn asked him to play it again but slower. Suddenly Cahn said, "I've heard that song before." Styne bristled until Cahn explained that it wasn't a criticism but a title.[23] In his autobiography, Cahn explained that when he hears a new tune, a title comes instantly to mind. Exaggerated? Perhaps. But Cahn did have a way of hearing words in the notes.

A few years later, he and Styne were writing a score for the movie *Romance on the High Seas*, starring Doris Day in her first movie. They needed a song for a scene in which actor Jack Carson takes Day to a nightclub in Cuba. Before starting to work, Styne always warmed up by playing the same waltz and tango that he'd made up some time earlier. Cahn writes about what happened next:

> Suddenly I began to listen to the tango, and I said: "What's that?" and Jule said, "Just something I've been playing for two years," and I said, "Play it again, slowly." And he did. "Once more, slower." He did, and we wrote "It's Magic."[24]

Beyond craft, many of these songwriters also worked by intuition. They had mastered all the devices of their trade, they understood the purpose of a song, and sometimes the writing was easy, sometimes hard. It was a rational process, marked by trial and error, but they often felt their way to the result. Cahn often said that once he had a title, everything else flowed naturally. Once he had, "I've heard that song before," it was only logical to explain: "It's from an old familiar score, / I know it well, that melody." For him, anyway, it felt inevitable.

Never underestimate the importance of a dummy melody or especially a dummy lyric. Dummy lyrics let composers hear how words fit their melody, but, more important, they help lyricists get the melody into their heads when they turn to writing. It shows them the patterns of sound and the emphatic notes or musical phrases. Nobody on either side expects the dummy to last; it's nothing more than a device. And then there was "Tea for Two."

In 1925, the composer Vincent Youmans and the lyricist Irving Caesar were collaborating on the score for a new musical to be called *No, No Nanette*. It would be the longest-running musical of the decade. Youmans was going to pick up Caesar because they'd both been invited to a party at Gertrude Lawrence's. He arrived early because he was excited about a new tune he'd just written and wanted Caesar to hear it. He pressed Caesar to write a lyric for it then and there, but Caesar wanted to nap before they left for the party. To stop Youmans's nagging, he dashed off a dummy lyric with a catch phrase for a title. In the end they used what Caesar had written without changing a word.

It was a common habit in songs from the Great American Songbook for lyricists to repeat the title line several times in their seventy-five or eighty words, sometimes with variations but always recognizably. For this song, though, the title appears only once. That's because Caesar never expected to use what he'd dashed off that afternoon:

> Picture you upon my knee,
> Just tea for two and two for tea.
>
> (Vincent Youmans and Irving Caesar, "Tea for Two," *No, No, Nanette*, 1925)

The song is more than it appears at a first listening. Although Youmans and Caesar wrote it as a duet, the boy sings the first verse and the girl the second. He's hoping to woo and wed her; she's just as charmed by him as he is by her but she'd like to wait a little while. A city boy, he envisions giving up "homes that are rented" for a move to the country or perhaps to the new suburbs that were so appealing to young married New Yorkers in the 1920s. The lyric is charming, simple, and inviting, but Caesar brings a dash of inventiveness to it, especially in his unusual triple rhyme. The first two rhymes are conventional, but the third requires an additional line for completion—"place is," "oasis," and "chase / Is":

> Darling, this place is
> A lover's oasis,
> Where life's weary chase
> Is unknown.

For Youmans's tripping melody, he provides an equally tripping lyric of one- and two-syllable words but has some clever two- and even three-syllable rhyme words that never slow the song's forward motion because he relies mainly a quick short vowels and crisp consonants:

> I'm discontented
> With homes that are rented
> So I have invented
> My own.

Mostly, though, Caesar follows where Youmans's music takes him. The lyric has to be lighthearted because the music is. Youmans had written two different verses, each with an identical AABA structure, as if each were a song complete in itself. That's not common in verses. Each of the verses here, though, uses the same structure—except that both B sections are a line shorter:

> Far from the cry of the city,
> Where flowers pretty
> Caress the streams.

For the refrain Youmans has teased out a melody that departs from the expected. He breaks the pattern invisibly, and Caesar joins him soft-shoe step by soft-shoe step. A typical refrain has an AABA structure with the same melody repeated in each of the A sections. Only the B—the release—is different. Here, though, the release sits between the song's only two A sections. Caesar adapts his rhymes, internal rhymes, repetitions, and use of assonance to wed words to music in a way that makes the finished song more complex, clever, and satisfying well beyond its likability.

The playfulness begins at the very beginning, with rhymes, internal rhymes, and alliteration:

> Picture you upon my knee,
> Just tea for two and two for tea

Youmans's refrain moves from the three-line A to a five-line B that Caesar uses to pick up the rhyme in the final line of A: "Just me for you and you for me alone." But he also moves the rhyme sound back a beat so that it's the next-to-last word in each line. Meanwhile, he's still using internal rhyme, reversals, alliteration, and assonance constantly. The song is weightless:

> Nobody near us to see us or hear us,
> No friends or relations on weekend vacations
> We won't have it known, dear
> That we own a telephone, dear.

Youmans then follows with two more choruses, another A and a new C. Each of them is three lines long, with different rhyme schemes to suit the feel of the music. The second A is a tour de force of rapid rhyming:

> Day will break and you'll awake
> And start to bake a sugar cake
> For me to take for all the boys to see.

It's exactly one breath long.

C is the most strikingly different section of the song. It is an assertive coda that uses a more insistent melody to suggest the shifting of desire to intention. It also borrows its single rhyme sound from the last line of the second A along with the assonant long "e" that's so important to C, especially in the final line. In both the rhyme words, Caesar precedes the final "ee" with the closed vowel "i."

> We will raise a family,
> A boy for you, a girl for me,
> Oh, can't you see how happy we will be?

That's the song's only question, as if to remind us that, even though they're both in love, his determination to marry her and her unwillingness to marry now aren't in alignment. The song is airy and simple, perhaps even a lesson in the skill it takes to create believable simplicity.

The working titles that Cahn handed to Styne in Styne's convertible as they drove to work were often catch phrases. They are familiar (or feel familiar). They are similar to the use of clichés that Ira Gershwin described (see chapter 2). That's also true for songwriters who, like the Gershwins, worked exclusively on Broadway (plus the occasional foray to Hollywood). When Frederick Loewe and Alan Jay Lerner collaborated, they would decide where in a new musical to place a song, for which character, and under what set of plot circumstances. They defined the song before they wrote it. They also started with a tentative title that was often a catch phrase, though sometimes altered slightly to make it more interesting. Such songs in Lerner and Loewe's shows number in the dozens, including "Almost Like Being in Love" from *Brigadoon*; "How to Handle a Woman" from *Camelot*; and "Get Me to the Church on Time," "A Little Bit of Luck," and "Wouldn't It Be Loverly?" from *My Fair Lady*. It's fair to say that no songwriter did without those phrases that immediately sound familiar.

It's easy to get caught up in the rhythm, wordplay, and sentiment of a song by the Gershwins, much of it given a jazzy drive by George's love for syncopation. Eventually, though, the song often deepens once you notice how George and Ira combined what they were doing. It wasn't as simple as George wrote the music and then Ira wrote the words.

It's just possible that what went on between the two of them was the most interesting collaboration of all. Deena Rosenberg believes that "George heard music in Ira's lyrics, Ira heard lyrics in George's music, and their songs sound as if music and lyrics emerge from a single source."[25] The brothers were very close to one another. At one point they shared a house on 103rd Street in Manhattan, but their personalities were strikingly different—Ira contented to stay in with his books, George the perennially eligible bachelor. George always wrote the music first, but they also had different ways of working together. The lines between writing music and words sometimes blurred. Ira might suggest something about the sounds of words for George to work with, or he might ask George to extend a line by a note or two to fit a lyric he was working on. George might revise a line of music once he heard Ira's tentative lyric.

One night, Ira was reading when George got home at about one in the morning. He took off his tuxedo jacket and asked Ira if he wanted to work. Ira answered that he'd been thinking about a spot in the movie they'd been working on. It was set in England so he thought that they ought to write something about fog. "How about a foggy day in London or a foggy day in London town?"[26] George preferred the use of "town." He also knew that it would lengthen the refrain's first musical line even slightly in this reflective, slightly meandering song.

That single word and note changed the song from something inviting to something memorable, something vaguely English rather than American (especially when sung by an American who's fallen in love with an English woman in the movie *A Damsel in Distress*). It also helped George to shape a flowing musical line. It was the kind of lyrical melody that he wrote more often in the 1930s, as opposed to his more percussive writing in the 1920s. The percussive titles include "I Got Rhythm," "Fascinating Rhythm," and "That Certain Feeling." Yet even in a lyrical melody like "A Foggy Day," George borrowed from his earlier syncopated composing style: "(Beat) A foggy day (Beat) in London Town" (George Gershwin and Ira Gershwin, "A Foggy Day (in London Town)," *A Damsel in Distress*, 1937). In an hour they'd written the refrain, words, and music; they'd never written a song so quickly—with the exception of the much simpler "Do, Do, Do" a decade earlier. Fred Astaire sings it in the movie as he wanders through a foggy rural setting late at night. He remembers that when he fell in love in "foggy London Town / The sun was shining everywhere" because he's in love. "Shining" ends the song with a dazzling surprise. The line rises musically to "shin" and then leaps up to "ing," a sign of his delight, before quieting to "everywhere." The passion of his memory lasts for only a moment but it suffices.

The Gershwins's way of collaborating, including occasional disagreements, extended through nearly all the songs they wrote together. Each of the short staccato lines for "Fascinating Rhythm" had only five or six notes (except for the release):

> Fascinating Rhythm,
> You've got me on the go!
>
> (George Gershwin and Ira Gershwin,
> "Fascinating Rhythm," *Lady, Be Good!*, 1924)

When Ira showed George the lyric, George said that the fourth ("I'm all a-quiver") and eighth ("Just like a flivver") lines should have a double rhyme. At that point, Ira had written one-syllable rhymes and had given equal weight to the word just before the rhyme words. He liked the forceful way the line ended. George couldn't see it, though. They argued for days. Eventually Ira gave in "after George proved to me that I had better use the double rhyme; because, whereas in singing, the notes might be considered even, in conducting the music, the downbeat came on the penultimate note."²⁷

From time to time, Ira would suggest to George that he'd like to work with certain sounds or words. One evening before dinner, he said that he thought they could do something with "do, do" and "done, done." They went up to George's studio on the top floor and, in half an hour, wrote the refrain to "Do, Do, Do":

> Do, do, do
> What you've done, done
> Before, Baby.
>
> (George Gershwin and Ira Gershwin,
"Do, Do, Do," *Oh, Kay!*, 1926)

George's music for the verse starts with a line that feels like the lead-in to a romantic ballad: "I remember the bliss." But then much of the lyric, with its play on "do" and "done," starts to feel silly until the release once again feels like a ballad thanks to George's sighing melody for which Ira places rhyme words at the start of the first three lines as well as at the end: "Let's try again, / Sigh again, / Fly again to heaven." As George's melody soars, Ira finds its ideal lyrical expression.

When George Gershwin was working on *Porgy and Bess*, he wrote a sixteen-bar tune that he thought might work as the basis of a song for the character of Sportin' Life. His brother asked for a lead sheet and wrote a dummy title across the top of the page. They were the first words to come to his head: "It ain't necessarily so." He later said, "I could just as well have written 'An order of bacon and eggs.' . . . The sense didn't matter. All I required was a phrase which accented the second, fifth, and eight syllables to help me remember the rhythm."²⁸

If you're one of those who thinks that song lyrics happen by a combination of good luck and faith in inspiration, you ought to treat Ira Gershwin's *Lyrics on Several Occasions* as required reading. Of course, accident plays a role, as it does in all the arts. What matters though is recognizing what you've stumbled upon and claiming it for your own. This taking of control is just the sort of thing that Ira Gershwin did very well. He was a mischievous writer. Yet his lyrics don't come across as the kind of showing off we came to expect from Lorenz Hart. In Gershwin's adept hands, they are clever and inventive but feel natural and effortless. And here we are, approaching inevitability yet again.

Ira Gershwin was a lyricist, not a writer of stories or essays, but he believed that "there are wonderful things you can do with words."[29] He read what he wrote as a lyricist would. He had to work with a composer and adapt language to music. He also pointed out that if you didn't know the melody, you might read two of his lines as if they were:

>Out-side-rs will not rate
>In our united state.

But the melody shifts the emphases, and Ira had to write to them. Here's how you sing it as the song ends up with a nice little play on "out" and "in":

>Out-siders will not rate
>In our united state.

>(Burton Lane and Ira Gershwin, "In Our United State," *Give a Girl a Break*, 1953)

For songs, you emphasize the rhyme more than you do in poetry. In a run-on line in a poem, you don't pause. You read or recite it right through the rhyme. In a song, though, the rhyme, in Ira Gershwin's words, "ought to be observed—or at least not negated—especially when the music calls for pause or breath." For the song "Things Are Looking Up," Gershwin had recently heard a singer perform the lines as if they read:

>And it seems that suddenly—
>I've become the happiest man alive.

"Personally," Ira said, "I'd rather hear:

>And it seems that suddenly I've
>Become the happiest man alive."[30]

>(George Gershwin, Ira Gershwin, "Things Are Looking Up," *A Damsel in Distress*, 1937)

In 2016, the Nobel Prize Committee gave the award for literature to Bob Dylan "for having created new poetic expressions within the great American song tradition."[31] It stirred controversy at the time. Should the Nobel

Prize in Literature have gone to a songwriter? We have great regard for Dylan, but to call him a poet is to do a disservice to both songwriters and poets. They may use the same devices, but lyrics aren't poems, certainly not during the years of the Great American Songbook. As Dylan said in his Nobel Prize address, "But songs are unlike literature. They're meant to be sung, not read."[32]

Ira Gershwin wrote of his own lyrics, "Any resemblance to actual poetry, living or dead, is highly improbable."[33] When a poet finishes a poem, he has written a new poem. When a composer and lyricist finish a song, they have written a new song. It's not music and it's not words; it's a song, a new third thing. As E. Y. Harburg wrote:

> Although lyricists employ many of the same tools as poets, the demands of their craft are significantly different. While lyrics and poetry both employ meter, rhyme, and sound, it is music which constrains and propels the ... lyric, shaping its form as well as its content with melody, harmony, and rhythm.[34]

The songs of the Great American Songbook were highly conventionalized in their use of structure, imagery, and subject matter. They innovated within those constraints. The composers relied heavily on syncopation and the lyricists on wordplay. If the music came first, the lyrics had to fit syllable to note, word to notes, and language to music, while always attuning themselves to the emotion suggested by the music. If the lyric came first, the same is true but in reverse: note to syllable, notes to words, music to language. Johnny Mercer said that "writing lyrics leaves you out there, exposed. Music can sit in the background." The music of poetry is the poet's own. A song must blend the music in the language with the composer's music. It's actually a harder task, partly because a lyric, unlike a poem, cannot stand on its own. It must match the emotion suggested by the melody. When the collaborators are in sync, melody and lyric become one thing.

Poets can write about any subject and can make their poems as challenging as they choose. Songs have a limited range of subjects and have to be accessible. Irving Berlin would have been a lousy poet, but he was a great songwriter. Poetry prizes originality. It's desirable in a song but not essential. Familiarity is every bit as important. Poets do everything possible to avoid cliches. Not songwriters.

For the king in *The King and I*, Oscar Hammerstein wrote an exuberant lyric for which Richard Rodgers composed a rousing polka that transformed Hammerstein's lyric into pure air: "Shall we dance? / On a bright cloud of music? / Shall we fly?" (Richard Rodgers and Oscar Hammerstein II, "Shall We Dance?" *The King and I*, 1951). The song does not have an original word or image. Its originality lies in its being the score's unlikely love song between the king and Anna Leonowens, the British schoolteacher who instructs his many children. That is, it's a theater song. Its originality also lies in the relationship between the characters and their clash of cultures and personalities. By the time the show gets to the song late in act two, audiences have come to know both of them and to suspect the deep affection they feel for one another. The song confirms it.

The lyric to one of Irving Berlin's most remarkable songs, "Cheek to Cheek," does not appear to be especially original at first glance. To hear the words is to discover a great lyric; to read them is to discover a second- or third-rate poem. The song's originality lies in the music, but Berlin also attuned the lyric to Fred Astaire's distinctive sensibility. Astaire played pretty much the same character again and again, defined by his ease of manner and his romantic readiness. He was always ready to fall in love, usually at first sight. Eventually, at his luckiest, he would get to dance with Ginger Rogers or Rita Hayworth.

Every time you think you've got his music pinned down, Berlin, this musical illiterate, confounds you by doing something apparently beyond him—except it wasn't. Even though it has no verse, the song is sixty-four bars long rather than the usual thirty-two, and he creates a musical and lyrical surprise after the first sixteen bars (Irving Berlin, "Cheek to Cheek," *Top Hat*, 1935).

Instead of AABA, Berlin tacks on another B section and writes a new C that feels like a very short song complete in itself: "Dance with me, / I want my arm about you." The song as finished is AABBCA.

The first two A sections begin, "Heaven, / I'm in heaven," while the release (B) begins, "Oh! I'd love to climb a mountain." The second release begins, "Oh! I love to go out fishing." Then the C section begins dramatically, "Dance with me, / I want my arm about you" before returning to a final A which ends, "When we're out together dancing / Cheek to cheek." Typical of Astaire's dance numbers, the music grows in intensity after the middle (if it were a story or lovemaking, this would be its climax) and then quiets at the end. The C is the most forceful part of the song. It begins with an imperative as the narrator expresses his ardor before gliding back into the song's smooth fox trot rhythm: "The charm about you / Will carry me through to heaven. / I'm in heaven."

Once Berlin establishes "heaven" in the song's first two lines—it's where Astaire's character finds himself when he dances with Rogers—he writes an ascending third line whose final note reaches the upper limit of Astaire's vocal range. A short line, a second short line, and then a long musical phrase for Berlin's musical innovation, small but telling:

> Heaven,
> I'm in heaven,
> And my heart beats so that I can hardly speak.

Berlin surprises the listener to create emphasis. In the first A section, he wants to emphasize the word "speak" at the end of the second line, not with a trumpet's blare but by making the note almost silent. He might have ascended the scale through the line or he could have jumped suddenly to reach the note he wanted. Instead the line, "My heart beats so that I can hardly speak," begins with a note on "my," moves up two steps to "heart," then down one to "beats," then up two to "so," down one to "that," and so on until he reaches "speak." When Astaire sings, "And my heart beats so that I can hardly speak," he can "hardly speak." The line is virtually mute, made only of breath, a suggestion of love as ineffable, graspable only through dance.[35]

"Cheek to Cheek" is a complete merging of word and note, lyrics and music, but it would not have made an especially impressive poem:

> Oh! I love to go out fishing . . .
> But I don't enjoy it half as much
> As dancing cheek to cheek.

The merging of music, words, singing, and dancing make this an extraordinary moment in a movie and in our musical memories, but it's far from being poetry. The originality of a great song lies in Berlin's mastery of everything from the extended structure to a single note wedded to the perfect word.

RECORDINGS

Robert Young, Ann Sothern, "Your Words and My Music," 1941.
Jason Danieley, "I Miss the Music," 2007.
Fred Astaire, "The Way You Look Tonight," 1936.
Julie Andrews, "The Last Time I Saw Paris," 1973.

Johnny Mercer, Jo Stafford, "Blues in the Night," 1943.
Deanna Durbin, "Lover," 1932.
Peggy Lee, "Lover," 1952.
Mary Jane Walsh, "I Like to Recognize the Tune," 1939.
Rita Hayworth, "I'm Old Fashioned," 1942.
Judy Garland, "Over the Rainbow," 1939.
Ethel Waters, "Happiness Is Just a Thing Called Joe," 1943.
Doris Day, "It's Magic," 1951.
Rebecca Luker. Jason Graae. "Tea for Two," 2011.
Fred Astaire, "A Foggy Day (In London Town)," 1937.
Cliff Edwards, "Fascinating Rhythm," 1924.
Gertrude Lawrence, "Do, Do, Do," 1926.
Gower Champion, "In Our United State," 1953.
Fred Astaire, "Things Are Looking Up," 1937.
Gertrude Lawrence, Yul Brynner, "Shall We Dance," 1951.
Fred Astaire, "Cheek to Cheek," 1935.

EPILOGUE

Suddenly, there they were. Songwriters, many of them Irish or Jewish, who were essential to the task of defining an American popular music a few decades into the twentieth century. They called where they worked Tin Pan Alley, Broadway, or Uptown, but what they wrote reached Americans all across the country, regardless of where their families had originally come from. The popular music business was one of those small but genuine things that bound us together. We all knew the tunes and we all knew the words. The Great American Songbook embraced composers with a keen ear for melody and lyricists with an equally keen ear for language. They also kept their eye on the bottom line.

The Songbook's era ended in the 1950s, replaced by rock and roll. Since then, popular music and the music business have endured many changes, and popular music now, in the 2020s, is a very different being. We set out to show that the music of that golden era combined the elements of music—melody, rhythm, harmony, form, and lyrics—in a way that was unique for its time, but also for all time. As Alexander Herzen wrote, "Geniuses are almost always to be found when they are needed."[1] The geniuses who did the writing cannot be duplicated. Theirs was artful work; they gave us a timeless music.

The writers of the Great American Songbook lifted the prosaic to the level of the sublime. They were fortunate to have had singers attuned to their work in rare ways. They ranged from the elegant Mabel Mercer in the tiny Manhattan *boites* where she appeared; to Alberta Hunter who sang the blues at The Cookery down in Greenwich Village; to Barbara

Cook who worked both supper clubs and concert halls, although she never lost the innate theatricality of her singing.

Because songwriters' essential subject was love, their songs have a way of making more of it than it can be but making us believe it at the same time. These songs travel from the depths of despair to the heights of ecstasy, shaped by masters of craft who knew how to aim the results at our hearts. And therein lies the legacy and the persistent appeal of the Great American Songbook. These songs may have had their day, but they "keep coming back like a song / A song that keeps saying, remember."

NOTES

INTRODUCTION

1. "E. Y. Harburg Quotes," *Brainy Quote*, July 287, 2021, https://www.brainyquote.com/quotes/e_y_harburg_389207.
2. Deena Rosenberg, *Fascinating Rhythm: The Collaboration of George and Ira Gershwin* (New York: Dutton, c. 1991), xiii.
3. Jody Rosen, "Willie Nelson's Long Encore," *New York Times*, August. 17, 2022, https://www.nytimes.com/2022/08/17/magazine/willie-nelson.html.
4. James T. Maher, in Alec Wilder, *American Popular Song: The Great Innovators* (London, Oxford, New York: Oxford University Press, c. 1972), xxiv.
5. Gene Lees, *Portrait of Johnny: The Life of John Herndon Mercer* (New York: Pantheon Books, 2004), 294.
6. Maher, in Wilder, xxviii.
7. Claudia Keelen, *American Poetry Review* (January/February 2007).
8. Paul Bloom, "Being in Time," *The New Yorker*, July 9, 2121, https://www.newyorker.com/culture/annals-of-inquiry/being-in-time?utm_source=nl&utm_brand=tny&utm_mailing=TNY_Daily_070921&utm_campaign=aud-dev&utm_medium=email&bxid=5eeb982d2e59087b007e4869&cndid=61442626&hasha=cd8d22f26cc60ee8d32b2c51d0aa01ad&hashb=52c631f112ee59a2f21859885d9c3b476dc4762c&hashc=7790a7094ab8b921668c4b20b67833c4b2b0d88ba12ce4b2d20bcf2af4ac3ab3&esrc=bouncexmulti_first&utm_content=B&utm_term=TNY_Daily.
9. William Butler Yeats, "Adam's Curse," in *The Collected Poems of W.B. Yeats* (Hertfordshire: Wadsworth Editions Limited, c. 2000), 64.

10. Joe Morton, script for "The Hollywood Style," *American Cinema*, November 17, 1994, https://test-learnermedia.pantheonsite.io/wp-content/uploads/2019/01/american-cinema-unit1-transcript-hollywood-style.pdf. The script does not list the name of the writer.

11. Marilyn Berger, "Irving Berlin, Nation's Songwriter, Dies," *New York Times*, September 23, 1989, https://www.nytimes.com/1989/09/23/obituaries/irving-berlin-nation-s-songwriter-dies.html.

12. Quoted in Aleandra Petri, "Stephen Sondheim Made Art That Made Life More Real," *Washington Post*, November 28, 2021, https://www.washingtonpost.com/opinions/2021/11/27/stephen-sondheim-songs-life-more-real/.

13. Petre, np.

CHAPTER 1

1. Terry Gross interview with Ken Emerson, "The *New York Times*, 'Lyrics and Legacy of Stephen Foster,'" *Fresh Air Archive*, April 16, 2010, https://freshairarchive.org/guests/ken-emerson.

2. Sue Roe, *In Montmartre: Picasso, Matisse and the Birth of Modernist Art* (New York: Penguin Books, c. 2014), xv.

3. Philip Furia, *The Poets of Tin Pan Alley: A History of America's Great Lyricists* (New York: Oxford University Press, 1990), 11–12.

4. James Kaplan, *Irving Berlin: New York Genius* (New Haven, CT, and London: Yale University Press, c. 2019), 41.

5. Kaplan, 48.

6. Philip Furia, *Irving Berlin: A Life in Song* (New York: Schirmer Books, 1998), 101.

7. Gershwin, 120.

8. Ira Gershwin, *Lyrics on Several Occasions* (London, New York, Sydney, Cologne: Omnibus Press, c1978), 320.

9. E. E. Cummings, "Quotable Quotes," *Goodreads*, May 9, 2021, https://www.goodreads.com/quotes/13990-like-the-burlesque-comedian-i-am-abnormally-fond-of-that.

10. Joan Acocella, "The Soloist," *The New Yorker*, January 11, 1998, https://www.newyorker.com/magazine/1998/01/19/the-soloist?utm_source=nl&utm_brand=tny&utm_mailing=TNY_Classics_Sunday_111021&utm_campaign=aud-dev&utm_medium=email&bxid=5eeb982d2e59087b007e4869&cndid=61442626&hasha=cd8d22f26cc60ee8d32b2c51d0aa01ad&hashb=52c631f112ee59a2f21859885d9c3b476dc4762c&hashc=7790a7094ab8b921668c4b20b67833c4b2b0d88ba12ce4b2d20bcf2af4ac3ab3&esrc=NYR_NEWSLETTER_TheNewYorkerThisWeek_217_SUB_SourceCode&utm_term=TNY_Sunday Archive.

11. Quoted in "Irving Berlin, Nation's Songwriter, Dies," *New York Times*, September 23, 1989.

12. S. N. Behrman, *People in a Diary: A Memoir* (Boston: Little, Brown, 1972), 256.

13. Jeffrey Melnik, "Tin Pan Alley and the Black Jewish Nation," in *American Popular Music: New Approaches to the Twentieth Century*, edited by Rachel Rubin and Jeffrey Melnick (Amherst, MA: University of Massachusetts Press, c. 2001), 31.

14. Melnick, 36–37.

15. James Weldon Johnson in Rubin and Melnick, 28.

16. Quoted in Dale Cockrell, *Everybody's Doin' It: Sex, Music, and Dance in New York, 1840–1917* (New York: W. W. Norton & Company, c. 2019), 125.

17. Jim Jarmusch, "Things I've Learned: Jim Jarmusch," *MovieMaker* #53, January 22, 2004, at *Redtree Times*, April 2, 2021, https://redtreetimes.com/2021/04/02/good-thievery/.

18. Frank Sinatra has one of the song's most popular recordings. It was also a regular part of his nightclub and concert appearances in his later decades. Sinatra, to his great credit, usually named both composer and lyricist in his introduction of each song, but then, for some unfathomable reason, he'd change the words. In various versions, he calls the "lady" a "chick" or a "broad," thereby undoing the irony and self-knowledge in Hart's lyric. Even great singers don't always have good judgment.

19. James Boswell, *Life of Johnson* (London and New York: Penguin Publishing Group, c. 1979), 153.

CHAPTER 2

1. Jeremy Wilson, "Someone to Watch Over Me (1926)," jazzstandards.com, June 2, 2021, https://www.jazzstandards.com/compositions-0/someonetowatchoverme.htm.

2. Wilson, https://www.jazzstandards.com/compositions-0/someonetowatchoverme.htm, YouTube link, https://www.youtube.com/watch?v=5QsqTIj-R4M.

3. Adam Kirsch, "The Classicist Who Killed Homer," *The New Yorker*, June 14, 2021, https://www.newyorker.com/magazine/2021/06/14/the-classicist-who-killed-homer?utm_source=nl&utm_brand=tny&utm_mailing=TNY_Fiction_061221&utm_campaign=aud-dev&utm_medium=email&bxid=5eeb982d2e59087b007e4869&cndid=61442626&hasha=cd8d22f26cc60ee8d32b2c51d0aa01ad&hashb=52c631f112ee59a2f21859885d9c3b476dc4762c&hashc=7790a7094ab8b921668c4b20b67833c4b2b0d88ba12ce4b2d20bcf2af4ac3ab3&esrc=subscribe-page&utm_term=TNY_Fiction.

4. Henry David Thoreau, *Walden* (New York: Thomas Y. Crowell, 1910), digitized June 27, 2007, https://www.google.com/books/edition/Walden/yiQ3AAAAIAAJ?hl=en.

5. Quoted in Michael Lasser, *City Songs and American Life, 1900–1950* (Rochester, NY: University of Rochester Press, c. 2019), 79.

6. Ira Gershwin, *Lyrics on Several Occasions* (London and New York: Olympia Press, c. 1959), 353.

7. Walter Rimler, *A Gershwin Companion: A Critical Inventory & Discography, 1916–1984* (Ann Arbor, MI: Popular Culture, Ink, 2015), 348.

8. Rosenberg, 179.

CHAPTER 3

1. Rimler, 368–39.

2. Alec Wilder, *American Popular Song: The Great Innovators 1900–1950* (London, Oxford, and New York: Oxford University Press, c. 1972), 170.

3. Rimler, 225.

4. Gershwin, 252.

5. Rimler, 183.

6. Quoted in Robert Wyatt and John Andrew Johnson, eds., *The George Gershwin Reader* (New York: Oxford University Press, 2004), 94.

7. Quoted in Alison, "Reel to Reel: Somewhere over the Rainbow," *Bowery Boogie,* January 7, 2016, https://www.boweryboogie.com/2016/01/motion-picture-capital-world-somewhere-rainbow-les/, 216.

8. Harold Meyerson and Ernie Harburg, *Who Put the Rainbow in the Wizard of Oz* (Ann Arbor: University of Michigan Press, c. 1993),76.

9. Meyerson and Harburg, 134.

10. Quoted in John S. Wilson, "E. Y. Harburg, Lyricist, Killed in Car Crash," *New York Times*, March 7, 1981, https://www.nytimes.com/1981/03/07/obituaries/ey-harburg-lyricist-killed-in-car-crash.html.

11. Meyerson and Harburg, 97.

CHAPTER 4

1. Noel Coward, *Private Lives* (New York: Samuel French, Inc., c. 1975), 17.

2. Noel Coward, *Sir Noel Coward: His Words and Music*, ed. Lee Snider (New York: Random House, 1981), np.

3. Furia and Lasser, 145–46.

4. Cockrell, 40.

5. Cockrell, 104.

6. Cockrell, 104.

NOTES

7. See Cockrell, 123.
8. Quoted in Furia and Lasser, 281.
9. Stephen Citron, *Jerry Herman: Poet of the Showtune* (New Haven and London: Yale University Press, c. 2000), 108.
10. Jonas Westover, "'Be a Clown' and 'Make 'Em Laugh': Comic Timing, Rhythm, and Donald O'Connor's Face," *Academia.edu*, retrieved May 2, 2021, https://www.academia.edu/34252083/_Be_A_Clown_and_Make_Em_Laugh_Comic_Timing_Rhythm_and_Donald_OConnors_Face.
11. Cited in Cecil Adams, "Aren't the Show Tunes 'Be a Clown' and 'Make 'Em Laugh' Suspiciously Similar," *The Straight Dope*, June 4, 1976, https://www.straightdope.com/21341497/aren-t-the-show-tunes-be-a-clown-and-make-em-laugh-suspiciously-similar.
12. William Baer, "Singin' in the Rain: A Conversation with Betty Comden and Adolph Green," *Michigan Quarterly Review* XLI, no. 10 (Winter 2002), https://quod.lib.umich.edu/cgi/t/text/text-idx?cc=mqr;c=mqr;c=mqrarchive;idno=act2080.0041.101;rgn=main;view=text;xc=1;g=mqrg.

CHAPTER 5

1. Penelope Green, "Gloria Vanderbilt's Beekman Place Apartment Is for Sale," *New York Times*, July 30, 2021, https://www.nytimes.com/2021/07/30/realestate/gloria-vanderbilt-home-sale.html.
2. Gertrude Stein, quoted in Roe, 139.
3. Rosenberg, xix.
4. Wilder, 103.
5. Philip Furia, *The Poets of Tin Pan Alley: A History of America's Great Lyricists* (New York: Oxford University Press, 1990), 55.
6. Rosenberg, xix.
7. Devin Gordon, *So Many Ways to Lose* (New York: Harper, c. 2021), 107.
8. Rimler, 373.
9. Bob Geller, "Dear Benjamin," *The English Journal* 58, no. 3 (1969): 423–25, accessed May 14, 2021, https://www.jstor.org/stable/811803?read-now=1&refreqid=excelsior%3Ae65e591a5825b7cf11fdfc33b1fd4465&seq=2#page_scan_tab_contents.

CHAPTER 6

1. Jackson R. Bryer and Richard Allan Davison, *The Art of the American Musical: Conversations with the Creators* (New Brunswick, NJ: Rutgers University Press, 2005), 102.

2. James Leve, *Kander and Ebb* (New Haven, CT: Yale University Press, 2009), 19, 17.

3. Ira Gershwin, np.

4. Meyerson and Harburg, 36–37.

5. Quoted in Dorothy Grace Winer, *On the Sunny Side of the Street: The Life and Lyrics of Dorothy* Fields (New York: Schirmer Books, c. 1997), 106.

6. Oscar Hammerstein, quoted in Max Wilk, *OK! The Story of Oklahoma!* (New York: Grove Press, c. 1993) 81.

7. See Wilk, 81.

8. Meyerson and Harburg, 2–3.

9. Meryle Secrest, *Somewhere for Me: A Biography of Richard Rodgers* (New York: Alfred A. Knopf, 2001), 300.

10. Quoted in Rosenberg, 76.

11. Theodore Taylor, *Jule: The Story of Composer Jule Styne* (New York: Random House, 1979), 105–6.

12. Taylor, 107.

13. Typescript of Johnny Mercer's unpublished autobiography, Johnny Mercer Papers, Popular Music Collection Special Collections Department, Pullen Library. Copyright owned by Georgia State University, XIII, 14.

14. Meyerson and Harburg, 132.

15. Taylor, 4.

16. Taylor, 85.

17. Quoted in Taylor, 85

18. John S. Wilson, "Harold Arlen Dead at 81," *New York Times*, April 24, 1986.

19. Michael Whorf, *American Popular Song Composers: Oral Histories, 1920s–1950s* (Jefferson, NC: McFarland & Company, Inc., 2012), 28–29.

20. Meyerson and Harburg, 176.

21. Meyerson and Harburg, 176–77.

22. Meyerson and Harburg, 181.

23. Sammy Cahn, *I Should Care: The Sammy Cahn Story* (New York: Arbor House, c. 1974), 74.

24. Cahn, 101.

25. Rosenberg, xviii.

26. Gershwin, 353.

27. Gershwin, 173.

28. Gershwin, 149.

29. Quoted in Rosenberg, xvi.

30. Gershwin, 346–47.

31. Bob Dylan, "Bob Dylan Banquet Speech," *The Nobel Prize*, December 10, 2016, https://www.nobelprize.org/prizes/literature/2016/dylan/speech/.

32. Dylan, np.

33. Gershwin, xvii.

34. Meyerson and Harburg, 32.
35. Furia and Lasser, 131–12.

AFTERWORD

1. Tim Britton, "This Winter in Mets: What Are Some of David Stearns's Biggest Off-Season Decisions," *The Athletic*, in *New York Times*, October 5, 2023, https://theathletic.com/4932301/2023/10/05/mets-winter-david-stearns-decisions/?campaign=5888993&source=dailyemail.

INDEX

A
Adams, Lee, 123
Adamson, Harold, 60, 124, 129
African American music, 1, 5, 6, 13–16, 38, 39, 41, 79, 106–7, 128, 159, 160.
    See also The Blues; Jazz; Ragtime
"After You, Who?," 108–10
Ager, Milton, xvi, 9, 103
"Ain't She Sweet," xvi, 20, 66, 103
Akst, Harry, 28
"Alexander's Ragtime Band," 2, 10, 16, 18, 92, 116
"All Alone," xvi, 16, 76, 116, 127
All-American, 123
"All at Once," 141
"All at Once You Love Her," 26, 141–42
"All by Myself," xvi, 33, 116
"All in Fun," 26
"All of You," 102–3
"All the Things You Are," x, 25–26
"Always," xvi, 125–27
Americana, 78–79
An American in Paris, xii, 114

Anticipation (in the Great American Songbook), xiv, 29, 34, 45, 55, 63, 75, 76, 88, 106, 123, 138, 140, 148
Anything Goes, 42, 99
"April in Paris," 12, 84, 119
Arlen, Harold, xii, xiii, 16, 33, 39–42, 48, 79–83, 84, 85–86, 86–87, 115, 144, 151, 152, 153, 155, 157, 159–60
Armstrong, Louis, x, 39
"As Long as There's Music," 60–61
"As Time Goes By," 132, 147
Assonance (in the Great American Songbook), 8, 43, 53, 54, 62, 69, 74, 85–86, 141, 161, 163–64
Astaire, Fred, 46, 58, 59, 66, 110, 152, 154, 156, 166, 170–71
Authenticity (in the Great American Songbook), xvii, 1, 9, 11, 12, 13–14, 16–17, 18, 21, 26–27, 104, 105, 144
"Autumn Leaves," 121

B
Babes in Arms, 17, 71

The Barkleys on Broadway, 66
"Be a Clown," 114
"Beautiful Dreamer," 18
"Begin the Beguine," 27, 108
Bells Are Ringing, xiii, 158
Berlin, Ellin Mackey, 12, 126–27
Berlin, Irving, x, xii, xiii, xv, xvi, 2, 4, 11, 12–13, 15, 16, 18, 19, 29, 33, 38, 49–50, 59, 61, 65, 76, 81, 92–94, 96, 107, 112, 113, 114, 115, 116–17, 119, 122, 126–27, 131, 136, 137, 147, 151, 160, 169, 170–71
Bernstein, Leonard, 124
"Bewitched, Bothered, and Bewildered," 72–73
"Bidin' My Time," 47
"Blah, Blah, Blah," 47–48, 135
Bloomer Girl, 79
"Blue Moon," 73–74
"Blue Skies," x, xvi, 49
The Blues, x, xvi, 1, 2, 13, 16, 37, 39, 41, 83, 105, 116, 128, 133, 142, 159–60, 173
"Blues in the Night," 39, 115, 128, 153
The Boys from Syracuse, 68, 70
"Breezin' Along with the Breeze," 28
Broadway, ix, x, xii, xvi, 5, 10, 14, 16, 19, 22, 26, 34, 36, 38, 49, 58, 61, 66, 68, 72, 77, 78, 81, 82, 84, 97, 106, 110, 111, 115, 123, 125, 128, 131, 133, 136, 148, 150, 151, 158, 159, 165, 173
"Brother, Can You Spare a Dime?," 10, 78–79, 119
Brown, Lew, 30
Brown, Nacio Herb, xii, 114–15, 149
Burke, Johnny, 53–54
"But Not for Me," 46–47, 101–2
"Button Up Your Overcoat," 30
"By Strauss," 49

C
Cabaret, 22, 133, 134, 151
"Cabaret," 133
Cahn, Sammy, xvi, 17, 52, 54–55, 60, 112–13, 159, 161–62, 165
"Call Me Up Some Rainy Afternoon," 19
Calloway, Cab, 140
Carmichael, Hoagy, 100, 128, 147, 155
Carousel, 12, 125
Castle, Irene, xi, 16
Castle, Vernon, xi, 16
"Cheek to Cheek," 170–71
"Chinatown, My Chinatown," 140
Cohan, George M., 19.
Collaboration (in the Great American Songbook), xii, xvii, 6, 9, 26, 36, 77, 78, 79, 82, 97, 98, 100, 105, 112, 114, 137, 144, 147–51, 152, 153, 156, 157, 159, 160, 161, 162, 165, 166, 169
Comden, Betty, xiii–xiv, 114–15, 124, 158
"Concentratin' on You," 142
Conversational Lyric (in the Great American Songbook), 19, 25, 26–27, 45, 47, 50, 51, 52, 53, 100, 102, 105–6, 142
Cook, Will Marion, 15, 39,
Coward, Noel, 91–92
Craft (in the Great American Songbook), ix, xii, xiv, xv, xvii, 2, 5, 9, 11, 12, 14, 21, 22, 27, 35, 37, 42, 43, 51, 62, 63, 74, 76, 87, 104, 109, 122, 128, 135, 144, 148, 151, 159, 161, 169, 174
"Cuddle Up a Little Closer, Lovey Mine," 20

D
A Damsel in Distress, 166, 168
"Dancing on a Dime," 61

"Dancing on the Ceiling," 74
"Dinah," 27–28
DeSylva, B. G., 30, 133
"Do, Do, Do," 157, 166
"Don't Get Around Much Anymore," 55–57
Donaldson, Walter, 143
Donen, Stanley, 114–15
"Down in the Depths," 28–29
"Down with Love," 86–87
Drama (in the Great American Songbook), 20–22, 23, 25, 36, 37, 45, 55, 57, 59, 74, 79, 86, 94, 96, 98, 102, 103, 104, 111, 119, 124, 125, 126, 127, 129, 132, 141, 148, 156–57, 170
Dramatic Monologue, 21, 22, 23, 86, 104, 117, 124, 134
Dubin, Al, 29–30, 140, 152
Duke, Vernon, 11–12, 79, 82, 129–30, 159, 160
Dylan, Bob, 106, 115, 168–69

E
"Eadie Was a Lady," 133
"The Eagle and Me," 79
Easter Parade, xii, 114, 119
Ebb, Fred, 22, 133, 149–51
Eliscu, Edward, 39, 58
Ellington, Duke, x, xvi, 55–56, 63, 115, 128, 160
"Embraceable You," 111–12
"Ev'rything in America Is Ragtime," 16, 18
"Ev'rytime We Say Good-Bye," 137–38

F
Face the Music, 29, 61
"Falling in Love with Love," 69–70
"The Farmer and the Cowman Should Be Friends," 12
"Fascinating Rhythm," 149, 166–67

Fields, Dorothy, 49, 50–52, 115, 152
Finian's Rainbow, 81, 83–84
The Firebrand of Florence, 48
"Five Foot Two," 68, 104
Flying Down to Rio, 58
"A Foggy Day (in London Town)," 34, 165–66
Follow the Fleet, xv, 59
Forrest, George, 66
Foster, Stephen, 1, 2, 18, 20, 115
Freed, Arthur, xi, 114–15, 149, 159
Freed, Ralph, 42
Funny Face, 76
Furia, Philip, xvii, 2, 127

G
Garrick Gaieties of 1925, xvi, 67
Garrick Gaieties of 1926, 67
The Gay Divorce, 108, 110, 138
The Gay Divorcee, 110
Gershwin, George, ix, xi, xiii, xv, xvi, 6–7, 10, 11, 33, 34, 38, 46–47, 48, 49, 55, 56, 75, 77, 101, 102, 111, 114, 115, 124, 137, 129, 131, 144, 148, 150, 151, 152, 155, 156, 165, 167
Gershwin, Ira, ix, xiii, 6–7, 10, 33, 34, 43, 46–47, 48–49, 55–56, 66, 75–76, 77, 78, 82, 84, 101, 102, 111, 114, 115, 124, 127, 129, 131, 141, 144, 145, 148, 150, 151, 152, 154, 155, 156, 157, 165, 166, 167, 168, 169
"Get Happy," 39
GiGi, 105
Gilbert, L. Wolfe, 5
Gilbert, W. S., 7, 66, 78
Gillespie, Haven, 28
"Glad to Be Unhappy," 70–71, 72
"The Glory of Love," 31
Goetz, Dorothy, 92, 116
Goetz, E. Ray, 92
Gordon, Mack, 124

Gorney, Jay, 78–79
The Graduate, 133
Great American Songbook, ix, x, xi, xii, xiv, xv, xvi, xvii, 1, 2, 6, 7, 8, 9, 10, 11, 12, 13, 16, 17, 27, 29, 31, 35, 37, 38, 43, 46, 48, 49, 53, 54, 57, 58, 59, 62, 63, 65, 72, 79, 80, 84, 89, 104–5, 106, 107, 111, 113, 115, 118, 119, 121, 123, 124, 128, 134, 135, 136, 141, 144, 147, 148, 162, 166, 69, 173, 174.
See separate entries for elements of the Great American Songbook: Anticipation; Authenticity; Collaboration; Conversational Lyric; Craft; Inevitability; Memory; Rhyme; Sentiment; Syncopation; Theatricality; Time; Unpredictability; Wit; Wordplay
Green Adolph, xiii–xiv, 114–15, 124, 158
Green, Johnny, 119, 129, 130–31
"Grizzly Bear," 15, 107
Gypsy, 12, 158

H

Hammerstein, Oscar II, 8, 11, 12, 23, 25–26, 47, 60, 70, 72, 81, 115, 125, 141, 144, 147, 153, 169–70
"Happiness Is Just a Thing Called Joe," 84, 159–60
"Happy as the Day Is Long," 39, 42
Harbach, Otto, 20, 26,
Harburg, E. Y., ix, xii, xiii, 6, 9, 11–12, 33, 48, 65, 78–87, 115, 144, 152, 154, 155, 157–58, 159–61, 169
Harlem, 17, 41, 82, 115, 140
Harlem Renaissance, xvi, 42, 140
Hart, Lorenz, xi, xii, xiii, xvi, 17–18, 33, 42, 47, 65, 66–74, 81, 87, 114, 115, 135, 141, 144, 151, 167, 153, 155

Hayward, DuBose, 6, 62
Henderson, Ray, 30, 104
Heyman, Edward, 130–31
Higher and Higher, 60, 129
Hill, Billy, 31
Hoschna, Karl, 20
"How About Me?," 117–18
"How Deep Is the Ocean?," 39, 119
Hupfeld, Herman, 132, 147

I

"I Concentrate on You," 143
"I Couldn't Sleep a Wink Last Night," 129
"I Cover the Waterfront," 129
"I Found a Million Dollar Baby (in a Five and Ten Cent Store)," 133–34
"I Get a Kick Out of You," 42–43
"I Get Ideas," 61
"I Hear Music," 58, 83
"I Love to Sing-a," 82
"I Remember It Well," 105–6
"I Sleep Easier Now," 99
"I Wanna Be Around," 62–63
"I Wanna Be Loved," 130–31
"I Wish I Were in Love Again," 71, 72
"If I Loved You," 125
"In the Still of the Night," 136–37
Inauthenticity (in the Great American Songbook), 1, 12, 13, 14, 16, 27, 144
Inevitability (in the Great American Songbook), 38, 51, 62, 63, 68, 74, 77, 96, 105, 110, 127, 135, 141, 158, 162, 167
"I'll Walk Alone," 54–55, 112, 158
"I'm in Love Again," 131
"I'm in the Mood for Love," 51–52
"I've Got a Crush on You," 75
"I've Got the World on a String," 39, 119
"I've Got You Under My Skin," 138

"I've Heard That Song Before," xvi, 112, 161, 162
"If I Only Had a Brain," 79–80
"If I Only Had a Heart," 79–80
"If I Only Had the Nerve," 79–80
"It's All Right with Me," 139–40
"It's Only a Paper Moon," 84, 119
"It's Time for a Love Song," 61–62, 83

J

Jazz, x, xvi, 1, 2, 5, 7, 13, 25, 38, 39, 49, 55, 83, 106, 110, 111, 116, 119, 128, 142, 154, 159, 165
"Jeepers Creepers," 30–31
Johnson, James Weldon, 14, 15
Johnson, J. Rosamond, 15
Jubilee, 27, 139
"Just in Time," xiii–xiv
"Just One of Those Things," 139

K

Kahn, Gus, xvi, 56
Kalmar, Bert, 36–37
Kander, John, 22, 133, 149–51
Kaplan, James, 2
Kelly, Gene, 72, 114
Kern, Jerome, 11, 23, 25, 26, 49, 60, 66, 71, 79, 114, 115, 116, 125, 152–53, 154, 155–57, 160
The King and I, 148, 169, 170
Kismet, 66
Koehler, Ted, 39, 42

L

"The Lady Is a Tramp," 17–18
Lady, Be Good!, xvi, 33, 77, 148–49, 153, 166
"The Land Where the Good Songs Go," x
Lane, Burton, 58, 61, 79, 81, 83, 84, 86, 150, 168

Lapine, James, 21
"Last Night When We Were Young," 84–86
Lawrence, Gertrude, 33, 162
Lees, Gene, xiii, 151
Lerner, Alan Jay, xii, 61, 105–6, 150, 154, 165
"Let It Snow, Let It Snow, Let It Snow," 113
"Let's Call the Whole Thing Off," 43
"Let's Do It," 99
"Let's Face the Music and Dance," 39, 58–59
Lewis, Sam M., 27–28, 104
Life Begins at 8:40, 48, 82
Link, Harry, 94, 96
Loesser, Frank, 58, 61, 100–101, 103, 113, 122–23
Loewe, Frederick, xii, 105–6, 150, 165
"Love Is Here to Stay," 102, 129–30, 132, 156
Love Life, 105
"Love Me Tonight," 119
Love Me Tonight, 155
"Lover," 119, 155

M

"Make Believe," 11, 23–25
"Make 'Em Laugh," 114–15
"The Man That Got Away," 39
"Manhattan," 67
"Manhattan Madness," 29
Maschwitz, Eric, 94–96, 104
"Maybe This Time," 22–23
McHugh, Jimmy, 49–52, 60, 129
Memory (in the Great American Songbook), x, xiv, xvi, xvii, 6, 13, 16, 21, 27, 47, 85–86, 93–98, 100, 104, 105, 106, 110, 111, 115–16, 122, 123, 124, 131, 132, 133, 135, 140, 158, 166, 171

Mercer, Johnny, xii, 12–13, 30–31, 38, 62–63, 115, 121, 128, 130, 148, 152, 153, 155, 156–57, 169
Merman, Ethel, 29, 42, 133
Mills, Irving, 55–56, 140
Minnelli, Liza, 22
"Minnie the Moocher," 140
Modernism (in the Great American Songbook), 2, 5, 16, 35, 137
"Mountain Greenery," 67–68
Muir, Lewis F., 5
Music Box Revue of 1921, 61
Music Box Revue of 1924, 76
"Music Maestro, Please," 60
"Music Makes Me," 58
"The Music Stopped," 60
My Fair Lady, xii, 165
"My Heart Stood Still," 141

N
"Never No Lament," 55
"Nevertheless (I'm in Love with You)," 36–38
Nichols, Mike, 133–34
"Night and Day," 108, 119, 138, 140

O
O'Connor, Donald, 114
Oh, Kay!, 33, 167
Oklahoma!, xi, 8, 12, 71, 153
"Ol' Man River," 147
"On the Sunny Side of the Street," 49–51
On the Town, 124
On Your Toes, 37, 70
"Once Upon a Time," 123
"One for My Baby," 39
Out of This World, 10, 99
"Over the Rainbow," 80–81

P
"Paddlin' Madeline Home," 88–89
Pal Joey, 72

Pipe Dream, 26, 141
The Pirate, 114–15
"Polka Dots and Moonbeams," 53–54
Pollyanna Song, 10, 49, 87
"Poor You," 86
Porgy and Bess, 6, 82, 167
Porter, Cole, xi, xii, 10, 23, 27–29, 33, 38, 42–43, 47, 49, 65, 81, 99, 102, 103, 106, 108–10, 113, 114–15, 126, 128, 135–42, 146, 151
"People Will Say We're in Love," 8
Private Lives, 91

R
Ragtime, 1, 2, 5, 13, 14, 15–16, 18, 19, 58, 92, 106–7, 108, 115, 116, 128
"Ragging the Baby to Sleep," 5
Razaf, Andy, xvi, 142
Refrain (in the Great American Songbook), 8, 18, 20–21, 22, 23, 25, 29, 30, 31, 37, 42, 50, 52, 53, 54, 56, 60, 67, 71, 74, 76, 79, 86, 95, 98, 100, 102, 103–4, 109, 117, 122, 126, 127, 130, 132, 137, 143, 163–64, 166, 167
Release (in the Great American Songbook), 8, 21, 22, 37, 43, 45–46, 50, 51, 53, 54, 55, 56, 58, 73, 77, 86, 88, 96, 106, 112, 156, 163, 166, 167, 170
Rhyme (in the Great American Songbook), xiii, xvii, 6–9, 19, 22, 27–28, 29–30, 35, 37, 42–43, 47, 48, 49, 50, 52–53, 54, 62–63, 65, 66, 67, 69, 71, 73, 74, 81, 85, 86, 87–88, 94, 96, 101, 109–10, 117, 141, 155, 159, 161, 163–64, 166–67, 168, 169
"A Rhyme for Angela," 48–49, 66
"Rhymes Have I," 66
Rock and roll, ix, xi, xii, 49, 118, 173

Rodgers, Richard, xii, xiii, xvi, 8, 12, 26, 33, 67, 68, 69–70, 72, 73–74, 114, 115, 125, 136, 141, 144, 147, 151, 153, 155, 160, 169–70
Rogers, Ginger, 46, 58, 59, 110, 111, 152, 154, 170–71
Romberg, Sigmund, 26
Rosenberg, Deena, ix, 46, 124, 127, 165
Ross, Shirley, 97–98
Ruby, Harry, 36–38
Russell, Bob, 55–56

S
"'S Wonderful," 76–77
"Sand in My Shoes," 103
"Say It Isn't So," 119
"Say It with Music," xvi, 61
Sentiment (in the Great American Songbook), ix, xii, xiv, xvii, 2, 5, 7, 12, 16, 19, 20, 26, 46–47, 61, 92, 94, 108, 110, 119, 127, 128, 129, 131, 133, 135, 151, 165
"September in the Rain," 29–30
"Shall We Dance?," 170
"Shoes with Wings On," 66
Show Boat, 11, 23, 26, 71, 147
"Side by Side," 89
Simons, Seymour, 28
"Simple Melody," 2
"Singin' in the Rain," xii, 114
"Soft Lights and Sweet Music," 60–61, 119
Soliloquy, 21, 22, 23, 42, 52, 73, 86, 104, 117, 124
"Some Other Time," 124
"Someone to Watch Over Me," 33–34
"Something Sort of Grandish," 83
"Something's Gotta Give," 130
Sondheim, Stephen, xii, xv, xvii, 21, 106, 131
"The Song Is Ended," 58–59, 122
"The Song Is You," 60, 119

"Spring Will Be a Little Late This Year," 122–23
Springsteen, Bruce, 9, 15, 115, 118
"Stormy Weather," 42
Strachey, James, 94, 96
Strouse, Charles, 123
Styne, Jule, xii, xiii, xvi, 54–55, 60, 79, 112–13, 155–56, 158–59, 161, 165
Sunday in the Park with George, 21
Syncopation (in the Great American Songbook), xvii, 4, 5, 13–17, 29, 34, 36, 53, 56, 75, 77, 96, 106–7, 111, 116, 117, 119, 156, 165, 166, 169

T
Take a Chance, 133
"Taking a Chance on Love," 131
"Thanks for the Memory," 96–98
"That Certain Feeling," 77, 166
"That Old Black Magic," 12–13, 39
Theatricality (in the Great American Songbook), xvii, 21, 84, 102, 128, 174
"These Foolish Things," 94–96, 104
"They Can't Take That Away from Me," 34, 46
They're Playing Our Song, 148
"Things Are Looking Up," 168
"This Can't Be Love," 68, 70
"Three Little Words," 37–38
Time (in the Great American Songbook), xiii–xiv, xvi, xvii, 10, 21, 22, 27, 34–35, 45, 47, 51, 56–57, 59, 61–62, 68, 77, 82–83, 84–86, 89, 93–94, 95–97, 97, 100, 103, 104, 109, 112, 116, 117, 118, 120, 121–23, 124, 125, 127, 128, 129–30, 131, 132–33, 134, 135–36, 137–38, 139, 141, 142, 144, 160
"Time on My Hands," 124

Tin Pan Alley, x, xii, xvii, 2, 4–6, 8, 13, 14, 15, 16, 19, 35, 43, 54, 72, 106, 128, 158, 173
Tip-Toes, 77
"Try a Little Tenderness," 89, 119, 147
"Two Sleepy People," 100–101

U
Unpredictability (in the Great American Songbook), xvii, 10, 30, 31, 38, 45, 46, 48, 53, 54, 55, 65, 67, 70, 74, 83, 87, 89, 99, 137, 141, 155

V
Van Heusen, Jimmy, 53–54
Verse (in the Great American Songbook), 20–21, 22, 23, 28–29, 30, 35, 45, 52, 55, 61, 74, 77, 101–4, 111, 119, 122, 126, 127, 129, 132, 138, 142, 162, 163, 167, 170
Vimmerstedt, Sadie, 62

W
Wake Up and Dream, 23
Walk a Little Faster, 12
Waller, Thomas "Fats," xvi, 115, 126, 142
Warren, Harry, 29–30, 39, 66, 115, 128, 134, 140, 152, 153, 155
Watch Your Step, 16
Weill, Kurt, 48–49, 105, 131, 141, 150, 154
"What Can You Say in a Love Song?," 48
"What Is This Thing Called Love?," 23
"What'll I Do?," xvi, 4, 38, 112, 116, 127

"When I Fall in Love," 130–31
"When I Lost You," 92–94
"When I'm Not Near the Girl I Love," 84
When the Red Red Robin Comes Bob, Bob, Bobbin' Along," 87–88
"White Christmas," 12–13
Whiting, Richard A., xvi, 28, 133
"Why Do I Love You?," 23
Wilder, Alec, xii, 67, 127
Wit (in the Great American Songbook), xii, xvii, 2, 7, 9, 22, 46, 49, 52, 66, 70, 76, 80, 84, 87, 99, 102, 105, 111, 114, 119, 128, 129, 156
The Wizard of Oz, 9, 79–81, 114, 157
Wodehouse, P. G., x, xii, 66, 125
Woods, Harry, 87–89
Wordplay (in the Great American Songbook), xvii, 19, 45–46, 49, 50, 61, 65, 66, 73, 76, 83, 84, 99, 102, 119, 165, 169
Wright, Robert, 66

Y
Yellen, Jack, xvi, 103
"You Are Love," 23
"You Never Knew About Me," 124–25
"You'll Never Know," 111
"You'll Never Walk Alone," 12
"You're a Builder-Upper," 82–85
"You're Driving Me Crazy," 143–44
"You're Getting to Be a Habit with Me," 140
"You're the Top," 99
Youmans, Vincent, 39, 58, 124, 162–64
Young, Joe, 27–28, 104
Young, Victor, 130–31

ABOUT THE AUTHORS

Michael Lasser is the author of three previous books on the Great American Songbook. His nationally syndicated public radio show, Fascinatin' Rhythm on WXXI Radio, won a George Foster Peabody Award and was on the air for over forty years. He has appeared at hundreds of museums and performing arts centers from New York to Los Angeles.

Harmon Greenblatt has spent his entire career teaching and working in the arts. He has worked as a presenter, agent/manager, and educator and as CEO of two arts councils. Harmon is most proud of his time teaching arts management at three universities: Columbia College Chicago, the University of Hartford, and the University of New Orleans.